Social Change and Economic Development in Nigeria

edited by
Ukandi G. Damachi
Hans Dieter Seibel

The Praeger Special Studies program—utilizing the most modern and efficient book production techniques and a selective worldwide distribution network—makes available to the academic, government, and business communities significant, timely research in U.S. and international economic, social, and political development.

Social Change and Economic Development in Nigeria

PRAEGER SPECIAL STUDIES IN INTERNATIONAL ECONOMICS AND DEVELOPMENT

Praeger Publishers   New York   Washington   London

Library of Congress Cataloging in Publication Data

Damachi, Ukandi Godwin.
    Social change and economic development in
Nigeria.

    (Praeger special studies in international economics
and development)
    Bibliography: p.
    1. Nigeria—Economic policy—Addresses, essays,
lectures. 2. Nigeria—Social policy—Addresses, essays,
lectures. I. Seibel, Hans Dieter, joint author.
II. Title.
HC517. N48D35   309. 1'669'05   72-92882

To Daphne and Helga

PRAEGER PUBLISHERS
111 Fourth Avenue, New York, N.Y. 10003, U.S.A.
5, Cromwell Place, London S.W.7, England

Published in the United States of America in 1973
by Praeger Publishers, Inc.

Printed in the United States of America

ACKNOWLEDGMENTS

We are grateful to the many people who helped us at various stages in the development of our ideas. To our mentors, on Damachi's part, Professor Frederick H. Harbison and Professor Wilbert E. Moore, and on Seibel's part, Professor Dieter Oberndörfer and the late Professor Arnold Bergstraesser, we are most in debt: their influences and early encouragement enabled us to initiate and execute this project. We are particularly thankful to Professor Frederick H. Harbison, Professor Wilbert E. Moore, Professor David W. Crabb, and Professor Gerald Breese for their thoughtful comments, which made us avoid many weaknesses and errors we might not have otherwise seen.

Our sincere thanks also to Egbe S. Egozi, Johnathan Hewitt, Austin A. Ihekwe, Justin Arinze, and Joan Maruhnic, who helped in one way or another to make this work possible.

For permission to reprint copyrighted material, grateful acknowledgement is made to the following sources: The Nigerian Journal of Economic and Social Studies for "An Analysis of the Management of Trade Union Finances in Nigeria" by M. O. Kayode.

CONTENTS

	Page
ACKNOWLEDGMENTS	v
LIST OF TABLES	xiii
INTRODUCTION	xv

PART I:
SOCIAL ASPECTS OF ECONOMIC DEVELOPMENT

Chapter

1   THE PROCESS OF ADAPTATION TO WAGE
LABOR
H. Dieter Seibel   3

     Attitudes to Work   4
       Changes in Attitude   4
       Positive, Neutral, and Negative Attitudes   6
     Labor Turnover   8
     Occupational Prestige   9
     Overadaptation   10
     Note   10

2   THE EARLY HISTORICAL EVIDENCE OF YORUBA
URBANISM
William Bascom   11

     Conclusion   31
     Notes   33
     Bibliography   36

3   THE WESTERN NIGERIAN COOPERATIVE AD-
MINISTRATION: AN OBSTACLE TO DE-
VELOPMENT
Michael Koll   40

     The Beginnings of the Nigerian Cooperative
       System   41

Chapter		Page
	Indigenous Cooperatives	41
	Cooperatives in Early Colonial Times	41
	The Introduction of State-Controlled Cooperatives	42
	The Structure of Present-Day Administration of Western Nigerian Cooperatives	43
	Structural Deficiencies in Administrative Staffing	43
	The Political Weaknesses of the Administration of the Cooperatives	44
	An Example: Craftsmen's Cooperatives	45
	State-Controlled Craftsmen's Cooperatives	45
	Cooperatives of Independent Craftsmen	46
	Conclusions	47
	Notes	49
4	SYSTEMS OF STATUS ALLOCATION AND RECEPTIVITY TO MODERNIZATION H. Dieter Seibel	51
	The Problem	51
	Methodology	52
	The Nigerian Case	52
	Hypothesis 1: There is a Relationship between Certain Structural Features and Receptivity to Change	52
	Hypothesis 2: There is a Relationship between Structural Complexity and Receptivity to Change	61
	Hypothesis 3: There is a Relationship between the System of Stratification and Receptivity to Change	62
	Hypothesis 4: There is a Relationship between the Amount of Social Mobility and Receptivity to Change	63
	Hypothesis 5: There is a Relationship between the System of Status Allocation and Receptivity to Change	65
	The Liberian Case	69
	The Societies Tested	70
	Testing Receptivity to Change	72
	Conclusion	72
	Notes	75

PART II: MANPOWER, TRADE UNIONS,
AND ECONOMIC DEVELOPMENT

5   MANPOWER IN NIGERIA
     Ukandi G. Damachi   81

        The Labor Force   83
        The Unemployment Trap   86
        Policy Considerations   93
        Notes   95
        Bibliography   96

6   INDUSTRIAL RELATIONS IN THE SAPELE TIMBER
     INDUSTRY: THE DEVELOPMENT OF COLLECTIVE
     BARGAINING
     Ukandi G. Damachi   98

        The Organizational Structure of the Timber In-
           dustry   98
        Labor-Management Relations   100
        Union Action in the Industry   105
        The Collective Bargaining Process   107
        Some Local Disputes and Solutions   111
        A Comparison of the Nigerian Situation with
           Some Aspects of Labor-Management Re-
           lations in the United States   112
        Conclusion: A Kaleidoscopic View of the Timber
           Industry   114
        Notes   116
        Bibliography   117

7   POLITICAL DILEMMAS OF NIGERIAN LABOR
     Robert Melson   119

        Labor and Politics in Nigeria   119
        Neutralist Labor in the Unitary Phase of Ni-
           gerian Nationalism   121
        Activists in the Regionalist Phase   124
           The UNAMAG Strike   125
        Dilemmas of the Polarized Phase   126
           The Neutralists   127
           The Activists   129

Chapter   Page

       The Activists, Neutralists, and the Dilemmas
          Fragmentation   131
             The Ironsi Coup   132
             The Gowon Coup   134
             The Lessons of the Political Dilemmas of
                 Nigerian Labor   135
          Notes   136

8   THE MANAGEMENT OF TRADE UNION FINANCES
    IN NIGERIA
    M. O. Kayode   138

       Introduction   138
       Methodology   139
       Findings   140
          Degree of Success of Financial Management   140
          Union Goals   140
          Other Uses of Union Funds   141
          Capital Expenditure Assets of the Unions   142
          Sources of Union Funds   143
       Conclusion   143
       Note   146

PART III:
EDUCATION AND ECONOMIC DEVELOPMENT

9   SOCIAL CHANGE IN NORTHERN NIGERIA: THE
    ACCEPTANCE OF WESTERN EDUCATION
    Alan Peshkin   149

       Introduction   149
       Procedure   152
       Findings   153
          Pro-Primary Education for Girls   153
          Pro-Primary Education for Boys   154
          Pro-Primary Education with Reservations   156
          Anti-Primary Education   156
          Pro-Koranic and Pro-Primary Education   159
          Pro-Koranic Education   160
          Anti-Koranic Education   161
       Discussion   162
       Conclusions   168

Chapter   Page

        Notes   171
        Bibliography   171

10   THE NIGERIAN UNIVERSITY: TOWARD MORE
     RELEVANCE
     Akpan Esen   173

        The Historical Background   174
        The Purposes of the Nigerian University   176
            The Concept of Liberal Education   177
            Goals of the University Revisited   179
        Bibliography   184

11   SEEDS OF RADICALISM AMONG AN ASPIRANT
     ELITE
     Pauline H. Baker   185

        Methodology   186
        Characteristics of the Samples   187
        Value Orientations   191
        Political Attitudes   194
            Political Alienation   194
            Political Liberalism   196
            Attachment to Democratic Principles   198
            Criteria for Leadership   199
            Causes of Political Difficulties   201
        Conclusion   203
        Notes   205

                    PART IV: POLITICS,
        COMMUNICATIONS, AND ECONOMIC DEVELOPMENT

12   NIGERIAN POLITICS: CLASS ALLIANCES AND
     FOREIGN ALIGNMENT
     Philip V. White   209

        Prewar Foreign Policy   209
        Factors Contributing to Military Intervention   211
            Vulnerability of the Political Economy   211
            Proximate Causes of Military Intervention   215
        The Establishment of Military Rule   218
            The Coup of January 15, 1966   218

Chapter   Page

      Countercoup and the Road to Secession   219
      The Soviet Union and the Civil War   221
    Postwar Policy and the Aperatura à Sinistra:
      An Assessment   222
        Postwar Foreign Policy   222
        Postwar Domestic Politics   225
    Notes   226

13   SOVIET INVOLVEMENT IN THE NIGERIAN CIVIL
       WAR
       George Obiozor   230

      Notes   234

14   MASS COMMUNICATIONS IN NIGERIA
       Alfred E. Opubor   235

      Media Content   238
      Media Costs   244
      Language and Access   245
      Training Media Personnel   247
      Recommendations   249
      Notes   251
      Bibliography   252

ABOUT THE AUTHORS   253

RELATED TITLES   256

LIST OF TABLES

Table   Page

4.1   Population of Major Tribes of Nigeria, by
       Region, 1952-53 Census   56

4.2   Relationship between Tribe and Twelve Vari-
       ables among Yoruba and Ibo Workers in
       Ibadan and Lagos, Nigeria   60

4.3   Scoring System, using Six Subindexes, for
       measuring Adaptation to Wage Labor among
       Kpelle and Kru Workers in Liberia   73

4.4   Moving Average of Scores of Adaptation to Wage
       Labor among Kpelle and Kru Workers in
       Liberia   74

5.1   Pattern of Total Gainful Occupation, 1969-74   83

5.2   University Graduates in 1966   85

5.3   The Labor Market, 1970-74   86

5.4   Federal and State Capital Expenditures on
       Education, 1970-74   87

5.5   Mean Annual Costs per Student from all Sources   88

7.1   Six Political Dilemmas of Nigerian Labor   122

9.1   Primary School Enrollment in Bornu, by
       Sex and Year   151

9.2   Primary School Enrollment in Northern Nigeria,
       for Selected Years   151

11.1   Prestige Ratings of Occupations   192

11.2   Desirability Ratings of Personality Character-
       istics   193

11.3   Political Alienation   195

Table		Page
11.4	Liberalism and Conservatism	197
11.5	Attachment to Democratic Principles	198
11.6	Criteria for Leadership	200
11.7	Responsibility for National Political Problems	202
14.1	Growth of Daily Newspapers	236
14.2	Growth of Radio Receivers	236
14.3	Growth of Television Receivers	237
14.4	Growth of Cinema Facilities	237
14.5	Language Use in the Media	246
14.6	Language Use in Radio Broadcasting in Mid Western Nigeria- N.B.C., Benin	246

Social change has characterized Nigeria's peoples throughout their known existence—usually as a process of gradual transitions (in no way linear, of course), but at times in the form of revolutionary upheavals. Everyone who has studied Nigerian history knows that the stability of pre-modern societies is but an anthropological myth. Even the ever increasing pace of social change in recent decades is more a parocentric prejudice than a substantiated hypothesis. Rapid economic development, however, is a more recent phenomenon, barely half a century old. It would not be very original to show that both social change and economic development are taking place in Nigeria; this is by now common knowledge. Yet very little is known about the interplay between social change and economic development. This collection of essays concentrates not on social change and economic development as separate tracks but on the crossroads between them.

In our first essay, "The Process of Adaptation to Wage Labor," H. Dieter Seibel shows how changes in the economic structure from extractive industry to manufacturing have been supported by simultaneous social changes. Four major stages of adaptation to wage labor are analyzed in terms of attitudes to work, labor turnover, and occupational prestige. During the first stage, attitude to wage labor is completely negative; as everyone was fully integrated into the pre-modern socioeconomic setup, workers could only be recruited through more-or-less coercive measures in the interest of the colonial administration. Labor turnover was extremely high as workers returned home immediately after having earned enough money to pay the hut tax (or the bride price during the second stage of adaptation). This high labor turnover was not entirely unwarranted; the colonial administration preferred the African not to become urbanized and pose a threat to its domination—a policy still followed today in South Africa. At the very beginning of the impact of new industries, only traditional occupations were prestige-ranked; modern ones were simply outside of that scale. Chinua Achebe brings this out quite clearly in his novel Things Fall Apart when he reports that

. . . the white men had also brought a court where the District Commissioner judged cases in ignorance. He had court messengers who brought men to him for trial. These court messengers were greatly hated in Umuofia because they were foreigners and also arrogant and high-handed. They were called <u>kotma</u>, and because of their ash-colored shorts they earned the additional name of Ashy-Buttocks. They guarded the prison, which was full of men who had offended against the white man's law. . . . They were beaten in prison by the <u>kotma</u> and made to work every morning clearing the government compound and fetching wood for the white Commissioner and the court messengers. Some of these prisoners were men of title who should be above such mean occupation. They were grieved by the indignity and mourned for their neglected farms.*

This changed within a short period of time, and the first occupations to gain high prestige were white-collar jobs—the jobs of the white man. Subsequently Africans continued to be quick in adjusting to the changing needs of a growing economy. In the present stage—the fourth one—the African is fully committed to wage labor. His attitudes to his job tend to be strongly positive, the main determinant being his interest in technical work. Labor turnover has been reduced drastically, and technical jobs enjoy the highest prestige. Industrial work has become a way of life. Recently, however, full adaptation has been changing to overadaptation, as Nigerians have adapted faster than the economy has grown. There is an overwhelming interest in education and occupational training and in rushing into modern occupations. As a consequence unemployment is becoming widespread in cities, while the rural areas are being depleted of their best young men and women. Thus urban overadaptation is being matched by rural maladaptation. It is suggested that only a thorough reform of two institutions could change this situation: rural education and rural cooperatives.

In our second selection, "The Early Historical Evidence of Yoruba Urbanism," William Bascom illustrates that change is in fact not a recent phenomenon in Nigeria that started with modernization. He gives an account of urbanization between 1485 and 1825 among the Yoruba, the most highly urbanized African society in both pre-modern and modern times. His description of early Yoruba cities and their colorful history demonstrates that city growth is not necessarily a by-product of modernization; it occurred in Yorubaland long before the British set foot there. This implies that bureaucratic structures, crafts, craft organizations, and trade have been developing for centuries.

---

*Chinua Achebe, <u>Things Fall Apart</u> (New York: Astor-Honor, 1959), pp. 180-81.

What has happened to these pre-modern structures, particularly to crafts and craft organizations? Michael Koll notes, in "The Nigerian Cooperative Administration-An Obstacle to Development," that pre-modern cooperative organizations existed in great numbers all over Nigeria as an integral part of traditional societies. Such cooperatives, both rural and urban, had vigorously started to respond to the new economic and social stimuli long before any colonial initiative had reached them. As they were part of pre-modern society and as the British administration had their own ideas of what cooperatives were supposed to look like, they were not even recognized as such. Thus the British were believed to have introduced cooperative societies to Nigeria. And as they passed laws about cooperatives, defining only their own creations as cooperatives, their beliefs found even legal support. A cooperative administration was then built up to encourage and supervise cooperative growth and development. All government success reports notwithstanding, this bureaucracy of colonial and later of independent Nigeria has stifled spontaneity and has hampered self-control. Once instruments of self-help, cooperatives have become objects of bureaucratic procedures. All efforts concentrate on a few legal token cooperatives, ignoring the many extralegal cooperatives of indigenous origin. According to Koll's sample census of 1967, there are about 14,000 craftsmen in Ibadan of whom only a few dozens are officially organized into cooperatives. Only one group has acquired definite shape: a group of some 10 tailors out of approximately 4,900. Their existence has filled fat files since 1955. Simultaneously there exist a great many indigenous cooperatives, usually with less than the legally required ten members. They operate without government control. None of them is entitled to badly needed loans and other types of governmental assistance. "Law and statute are like a strait jacket which doom free enterprise and any experiment to failure," concludes Koll. An overall reform of cooperative administration is needed if it is ever to become a tool for development.

In his essay, Koll indicates that modern institutions may have a negative impact on development. The next essay, "Systems of Status Allocation and Receptivity to Modernization" by H. Dieter Seibel, examines the impact traditional institutions or aspects of traditional structures may have. This study has been provoked by the observation that there are considerable differences in the pace of modernization among various Nigerian peoples that cannot be fully explained by differences in the extent of exposure to agents of change. Could there be certain variables in the social structure and value system of traditional societies that determine receptivity to modernization today, including a society's willingness to expose itself to agents of change? Seibel finds the traditional system of status allocation to be of crucial importance. Societies that traditionally allocate social positions predominately on the basis of achieved criteria tend to be receptive to change; societies that traditionally allocate positions predominately by ascription (birth, etc) tend to' resist change.

While the first group of four essays (discussed above) deals with general social aspects of economic development, the next section is more specific, examining manpower and trade unions in their relationship to economic development.

In "Manpower in Nigeria," Ukandi G. Damachi examines the manpower situation in Nigeria. He concludes that unemployment, underemployment, and shortage of critical skills are the major manpower problems in Nigeria. Vaste amounts of money are being spent on education—an academic type of education that is useless for the masses and only of limited practical use for that 5 percent of the labor force employed in the modern sector of the economy. Moreover this type of education is not only useless for the masses, it is even harmful in that it hampers economic development. Instead of training millions of young Nigerians to become good farmers and cope with their (rural!) environment, it alienates them from their social and natural environment; the young get a "modern" education and leave to go to a "modern" city for a "modern" job. Instead of improving their farms at home, they become unemployed in the cities—an enormous double waste of manpower. Damachi follows Nyerere's suggestion that only when rural schools have been turned into "economic and social communities" will there be a chance for real development.

Trade unions have existed in Nigeria for several decades to represent the workers' interests in a modernizing economy. What have they contributed to Nigeria's development and/or to the betterment of the workers' lot? Very little, if Ukandi G. Damachi's study of trade unionism and collective bargaining in a major company in Nigeria, "Industrial Relations in the Sapele Timber Industry: The Development of Collective Bargaining," is in any way indicative. With a remarkable lack of militancy, it is shown that there is a wide communication gap between union and management, that discussions concentrate on trite matters, and that, in the last analysis, unions serve as a last-resort job opportunity for university graduates who cannot find a better job. Instead of pushing Nigeria's progress and the workers' well-being forcefully ahead, unions are leading a pallid existence.

While Damachi points to the economic powerlessness of trade unions, Robert Melson in "Political Dilemmas of Nigerian Labor" strikes a similar note—the note of political powerlessness of trade unions throughout the history of Nigeria. Examining the political dilemmas of neutralist and activist labor unions during the unitary phase (1945-50), regional phase (1950-62), polarized phase (1962-66), and fragmented political phase (after 1966), Melson concludes that while it is virtually impossible for trade unions to keep out of politics, it is never trade unions that determine the course of politics in any way. The failure of the general strike of December 1964, which was essentially political in nature, may stand as a symbol. At no point in Nigerian history has labor played a decisive political role.

Trade unions are not only unable to exert any influence on external political and economic affairs; they are also incapable of managing their internal affairs. M. O. Kayode's analysis, "The Management of Trade Unions Finances in Nigeria," presents Nigerian trade unions as an illustration of Parkinson's Law. Most of their funds are swallowed up by administrative expenses that grow as positions proliferate. As unions appear to serve no other purpose, one could at least expect that they render "friendly benefits" to their members, as do almost all voluntary associations of indigenous origin. But even that is only done to a negligible extent.

Failure of the educational system to prepare people for real life with economic development as a goal to be accomplished has been a recurrent theme so far in this book. Our third section concentrates therefore on schools and universities.

As Seibel has indicated in his essay on systems of status allocation, various Nigerian societies have responded unequally to the stimuli of modernization. One consequence of this unequal response is an unequal distribution of modern educational institutions and of popular reactions to modern education. In southern Nigeria there has been overwhelming striving for modern education in virtually every village—matched by strong political support. In Northern Nigeria however, where Koranic schools have offered formal religious instruction for centuries, the spread of modern education has been severely hampered until recently by the traditional elite. In "Social Change in Northern Nigeria: The Acceptance of Western Education," Alan Peshkin demonstrates that this has had strong effects on popular opinions, which have just started to change. Preference for Koranic school education is now clearly shifting toward preference for primary school attendance, although attitudes toward modern education remain highly ambiguous. Modern education is considered as a curse and a blessing at the same time; it is becoming a prerequisite for a well-paid job, but unemployed school-leavers are common. It helps adapt to changing times but simultaneously alienates children from their parents. Educated girls find it easier to get a husband, but they may not be allowed to leave school when they reach marriage age. Children receive religious instruction in primary schools, but they may abandon their faith. Academic and occupational attainments enhance family honor, but students may loose their respect for authority and shame their families. Two reasons for getting an education are altogether absent—national development and political socialization—thereby indicating a perfectly rational attitude, as we have pointed out, that modern education does in fact not serve these two functions very well. All pros and cons given by those interviewed were highly instrumental and of a very immediate nature.

In "The Nigerian University: Toward More Relevance," Akpan Esen contributes a new insight to the problem of educational failure in Nigeria: Nigeria's universities have been, from their beginnings, "universities in Nigeria" rather than "Nigerian universities." As "universities in Nigeria," they have been British brain-children educating a gentleman-elite for leadership. As "Nigerian universities," they would be people's universities; i.e., training institutes "dedicated to grappling with Nigeria's problems with a view to raising living standards for all Nigerians." In other words they would be fully and realistically oriented toward economic development. The demise of departments of classics at Nigerian universities may be indicative of an educational awakening. Yet defining the purposes of higher education in Nigeria in terms of its "close relevance to the needs of the society" still appears for the most part to be mere lip service to the overall goal of development. Ultimately, Esen suggests, there needs to be a shift of all research and teaching emphasis to very concretely "applied disciplines," including, however, those fields that in some other parts of the continent have emerged out of the clouds of a falsely asserted dark past into the bright African sunlight of négritude: indigenous languages, institutions, attitudes, values, perceptions, etc. that are worth preserving—not only for their own value but also for their direct or indirect developmental function. Take as an example the traditional positive attitude to hard work, rarely found among educated Nigerians. Esen regrets that Nigerian universities do not give their students an opportunity to engage in manual work—e.g., in construction, or even dishwashing after their own meals. There is no doubt that there is a tremendous thirst for education; whether it can be satisfied by the educational institutions so that it will contribute to development remains an open question.

In "Seeds of Radicalism among an Aspirant Elite," Pauline H. Baker deals with the most conspicuous group in modern education—university students. In two studies in 1966 and 1971, she examined the social background and the aspirations and the political attitudes of students at Lagos University. More than half of them are of peasant origin, coming from families without any formal education. They aspire to become medical doctors, university lecturers, government ministers, building contractors, civil servants, and lawyers—in the order of their occupational prestige ranking. Personality characteristics highly valued by them are hard work, honesty, intelligence, and courage; these are followed by success, respect for authority, higher education, and integrity. An analysis of the students' political attitudes reveals that the majority of them are highly alienated, the greatest source of alienation being citizen impotence. Their disillusionment was found to be much stronger in 1971 than in 1966. In their view, politics are run by a small group of notables who owe their positions of influence to personal connections and exclude any public participation. Most important characteristics of a good politician are, in their opinion, sympathy for common people and "leadership capabilities." Tribal and regional origins are roundly rejected, indicating a clear tendency to universalistic values. On the whole they tend to be pro-democratic, which includes a tendency to favor a democratic one-party system. The civil war, however, seems to have led to a decrease in attachment to democratic values. They see the country's main political problems vested in (1) the irresponsibility and corruption of politicians; (2) the illiteracy and ignorance of the masses; and (3) the existence of an irreconcilable cultural conflict. Factors such as modernization or class conflict are dismissed as possible determinants of political dilemmas. The main determinant of student reactions seems to be their class position as an aspirant elite, not ideological orientations in politics or economics. The students appear to be a highly visible interest group that is yet unabsorbed by the establishment. While they were welcomed by politicians as freedom fighters in the pre-independence era, a new attitude has been emerging toward students: they are being considered as a political threat—opposition to be crushed. Students pose a personal threat to personal power, not an ideological threat. They are not revolutionaries, and there is no evidence that some major political or economic or even educational reform may be instigated by them. In the future, student nationalism is likely to grow—not as an expression of new political, social, or economic ideas, but as a consequence of consolidating class interests among an aspirant elite.

Social change and economic development do not occur in a political vacuum. Our last section, therefore, deals with the political framework. In "Seeds of Radicalism among an Aspirant Elite," it was pointed out that economically based class interest is the strongest determinant of political attitudes and actions among university students. Philip V. White places this issue in a broader setting, examining the changing economics of class interests as a basis of changes in politics and relating these internal shifts to Nigerian foreign policy. In a historical approach, "Nigerian Politics: Class Alliances and Foreign Alignment," he presents a picture of Nigerian politics dominated by the interests of wealth and power rather than ethnicity. These interests determine new class alliances, which in turn lead to new trends in the pattern of foreign alignment. White considers Nigeria more truly nonaligned now than before the civil war, arguing that her orientation toward the West is now being balanced off by her ties with the Soviet Union and other socialist states. However, one can just as well suggest that Nigeria is now in a phase of dual alignment. It appears to be not unlikely that socialist influences will have an impact in Nigeria not only on the pattern and speed of economic development but also on the direction of social change—in ways that are much more complex than any naive ideologues may imagine. As an example one may think of the nationalization of the oil industry, and the subsequent movements into the new top positions that would be open to Nigerians.

George Obiozor, in "Soviet Involvement in the Nigerian Civil War," takes a more concerned and accordingly less calm position toward these changes. What enrages him is the pragmatic but amoral carpet-crossing of the Soviet Union, which was first a proponent of the progressive forces to which the Ibo belonged, then of the reactionaries, including the emirs and the military bureaucracy. However, when infuriated by the Soviet Union's "shameless inconsistency" that "leaves little room for confidence or predictability," he may at least be reminded of Marion J. Levy's fourth law: "In wickedness there is a strong strain toward rationality. . . . Good intentions randomize behavior."

In "Mass Communications in Nigeria," Alfred E. Opubor presents a comprehensive view of Nigeria's mass media—the press, radio, television, film, "high" and "low" literature, and folk operas and dramas—both in the English language and in Nigerian languages. So far the mass media have catered mainly to the urban elites, mostly ignoring the masses. Hence an increase in the quantity of media has usually not been accompanied by an increase in access. Certain government practices—e.g., imposing import duties on radios—have tended to support this limitation of access. Even though the media themselves have grown considerably, they have contributed very little to economic development, and they are hardly being systematically used as agents of change.

A few conclusions emerge. In most cases the Nigerian people themselves are very open to change. They are eager to undergo a new education, migrate to cities for jobs, and adapt quickly to city life and wage labor. Indigenous cities and indigenous organizations, such as cooperatives, have demonstrated considerable vigor when coming into contact with the new modernizing economy. Individual adaptability appears to be astonishingly unproblematical. However, the more problematical is the adaptability of modern institutions—be it that of regional or national governments, cooperative bureaucracies, trade unions, the educational system, or the mass media—in all aspects they appear to be out of step with the requirements of economic development. We strongly agree with Clark Kerr who has said: "The real problem is not the adaptability of man, which is almost infinitely greater than we once supposed, but the suitability of institutions and their politics. The contact of civilizations, the traditional and the industrial, can be managed well or managed badly. The social management of this contact, not the adjustability of individual man, is the heart of the matter. . . . [it] can vastly affect both the liberty and the welfare of the new industrial man."*

Development has only a chance of speeding up by making develop-ment from below its maxim. It has to start at the grass-roots level supplementing and at the same time reforming development from above.

H. Dieter Seibel
Ukandi G. Damachi

---

*Clark Kerr, "Changing Social Structures," in Wilbert E. Moore and Arnold S. Feldman, eds., Labor Commitment and Social Change in Developing Areas (New York: Social Science Research Council; 1960), p. 359.

SOCIAL ASPECTS
OF ECONOMIC
DEVELOPMENT

1

THE PROCESS
OF ADAPTATION
TO WAGE LABOR
H. Dieter Seibel

A cursory look through the literature, conversations at cocktail
parties in Africa, and more serious types of investigations legitimized
by the use of prestructured questionnaires reveal that there are some
widespread stereotypes about African workers. One crucial ster-
eotype, very similar in fact to beliefs held about workers in countries
that started to modernize some one or two centuries before Nigeria,
maintains that African workers are neither capable of adapting nor
willing to adapt fully to industrial labor within reasonable time. It is
believed, for example, that workers work only for money and that they
have no interest at all into their work as such. As a consequence it
is assumed that labor turnover has been high. In addition, interest
in modern work is supposedly limited to white-collar jobs.

These opinions are in fact not entirely wrong; they do characterize an early stage of adaptation to wage labor. But it is certainly
wrong to assume that they are an expression of an "African mentality."

These stereotypes are not without social consequences. If
management believes that workers will not adapt, that they do not like
their jobs, that they are not able to assume responsibilities, and that
they are not able to understand what goes on in the production process,
then these beliefs may turn out to be self-fulfilling prophecies; i.e.,
the prediction tends to bring about the predicted event. According to
its assumptions, management does not teach the workers to understand
the process of production and does not give them any opportunity to
take up responsibilities. Hence workers cannot learn any of these,
which eventually may result in the predicted situation. An accurate
analysis of the process of adaptation to wage labor and its stages is
therefore not only of theoretical value but also of practical concern.

The following analysis is based on published sources and on an
interview study of a random sample of 509 blue-collar workers in

ten companies in Ibadan and Lagos in 1963-64. Three indicators have been chosen in terms of which the process of adaptation will be analyzed: (1) attitudes to work, (2) labor turnover, and (3) occupational prestige.

ATTITUDES TO WORK

Attitudes to work is the first and probably most important factor influencing worker adaptation to labor and being influenced in turn by the adaptation process. Such attitudes are of crucial relevance even before wage employment is taken up for the first time, for they are likely to influence migrations to employment sites in a positive or negative manner. They are expressed in the reasons given for taking up wage employment, although of course there may be some discrepancy between the actual reasons that led to the decision to take up a paid job and the reasons given ex post facto.

Changes in Attitude

Over the last two or three generations, the underlying attitudinal structure has changed considerably. Four stages of change are discernible.

First Stage

In the first stage the colonial administration needed cheap unskilled labor in the primary sector of the economy; i.e., in mines and plantations. As the products were to be exported, roads and railways had to be constructed—a second area where unskilled labor was used. As people were fully integrated into their traditional socioeconomic system, there was, from their perspective, nothing to be gained from being hired by these intruding white men. Thus it turned out to be extremely difficult for the colonial administration to find wage laborers. Hence labor was recruited by force—sometimes through very subtle, sometimes through overt, forms of coercion.

A second technique of recruitment had very similar results. At roughly that time the colonial administration started to introduce taxes to be paid in cash. This was nothing new in principle for many societies, as they had been paying taxes before—in kind, in labor, in cowry shells, or in other forms of primitive money. But as the new law required them to pay taxes in British money, one of the very few ways of obtaining the needed money was through wage labor. Taxes thus had an effect very similar to labor recruitment by force. As a matter

4

of fact, instances have been reported where taxes were introduced solely to induce people to work for money.

Hence the typical pattern of this first stage was involuntary work or work for motives entirely external to the job. Very little adaptation took place, and workers returned to their home village as soon as they could.

Second Stage

The second stage was marked by a new motive for working and for staying in town or at some other employment site: work for bride wealth, the first genuinely voluntary motive. It is customary in African societies to work for a prospective father-in-law—in some ethnic groups for as long as seven years. When young men started to be sent to town to earn money for taxes, they experienced a "comparative disadvantage" as they could not work on their father-in-law's farms like those who stayed home. However, as some kind of bride wealth was usually given in addition to labor services, a solution was quickly found: money was substituted for work. Both parties found this advantageous—the young men liked it because it took much less time to earn the money than to do the farm work; the in-laws found it advantageous because it allowed them to satisfy some of their newly arising needs and wants, such as the need to buy some imported commodities or a zinc roof to replace the old thatch roof.

Third Stage

As part of the wages have to be consumed in town, workers have to stay there beyond the point in time where the amount of wages equals the amount of money needed for taxes and bride wealth. And as needs and wants increase and prices rise, the period spent in town has to be extended further and further. Thus a third stage is gradually developing through prolonged and intensified contact with modern money, modern commodities, and the amenities of city life.

The structure of needs and wants changes—first in the city and then in the rural areas. Tax and bride price are no longer the only motives for wage labor. They are supplemented and eventually replaced by motives that aim at the purchase of certain goods, such as bicycles, radios, and clothing. The first two stages may be called phases of specific target work, the targets being few and well-defined. The third stage is a phase of diffuse target work, the targets being many and variegated in composition.

When the worker has earned enough money for tax, bride price, and a variety of objects for himself and his relatives, he usually returns home to his family. But workers usually stay only for a short while until they find themselves in need of some other objects or until they get bored by village life. Toward the end of this third stage, the periods of staying at home become increasingly shorter and more infrequent. This trend is then reinforced by the fact that it becomes customary to take one's wife and eventually also one's children to town and start settling down there.

In this context an issue may be discussed that has found much attention in economic literature on development. In the first and second stages of adaptation, people are target workers accumulating a specific amount of money for certain purposes. If wages are increased, the target amount is earned in a shorter period, and workers leave their jobs sooner than before. Thus what is meant to be an incentive to increase the duration of employment actually works in reverse order. However the likelihood that employment periods are shortened because wages have gone up decreases considerably in the third stage and is negligible in the fourth stage, as needs and wants have increased to the extent that their satisfaction is anyway far beyond actual means.

Fourth Stage

Finally, in the fourth stage, needs and wants develop to a degree where a more or less permanent stay in town becomes necessary. Wage labor becomes fully integrated into the normal life of the African worker. For a great many Africans, wage labor has replaced agricultural or craft work carried out on an extended family basis. Wage labor has become a socially recognized section of life. It is regarded as a substitute for life and work in village, not only among people in town but also among villagers. Three quarters of the people the author interviewed in five villages in southern Nigeria expressed positive attitudes to migration to cities. For many, wage labor is not only a means of earning one's living but has become an end in itself.

Positive, Neutral, and Negative Attitudes

In this fourth stage the motivational structure has become most complex. This is indicated by the mere fact that the 509 workers interviewed in southern Nigeria gave about 1,700 answers when asked why they worked. These answers were summarized in the questionnaire in approximately 40 groups.[1] The stage where people worked for taxes or bride wealth has passed; in fact bride price as a reason for work was not given at all, and tax was given only in two instances.

Attitudes to work are not only motivationally complex but also tend to be positive. The workers' attitude to their present job is as follows: positive, 63 percent of all the interviewees; neutral, 19 percent; and negative, 18 percent.

The main reasons given for a positive attitude to work are to learn something new, to gain experience, and to have a technical job; these reasons amount to 40 percent of positive answers given. This means that the opportunity of learning something by experience at the work place is a most important factor influencing the worker's attitude toward his work and employer.

Other aspects of the study strongly indicate that the workers also act according to this attitude. For instance 42 percent of the workers are enrolled in evening classes or correspondence courses, with more than half of these courses being of a technical nature. The workers spend nearly 10 percent of their wages on course fees—a considerable financial burden for people at relatively low wage levels. It may be surprising to find such a strong and deep interest in one's work among Africans (the relationship of European workers to their work in the 19th century was much more alienated). Only 13 percent give "earning money" as a reason for a positive attitude to work. This shows again of what little importance money is as an incentive to work (it becomes only important if one does not have it). A total of 12 percent of the workers state they would like any job—a consequence of the unemployment problem in Nigeria; as it is very hard to find another job, workers adapt to that no-choice type of situation. A total of 6 percent indicate they regard their job as an opportunity for advancement and promotion. Further reasons given for a positive attitude are good labor conditions, security, and good treatment of workers.

If it is right that the ideal worker considers his work as an end in itself, these workers come quite near to the ideal: their main reason for a positive attitude to work is that they are interested in the job.

This result is indirectly confirmed by the reasons given for negative attitudes to work. More than half the complaints are related to low wages: the workers simply cannot manage to live on them, particularly when they have families. Bad working conditions—which is understood to refer to a lack of security and of social services—are the second-most common cause of complaints. There are companies where all workers are "daily paid" (meaning they may be dismissed without notice, are given no vacation, etc.), even though some of them have worked at the same place for as long as ten years.

Most of the reasons given do not reveal a negative attitude to work in general. Rather, they represent real grievances about conditions of work that are far from humane.

7

LABOR TURNOVER

A second indicator of adaptation to work is labor turnover, or labor mobility. Turnover is often said to be so high in Africa that it seriously interferes with the production process. High turnover is actually related to the first and second stages of adaptation—stages that Nigeria and most other African countries have left behind. The type of labor needed during the early stages (in mines, plantations, road and railway construction) is mainly unskilled; frequently—particularly in any type of construction—workers are given only limited contracts and are dismissed after their contracts have expired. In some countries (South Africa, for instance), this is even today an explicit policy to prevent the workers from becoming permanent city dwellers. This policy was much more widespread during the early period of industrialization. During these early stages, though, workers are not really interested in staying permanently in town. They do not in any way sever their family ties, working in town being considered as a short, transitory period. However, as workers adapt to town life in general and industrial labor in particular, wage labor becomes an economic necessity for them and becomes fully integrated into their lives. This explains why labor mobility has been drastically reduced in virtually all African countries. On the average the 509 workers in southern Nigeria have stayed at their present place of work for approximately 1.7 years. This mean is so low because most of the companies in which the study was conducted opened up within the last two years (this shows how easily statistics can be misinterpreted whenever no detailed knowledge of a situation is available). On the average, every worker has had 1.5 previous occupations. If they are taken into account, the mean employment period goes up to 3.2 years. More exact knowledge about turnover, however, can only be gained if the figures are broken down by age groups. Among the workers below eighteen years of age, the mean employment duration per job is 0.9 years; this number increases with age up to 6.2 years among those above forty five years of age. One has further to take into consideration that the majority of jobs were not voluntarily left by the worker but were terminated by the employer—usually because of end of contract. This indicates that any tables about labor turnover have to be read very carefully if any conclusions are to be drawn about underlying motives and attitudes; such tables do not allow for any direct inferences. Particularly in an economy where construction companies employ a high proportion of labor, turnover tends to be statistically high—not because of the workers' habits of leaving their jobs but because of the companies' habits of dismissing workers at the end of their contract.

It has to emphasized that labor turnover is no problem for companies in southern Nigeria. In those few cases where it is a problem,
this should give rise to a thorough revision of the company's policies
toward workers. For it is much more likely that there is something
wrong with these policies than with the workers.

OCCUPATIONAL PRESTIGE

A third indicator of adaptation to wage labor is occupational
prestige. According to conventional wisdom about Africa, white-collar
jobs have the highest prestige everywhere in Africa, while manual and
technical jobs are generally rejected. This, though, is true for the
situation that prevailed many decades ago. In this past stage the high
prestige of white-collar jobs was really in harmony with the economic
structure, when senior work could be found only in government and
administration, when strong incentives were needed to attract people
for positions in the bureaucracy, and when industry provided only
unskilled jobs for Africans. But it has to be strongly emphasized that
even this expresses a tremendous change—the change from a traditional society where white-collar jobs were nonexistent and accordingly
had no prestige. Today, as the structure of the economy has changed
and the number of technical and other jobs in industry has greatly
increased, occupational prestige has changed accordingly. In rural
areas where changes usually occur later than in towns, the old attitudes
still prevail. Out of 182 people interviewed in five villages in southern
Nigeria (in the former Western, Midwestern, and Eastern regions),
42 percent wish their sons to take up nontechnical academic jobs and
38 percent favor other white-collar jobs—a total of 80 percent. Only
10 percent give technical or craft jobs as their choice.
Occupational prestige as expressed in these preferences by
villagers is related to the first stage of adaptation. The workers have
left this stage behind. For themselves 47 percent prefer a technical
job; only 11 percent favor a white-collar job. A total of 18 percent
want to become independent and to establish a business or trade of
their own. This could be interpreted as an indication of latent
entrepreneurial initiative.
However, as these preferences may be determined to some
extent by the probability of getting access to these jobs, a more accurate picture of occupational prestige emerges when the workers are
asked which jobs they prefer for their sons. By answering this
question, practical aspects such as whether or not their sons have a
chance of achieving the goals set by their parents, are not being
considered. A total of 68 percent of the workers want their sons to
become engineers, technicians, or mechanics, and 2 percent give

9

preference to workers or craftsmen—altogether 70 percent. And 28 percent would like their sons to become medical doctors—a profession that has had a high prestige from the beginning of changes in the occupational prestige structure. Only 8 percent want their sons to become clerks or civil servants.* This is almost a reversal of the occupational prestige rankings found in the villages.

On the whole it appears that occupational prestige has adapted well to the changing economic and occupational structure. By no means can it be seen as an impediment to to further adaptation to a changing economy in general and wage labor in particular.

OVERADAPTATION

Southern Nigeria and other parts of Africa are presently experiencing not a problem of adaptation but rather a problem of over-adaptation. There is an overwhelming thirst for general education as well as for further technical training, a striving for occupational advancement, and a rush into any type of modern occupation. This is now presenting serious problems in that many more people are being educated and trained than can find jobs. As a consequence there is hardly any African city without major unemployment. The problem of the unemployed school leaver is looming larger and larger everyday. The extent of adaptation has far exceeded the economy's need for adaptation. This has had severe repercussions in the rural areas where production has not been very progressive; in some cases, production has even gone down as a consequence of the rural exodus.

Urban overadaptation is matched by rural maladaptation. This will remain Africa's number one economic problem as long as agricultural production has not been thoroughly reformed. There are two social institutions that are crucial in determining the process of adaptation to modern agriculture: rural education and rural cooperatives. Both have to be revolutionized as a prerequisite for agricultural adaptation among farmers and rural youth.

NOTE

1. Hans Dieter Seibel, Industriearbeit und Kulturwandel in Nigeria (Köln & Opladen: Westdeutscher Verlag, 1968).

---

*The total exceeds 100 percent because the number of answers exceeds the number of respondents.

2

THE EARLY
HISTORICAL EVIDENCE
OF YORUBA URBANISM
William Bascom

In this author's 1955 paper entitled "Urbanization among the Yoruba"[1] the historical documentation of the existence of Yoruba cities prior to European contact was summarized in two brief paragraphs. It is expanded here both to substantiate the statement that Yoruba cities existed prior to European penetration and to bring together what was known of the Yoruba people before 1825.

The first issue is whether or not urbanism was a traditional part of the way of life of a nonliterate, nonindustrialized people, who in 1952 had a city of half a million inhabitants and an index of urbanization exceeding that of France and most European countries. An attempt is also made to answer the question of whether or not these cities developed as defensive centers as the result of warfare.

The materials examined cover the period prior to the exploration of Yoruba territory in 1825, and consist largely of reports from Benin to the east and Dahomey to the west. Understandably estimates of size are lacking, but Yoruba cities are mentioned as early as 450 years ago. Before the exploration of the interior began, several Yoruba subgroups were known, including the Oyo or Yoruba proper, the Ijebu, the Ketu, the Nago, and possibly the Ife, the Ondo, and the Ifonyin.

Yoruba territory remained terra incognita until Clapperton and Lander's expedition in 1825, although Abomey, the capital of Dahomey, had been known for a century, and the powerful city of Benin for more than three centuries. From 1724 to 1726 Bulfinch Lambe, a British trader, was held captive in Abomey, and in 1793 Dalzel described the road from the coast to Abomey as "perhaps the most beaten track, by Europeans, of any in Africa." Benin had been visited by the Portuguese in 1485:

For at the time of Diogo Cam's first return from Congo,
in the year fourteen hundred and eighty six, this king of
Beny (Benin) also sent to solicit the King (D. João III of
Portugal) to despatch thither priests who might instruct
him in the Faith. This country had already been visited in
the previous year by Fernão do Po, who had discovered
this coast and also an island near the land, now known by
his name. . . . This emissary of the king of Beny came
with João Affonso d'Aveiro, who had been sent to explore
this coast by the King, and who brought back the first pep-
per from these parts of Guinea to the Kingdom. . . .

Among the many things which the King D. João learnt
from the ambassador of the king of Beny, and also from
João Affonso d'Aveiro, of what they had been told by the
inhabitants of these regions, was that to the east of Beny at
twenty moons' journey—which according to their account,
and the short journeys they make, would be about two hundred and fifty of our leagues—there lived the most powerful
monarch of these parts, who was called Ogané. Among the
pagan chiefs of the territories of Beny he was held in as
great veneration as is the Supreme Pontif with us. In accordance with a very ancient custom, the king of Beny, on
ascending the throne, sends ambassadors to him with rich
gifts to announce that by the decease of his predecessor he
has succeeded to the kingdom of Beny, and to request confirmation. To signify his assent, the prince Ogané sends
the king a staff and a headpiece of shining brass, fashioned
like a Spanish helmet, in place of a crown and sceptre. He
also sends a cross, likewise of brass, to be worn round the
neck, a holy and religious emblem similar to that worn by
the Commendadores of the Order of Saint John. Without
these emblems the people do not recognize him as lawful
ruler, nor can he call himself truly king. All the time this
ambassador is at the court of Ogané, he never sees the
prince, but only the curtains of silk behind which he sits,
for he is regarded as sacred. When the ambassador is
leaving, he is shown a foot below the curtains as a sign that
the prince is within and agrees to the matters that he has
raised; this foot they reverence as though it were a sacred
relic. As a kind of reward for the hardships of such a
journey the ambassador receives a small cross, similar to
that sent to the king, which is thrown round his neck to
signify that he is free and exempt from all servitudes, and
privileged in this native country, as the Commendadores
are with us. I myself knew this, but in order to be able to

write it with authority, (although the King D. João in his time had also enquired well into it) when in the year fifteen hundred and forty certain ambassadors of the king of Beny came to this Kingdom (Portugal), among whom was a man about seventy years of age who was wearing one of these crosses, I asked him the reason, and he gave an explanation similar to the above. And as in the time of the King, D. João, whenever India was spoken of, reference was made to a very powerful king called Preste João (Prester John) of the Indies, who was reputed to be a Christian, it seemed therefore to the King that it might be possible to enter India by way of this kingdom. . . . Wherefore the King and his cosmographers, taking into consideration Ptolmey's general map of Africa, the Padrões on the coast which had been set up by his discoverers, and also the distance of two hundred and fifty leagues to the east where according to the people of Beny the country of prince Ogané lay, concluded that he must be the Preste João, for both were hidden behind curtains of silk and held the emblem of the cross in great veneration. And it also appeared to him that if his ships continued along the coast they had discovered, they could not fail to reach the land where the promontory Praso was, that is, the limit of that country. Therefore taking into consideration all these facts which increased his ardour for the design of discovering India, he determined to send immediately in the year 1486 both ships by sea and men by land in order to get to the root of this matter which inspired so much hope in him.[2]

In 1486 Antonio de Lisboa was sent to find a way to India by land, but he returned after having reached Jerusalem; in the same year Bartholomew Dias set sail, passing the Cape of Good Hope in 1487. In 1487 Pedro de Covilham and Afonso de Payva set out by way of the Mediterranean and Egypt, eventually reaching India and Abyssinia,[3] and in 1498 the sea route to India was discovered. The search for Prester John was ended without establishing the identity of Ogané (Hooguanee, as he is called by Pacheco Pereira): "A hundred leagues to the east of this kingdom of Beny in the interior we know of a land which in our time has a king called Licosaguou; he is said to be the lord of many peoples and very powerful. Close by is another great lord of the name of Hooguanee, who among the negroes is as the Pope among us."[4]

Disregarding east and west, which in fact are often confused and internally inconsistent in the early records, Talbot[5] identifies Licosaguou as the King, or Alafin, of Oyo; the evidence for this is the Alafin's power, the size of his kingdom, and his proximity to the King, or Oni, of Ife, whom, with greater reason, Talbot identifies as Hooguanee. As Talbot writes, "There is little doubt that by Ogane the Bini meant the Awni (Oni) of Ife, or Awgenni (Ogeni) of Ufe, as they termed him, whose suzerainty is still acknowledged at this time."[6] This is confirmed by Bradbury, who notes the use of "Ogana n'Uha, the Edo name for the Oni of Ife" in Benin. Benin and Yoruba traditions agree that the Benin dynasty derived from Ife, and that it was only because of the distance involved that the King of Benin in later times was not required to send to Ife for confirmation of his coronation. References to the Oni of Ife as "the spiritual head of the Yoruba people" are common in the literature of the twentieth century, as are comparisons of his position to that of the Pope.

Talbot notes that Portuguese maps (c. 1500) show the Ciudade de Jabu, which is Ijebu-Ode, the capital of the Ijebu or 'Jebu Yoruba.[7] The city is mentioned again as the "very large city called Geebuu, surrounded by a great moat" by Pacheco Pereira, whose work, first published in 1892, was written in 1505-08 (although the portion cited below was written in 1507-08). Although Kimble mistakenly identifies Geebu with Abeokuta, 36 miles up the Ogun River, Geebu clearly refers to Ijebu-Ode, which lies somewhat inland from the lagoon north of a point some 30-35 miles east of the lagoon entrance. This identification is confirmed beyond question by later reports and maps, while Abeokuta was not founded until the nineteenth century. Describing the entrance to the Rio do Laguo (the lagoon at Lagos), Pacheco Pereira states:

> The channel has two fathoms at high tide, but its entrance is very dangerous, with shallows of sand on which the sea breaks during the greater part of the year, so that the channel is scarcely seen; only small vessels of thirty to thirty-five tons can enter it. Once inside the mouth it broadens out into a great lake over two leagues wide and as many long. Twelve or thirteen leagues up this river is a very large city called Geebuu, surrounded by a great moat. The river of this country in our time is called Agusale, and the trade is mainly in slaves (who are sold for twelve or fifteen brass bracelets each) but there is some ivory. . . .
>
> Rio do Laguo and Rio Primeiro lie W by N and E by S and occupy twenty-five leagues of the route. Rio Primeiro has a fairly wide mouth half a league across, with a dense wood on its SE side. Four leagues beyond this river are three canals, and the coast of these canals along the sea to Rio Primeiro is all mud, there being no

sand. This country yields no trade or profit. The whole
of the territory from the aforesaid Rio do Laguo to this
Rio Primeiro and for more than 100 leagues beyond is
intersected by many other rivers, so that it is cut into
islands. It is greatly subject to fever and is very hot
throughout nearly the whole of the year, because it is so
near the orb of the sun; the principal winter season falls
in the months of August and September, when there is
much rain. The negroes of this country are idolators and
are circumcised without having any law or reason for their
circumcision, but as these matters are irrelevant we will
not write of them.[8]

Although trade in slaves is mentioned, the export of slaves
from this region to the Americas could hardly have begun by 1508;
and although the surrounding moat was probably built for defensive
purposes, the intertribal wars could not yet have reached the proportions of the slave war period, when they were intensified by
increasing demands for slaves, rising prices, and supplies of gun-
powder and firearms. It is clear that Ijebu-Ode and other ancient
Yoruba cities did not develop as the result of the slave wars. There
is no reason for concluding that Yoruba urbanism was the result of
warfare, and no reason to hope that its causes can ever be determined
from historical documents. On the other hand, Ijebu-Ode, Oyo, Ife,
and Ketu were capitals of independent kingdoms, and important as
governmental and ritual headquarters.
In 1604 "D. R.," whom Naber identifies as Dierick Ruyters,
described the town of Jabu as surrounded with a wooden wall, and
located thirteen leagues eastward of Kuramo (Lagos) on the west side
of the entrance of the River Palmer.[9]
A small lagoon in the Victoria Beach area of Lagos, connecting
with Five Cowrie Creek, is still known as the Kuramo Waters. The
River Palmar (Palmer, or Agusale) appears to be the River Ona,
which flows southward into the lagoon from Ijebu territory. The
River Primeiro (or Primero) may be the River Siluko (Mahin), which
marks the boundary between the Yoruba and Benin, but on later maps
it appears to be the River Oni that flows into the lagoon and that is
still recognized by the Yoruba as the boundary between Ijebu and
Ondo territory.
In 1623 Dierick Ruyters described Iabum as ten miles up the
River Lagoa (the lagoon): "Jn dit landtschap van Arda [Allada, in
southern Dahomey] is gheleghen de Riviere van Lagoa: al waer veel
Olyfants-Tanden vallen: 10. mylen de Rivier op, aen een plaetse
ghenaemt Iabum; die verhandelt werden voor Slesigher Lijwaet,
ghebranden Wijn, Blaeuw, Geel, ende Root Laken, Naems-yser, veel

15

sorteringe van cralen, veel Neurenburgerye bylen en messen, copre
ende tinne armringen."10

In 1627 Alonso de Sandoval wrote: "A ocho o nueve leguas
adelante de estos ardas [Allada] está el río de Lago, en donde no
puede entrar embaracación, que pase de treinta toneladas: por él
se va a una población grande, que llaman Iabu, cercada de foso.
Veinticinco leguas adelante se da en el río llamado Primero."11

Sandoval makes the earliest known reference to the "Lucumies,"
who, under various spellings, are frequently mentioned for over a
hundred years following Sandoval. As Sandoval works: "A un lado
de estos ardas están situados, la tierra adentro, los lucumies, gente
de gran fidelidad, así para las guerras (cuando sus vecinos se quieren
ayudar de ellos) como para el servicio de sus amos, que los cautivan."12
Talbot identifies the Ulkami as Oyo, and they probably are a subgroup
of the Yoruba or perhaps the Nupe, both of whom are known in the
New World as Lucumi.13

Two maps in Dapper's compilation (1668) place Ulcuma (or
Ulcumi) east of the River Curamo (Ogun), just north of Lago de
Curamo (the Lagos lagoon). The mighty Kingdom of Ulkami (or
Ulkuma) stretches eastward of Arder, between the kingdoms of Arder
and Benijn (Benin), but does not reach the coast.14 The people of
Arder have little respect for their mother tongue, which they seldom
speak; but they esteem most Alkomijs, which is held to be a noble
language.15 Every four days a free market is held at the town of Ba,
mostly in salt, which is brought from Jojo in great quantities by
canoes, and taken to the territory of Ulkuma in trade.16 Many slaves
are brought to Little Arder from Ulkami (or Ulkuma), where boys
are circumcised and where girls are excised by being bitten by ants.17

Dapper says that Benijn (Benin) borders in the northwest on
Ulkami, Jaboe, Isago and Oedobo, in the north on Gaboe, in the east
on Istanna and Forkado or Ouwerre, and in the south on the sea.18
These directions are misleading, as the coastline here runs southeast
and more south than east. Jaboe, Oedobo, and Isago are tributaries
to kingdoms in the west; Isago, rich in horses, was the most power-
ful.19 Jaboe is again probably Ijebu, as Talbot notes,20 but while he
suggests that Oedobo, Oedebo, Odobo, or Udobo may be the Sobo or
Uzobo (Urhobo), who live south of Benin, it may refer to the Yoruba
city and kingdom of Ondo—a possibility supported by later maps.
Isago may be the Etsako, or perhaps the Kukuruku as a whole, who
live northeast of Benin, bordering on the Yoruba kingdom of Owo,
the Igbira, and the Niger River.

The Bagoe, described as living eight days up the Benin River
from Benin city,21 may be the Jaboe (Ijebu) again, or possibly the
Aboh, an Ibo group, as Talbot says.22 The Istanna may be the Ishan,
who live east of Benin, south of the Kukuruku. The Kingdom of

Ouwerre (or Forkado) clearly refers to the Itsekiri, who also call themselves Iwere and are commonly referred to as the Warri. The Rio Forkado is clearly the Forcados River, but the town of Ouwerre, which is described as about 27 miles up this river,[23] is probably not the new town of Warri, but the nearby traditional capital, Ode Itsekiri. According to Dapper, Istanna and Forkado were tributary to Benijn, as well as Jaboe, Isago, and Oedobo. Dapper's work was translated into German (1670) and French (1685), and the material cited was repeated by Ogilby (1670), de la Croix (1688), and Barbot (1732).

Bosman (1705), who visited Fida (Whydah) in 1698 and 1699, wrote:

> The King of Great Ardra with all his dependant Countries, is twenty times as strong as he of Fida, and yet hath not the Courage to make War against him, tho' they live in perpetual Enmity.
>
> Farther In-land are yet more potent Kingdoms than this; but I know nothing, or at most but very little of them; except that while I was here one of their Ambassadors came to the King of Great Ardra, to advertise him from his Master, That several Ardrasian Negroes had been with, and made Complaints to him: And to advise him to take Care that his Viceroys treated these poor Men more gently; or else much against his Will, he should be obliged to come to their Assistance, and take them into his Protection.
>
> The King of Great Ardra, instead of making a proper use of this wholsome Advice, Laughed at it, and in farther despight to that King, Murthered his Ambassador; upon which he was so violently as well as justly Enraged, that with utmost Expedition he caused an Army (by the Fidasians augmented to the number of Ten Hundred Thousand Men) to fall into their Country; and these being all Horsed and a warlike Nation, in a short time Mastered half the King of Ardra's Territories, and made such a Slaughter amongst his Subjects, that the Number of the Dead being innumerable, was commonly express'd by saying they were like the Grains of Corn in the Field. . . .
>
> This Nation strikes such a Terror into all the circumjacent Negroes, that they can scarce hear them mentioned without Trembling.[24]

Although Burton and Herskovits identify these invaders as Dahomeans, Talbot, Parrinder, and earlier writers as well, identify them as Oyo or Ulkami, with Snelgrave and Dalzel pointing out that

Dahomey had few if any horses and no cavalry.[25] Dalzel says that Eyeo (Oyo) "seems to have been the first inland nation in this part of Africa, of which the Europeans had any intimation. Bosman speaks of an invasion of Ardra, in 1698, by a potent inland people, which could, from his description, be no other than the Eyeos."[26]

Barbot's work, based on two visits in 1678 and 1682, refers to this incursion of Ardra:[27] "They are commonly beaten by the inland nations, assisted by auxiliaries from Fida; sometimes bringing down an army of several hundred thousand men, most of them cavalry, and a warlike people, who now and then overrun one half of the kingdom of Ardra, making a mighty slaughter of men, and commit all manner of outrages and devastations. That remote inland nation, which I suppose to be the Oyeos (Oyo) and Ulkami, strikes such a terrour at Ardra, and all the adjacent countries, that they can scarce hear them mentioned without trembling."[28] "The Ardrasians do so little value their own, that they rather use the Ulkami language; which they are studious to learn, as being in their opinion far more elegant and sweet."[29]

Ardra reaches "to the kingdom of Ulkamy on the north, which is under ten degrees of north latitude.* Ulkamy, according to a very modern author, borders northward on the country of Lamtem, which reaches the same way to the kingdom of Guber (Gobir), and that again to the Sigismes lake, or the Niger."[30]

Some authorities, Barbot states, will have Ardra reach "to Oyeo, a large populous country, and to other potent kingdoms situated towards the Niger."[31]

Fida can supply 1,000 slaves a month, brought to the coast from about 200 leagues inland; "among the many slaves we carry thence to America, there are many of the Oyeo and Benin Blacks, implacable enemies to those of Ardra."[32] Barbot repeats Dapper's account of the Kingdom of Ulkamy and its circumcision, and, with some discrepancies, Dapper's information on Jaboe, Isago, and Oedobo. Benin "borders to the northwest, on Alkomy, Jaboe, Isago, and Oedobo"[33]; yet the kingdoms of Jaboe and Oedoba join Benin on the northeast,[34] and it was the cavalry of Issabo, which borders on Benin at the west, which attacked Benin unsuccessfully.[35]

Barbot adds that "The Portuguese geographers place Ciudade du Jubu, or city of Jubu, several leagues inland" from the lagoon, which is known as Lagoas, Rio Lagos, or Lago de Curamo.[36] Talbot cites a Portuguese map printed in Amsterdam in 1700, showing the Cidade de Iubu.[37]

---

*Old Oyo was situated at latitude 9 degrees north. Bida, the Nope capital, is at about the same latitude.

In an account of a visit to Juda (Whydah) in early 1725, Labat describes the kingdom of Ardra (or Adres) as reaching from the Volta to the Benin rivers. Juda, Popo, and Cotto are subject to the King of Ardra, who is subject to the King of Benin, who in turn is subject to Biafara (Biafra). North of Ardra are the two small kingdoms of Fouin and Oulcoumi, and Dahoume or Dahoma (Dahomey), which is larger.[38] Among the slaves exported from Juda, Ardra, and Jaquin (Godome) are the Foin, Tebou ('Jebu?), Nago, and the warlike and hard-working Ayois (Oyo).[39] Nago is a term both for a western Yoruba group and for the Yoruba as a whole. Fuoin and Foin may refer to the Fon, another name for the Dahomeans, or to the Ifonyin, a western Yoruba group.

Labat's work contains a map by Sr. d'Anville dated 1729 with information that is not contained in the text but is apparently derived in part from Dapper's account.[40] Between "Ardra détruit par Dahomé" on the south and Dahomé on the north is the Kingdom of Fouin. "Les Ayos, Nation Guerriere dont le pays est fort eloigne, et qui on't fait une irruption dans les pays de Dahomé pour faire diversion" are placed to the northwest of Dahomé, rather than to the northeast where Oyo belongs. To the east of Fouin, about where the province of Abeokuta is today, is the Kingdom of Oulcoumi, with the town of Daroura on a river that may be the Ogun, flowing into the western end of Lac de Curamo (the Lagos lagoon). The town of Curamo (Lagos) is situated on an island at the west end of the lagoon. East of Oulcoumi and inland from Lac de Curamo is the Kingdom of Jabou, where Ijebu province is now located. To the east of Jabou and again inland, in Ondo province, is the Kingdom of Oudobo. The Kingdom of Isago lies to the east of Ondo, to the northwest and north of Benin, which is the area of the Yoruba kingdom of Owo. Rio Palmar flows southward into Lac de Curamo from Jabou, as Rio Primeiro does from the boundary between Jabou and Oudobo; from their locations these would seem to be the rivers Ona and Oni, the latter having marked the boundary between Ijebu and Ondo according to my Yoruba informants.

Another map based on d'Anville and Labat, dated 1743, is reproduced in Foa.[41] To the north of Ardra kingdom lie the kingdoms of Assem, Calmina, and Fouin. To the east of these, inland from the lagoon, lies the kingdom of Ayos (Oyo), with Oulcoumi kingdom to the north, Jebou kingdom to the east, and Bodagri (Badagry) kingdom to the southeast.

In 1727 Snelgrave visited Whidaw (Whydah), which Dahomey had destroyed less than a month before, and Jaqueen (Godome). In 1724 Dahomey had captured Ardra (Allada), taking Bulfinch Lambe a prisoner, but before their armies had returned home Dahomey was invaded by J-oe (Oyo) cavalry. Snelgrave learned that some princes from countries conquered by Dahomey had taken refuge in J-oe and had persuaded its king to

make War on the King of Dahomè, which he did soon after
the latter had conquered Ardra. The King of J-oe sent,
under the Command of a General, a great Army of Horse,
consisting of many Thousands, (for they never use Infantry)
wherewith he invaded the Dahomes in their own Country:
On this sudden and unexpected Invasion, the King of
Dahomè marched immediately from Ardra into his own
Kingdom, and made Head against the J-oes. But as he had
none but Infantry, whose Arms were Guns and Swords, he
was hard put to it: For the Country being open and without
Inclosures, the Horsemen, who were armed with Bows and
Arrows, Javelins and cutting Swords, had certainly con-
quer'd, if the unusual noise of the Dahome's Fire-Arms
had not so frightened the Horses, that their Riders could
never make a home-Charge on the Enemies Foot.[42]

The Dahomes routed the J-oe cavalry through a ruse, capturing
many horses. Snelgrave was told

That tho' the Dahomes were exceeding proud of this
Victory, they were still much afraid of a second Invasion,
an Army of Horses being very terrible to them: And that
the King had lately sent great Presents to the King of J-oe,
to prevent his attacking him a second time. However, in
case he did it, and they should not be able to withstand
them, they comforted themselves with this Thought, that
they might save their Persons, by flying to the Sea Coast,
to which the J-oes durst not follow them. For as their
national Fetiche was the Sea, they were prohibited by their
Priests from ever seeing it, under no less a Penalty than
Death; which they made the People believe, would by their
God, if they were so presumptuous, be inflicted on them.[43]

An account of this ruse and of the "fetiche" of the sea of "les
Ayos, nation très nombreuse, située au nord du royaume de Dahomet,
qui n'a de troupes que de la cavalerie" is repeated by Isert in a letter
written at Whydah in 1785.[44]

Visiting the war camp of the king of Dahomey in 1727, Snelgrave
saw two of the horses captured in this battle. He was told that "They
came from the Kingdom of J-oe; which lies towards the North-East,
many days Journey off, beyond a great and famous Lake, which is
the Fountain of several large Rivers, that empty themselves into the
Bay of Guinea."[45]

[In 1727] the King of Dahomè being desirous of the
Portuguese Gold, which they bring to purchase Negroes

with, his Majesty sent a great many Slaves down to
Whidaw, which made Trade dull with us at Jaqueen. For
tho' formerly great Numbers came to this place, from
other Nations now destroyed by the Dahomes, there remains at present only one Country called Lucamee, lying
towards the North-East, for the Jacqueens to trade to.
Which Nation, by means of a wide River, has escaped being
made a Conquest to the barbarous and cruel Dahomes.[46]

Snelgrave's map shows the kingdom of Ulcama (or Ulcami) southeast
of the Dahomey kingdom and north of the Lagos lagoon. North of
Ulcama is the kingdom of Guber (Gobir), north of which the River
Niger spreads into a large inland lake, "the great Lake of the I:oes
forded over in a dry season."

In 1730 Snelgrave returned to Jaqueen, where he learned that
sons of the King Weemcy (Weme or Oueme) who had "fled to a far
Inland Potent Nation called the J-oes" had succeeded in convincing
its king to send his army to avenge the execution of their father and
the destruction of Weemey by Dahomey in 1727.[47] "This Nation of
J-oe fight all on Horseback, and living a great way on the North
towards Nubia, they can at no other time march to the Southward, but
when the Season for Porage, and the dry Weather sets in. The King
of Dahomè had notice of their coming, a few days before they reached
his Country; and he having formerly experienced how terrible such
Numbers of Horse had been to his Army, which consists of none but
foot Soldiers; he resolved to bury his Riches, burn his Towns, and
then fly into the Woods and Thickets with his People."[48] The Dahomes
were besieged in the forest until the J-oe had to return home with
their horses before the beginning of the rains in the spring of 1729.[49]

Sometime after this the King of Dahomè considering he
should certainly be invaded again by the J-oes, as soon
as the Season permitted them to march, and dreading very
much their power, he sent Embassadors with large Presents to their King, together with one of his handsomest
Daughters. These were civilly received, and had the good
fortune to succeed in their Negotiations. For they so
gained some great Men about the King, by presenting them
with large pieces of Coral (which the J-oes esteem above
all things) that by their means an advantagious Peace was
obtained for their Master, and they were civilly dismissed
with handsome Rewards. For a Confirmation of the Peace,
the King of J-oe sent, a little while after, one of his Daughters to the King of Dahomè for a Wife; and she was received with great Joy by the King and his People.[50]

21

Pruneau de Pommegorge, director of the French fort at Whydah in 1763 and 1764, describes how the king of Dahomey had several times avoided payment of annual tribute to the king of the Ayeots (Oyo), to whom ten other kings were said to pay tribute [51]:

> Le peuple dahomet, dont il vient d'être parlé, malgré sa réputation de bravoure, a plusieurs fois été obligé, dans le temps même de sa plus grande prospérité, de fuir de son pays pendant trente ou quarante jours, lorsque son roi ne pouveit payer le tribut annuel à un autre roi beaucoup plus puissant que lui, qui se nomme le roi des ayeots et qui, dit-on, met cent mille hommes sur pied, et à qui dix autres rois paient aussi tribut. Il réside à cent cinquante ou à deux cens lieues dans les terres. Lorsque ses ambassadeurs viennent recevoir ce qui est dû à leur maître, s'il se trouve alors un blanc chez le roi des dahomets, on a grand soin qu'il ne puisse parler à ces ambassadeurs.
>
> Les ayeots ne font point de captifs, les prisonniers sont attachés à la queue de leurs chevaux avec lesquels ils galoppent jusqu'à ce qu'ils soient morts.
>
> Il est encore une autre nation, inconnue aux blancs, qui viennent chez le roi des dahomets: ce sont des marabous mahométans, d'un pays fort éloigné dans les terres, qui apportent des tapis de coton et soies fabriquées chez eux, qu'ils échangent contre d'autres marchandises. Ces négres paroissent beaucoup moins ignorans que tous ceux des bords de la mer; aussi nous ne connoissons que les nations qui avoisinent les dahomets. Ce sont les mailleys et les nagots qui sont sans cess pillés et vendus dans nos établissemens.[52]

Unfortunately there is no way of knowing whether the evasions of tribute occurred before 1763, in 1763-4, or afterwards—1764-89. The Nagots (Nago) are again a Yoruba group, while the Mailleys (or Malays, according to other writers) are Muslims, known in Yoruba as Male.

Norris, who visited Abomey in 1772, estimated its population at 24,000. He says:

> To the northeast of Dahomy lies a fine, fertile, and extensive country, inhabited by a great, and warlike people, called the Eyoes; the scourge and terror of all their neighbours. These Eyoes are governed by a king; but not by one so absolute as the tyrant of Dahomy. If what report says of him be true, when his ill conduct gives just offence

to his people, a deputation from them wait upon him, it is
said, and represent to him, that the burden of government
has been so fatiguing, that it is full time for him to repose
from his cares, and to indulge himself with a little sleep.
He thanks his people for their attention to his ease, retires
to his apartment as if to sleep, where he gives directions
to his women to strangle him; which is immediately exe-
cuted, and his son quietly succeeds him, upon the same
terms of holding the government no longer than his conduct
merits the approbation of his people.

    The Dahomans, to give an idea of the strength of an
Eyoe army, assert, that when they go to war, the general
spreads the hide of a buffaloe before the door of his tent,
and pitches a spear in the ground, on each side of it; between which the soldiers march, until the multitude, which
pass over the hide, have worn a hole through it; as soon
as this happens, he presumes that his forces are numerous
enough to take the field. The Dahomans may possibly
exaggerate, but the Eyoes are certainly a very populous,
warlike and powerful nation.

    They invaded Dahomy in 1738 with an irresistible
army, and laid the country waste with fire and sword to the
gates of Abomey; here the Foys had collected their whole
strength, and waited the arrival of the enemy, who were
advancing with an incredible multitude.53

The Foys (Fon), or Dahomans, evacuated Abomey, their capital,
after their king had fled to a secret hiding place near Zassa, accompanied by Mr. Gregory, governor of the English fort at Whydah. The
Eyoes remained in Dahomey, plundering and burning Abomey, Calmina,
Zassa, and the surrounding countryside until food became scarce.54

    The Eyoes continued for several years to harrass Dahomy
with an annual visit: the Foys never thought it prudent to
engage them afterwards; but when apprized of their coming,
used to evacuate their towns, divide into small parties, and
shelter themselves as well as they could in their fastnesses
and woods. The king used all his efforts to obtain an accomodation, and offered them any reasonable compensation
to refrain from hostilities; but it was difficult to satisfy
their demands. They claimed, in consequence of an old
treaty, an annual tribute; the payment of which had been
omitted in the prosperous days of King Trudo. These
arrears were considerable; and fresh demands were also
added, on account of the conquest of Whydah, which the

Eyoes looked upon as an inexhaustible source of wealth to
the king. Their expectations, upon the whole, were so
exorbitant that (King) Ahadee found it impracticable to
satisfy them; and the Eyoes continued to ravage the country for several years, burning their towns, destroying
their crops in harvest, killing many people, and carrying
numbers away into captivity. In the year 1747, however,
the Eyoes consented to an accomodation, and compromized
the matter for a tribute, which is paid them annually at
Calmina, in the month of November.[55]

Norris says that in 1788 the Eyos attacked the Mahees (Mahin)
and by May "had ravaged no less than fourteen districts; and, burning
and destroying multitudes of towns and villages, continued their
progress with such devastation and horror, that the tyrant of Dahomy
was not without violent apprehensions for his own safety."[56] Bordering
on the kingdom of Dahomey "are the Eyos or Eyoes on the eastern
side, between Dahomy and Benin; the Mahees, on the western; and
the Tappas, whose country lies contiguous to the Eyos."[57] Norris
believes that the Tappas (Nupe), who "drew a regular tribute from
the Eyos",[58] are Snelgrave's Yahoos or Tuffos,[59] but Tapa is the
Yoruba name for the Nupe, who border Yoruba territory to the north-
east.
    On Norris' map the Mahees are placed west and the Fouin
southwest of Abomey. The Ayoes (or Eyoes) are east and somewhat
north of Abomey, due north of the town of Lagos, which is correctly
located on an island at the west end of Cradoo Lake (the Lagos lagoon).
Opposite Lagos, the Doo (Ogun) River flows south through the "Kingdom of Lagos, which is tributary to Benin." Cradoo (Ikorodu), however, is located farther east, on the north bank of the lagoon, just to
the west of the River Palmer (Ona), which rises towards Jaboo
('Jebu). Quasee (Ikosi) is also located too far east, on the east side
of an unnamed river (Oni), which rises east of Jaboo and flows into
the lagoon near its eastern end.
    In 1793 Dalzel, who had been governor at Whydah from 1766
to 1770, reproduced Norris' map with modifications, identifying the
Fouin as Foy (Fon), "the antient Country of the Dahomans then called
Foys," the Ayoes or Eyoes as "perhaps Gagoes," mentioned by
Dapper[60] and Barbot[61] as lying north of Benin and located on d'
Anville's map as being east of Isago. To the northwest of Abomey,
Dalzel places the "Tappa's supposed to be the In-tas a formidable
people." In his text, however, while suggesting that the Tappahs
(Nupe) may be the Intas or the Assienta (Ashanti),[62] he says that
Eyeo is northeast of Dahomey and that "The Tappahs, to the north-
east of Eyeo, were unknown in his (Snelgrave's) time; and indeed

till very lately, when they made themselves as formidable to the Eyeos, as these to all the southern nations."[63]

Drawing heavily on Snelgrave and Norris, Dalzel brings together the earlier references to the Eyeo before adding subsequent developments. To Norris' account of the strangling of a rejected king, Snelgrave adds that the deputation to the king carried "a present of parrots eggs, as the mark of its authenticity,"[64] which is confirmed by Yoruba informants today. In about 1774 the king of Eyeo was presented with parrot eggs, but refused to allow himself to be strangled. A party led by "Ochenoo, the prime minister" then rebelled openly, but was defeated and killed.[65] Upon this occasion Adahoonzou, the king of Dahomey, sent an embassy of congratulations to the king of Eyeo.[66] In 1778 Dahomey entered into an alliance with Ardra to attack Apee, whose king fled to Wemey (Weme or Oueme); Dahomey did not dare attack Wemey, dreading "the resentment of the King of Eyeo, with whom the state of Wemey was then on a friendly footing."[67]

In 1781 the Eyeo ambassadors in Dahomey demanded that the annual tribute be increased, insisting that they would not depart without one hundred of the widows of Mayhou, an important chief who had recently died. They were given some of the women to take to Eyeo, but three months later "a messenger arrived from the King of Eyeo, with a demand of the rest of Mayhou's women; accompanied by a threat that, in case of non-compliance on the part of Dahomy, the Eyeo general Banchenoo should be sent to fetch them."[68] Dahomey attacked Agoonah (Aguna, a Yoruba town) to obtain captives to substitute for the Dahoman women.[69]

In 1783 the Dahoman army was ambushed and routed when it attacked Badagree (Badagry). In 1784, aided by the king of Lagos and augmented by numerous auxiliaries from "the inland countries of Mahee (Mahin) and Nago," their general attacked again "conducted by guides, which had been provided by the King of Eyeo. He laid waste the whole country in his progress, making many prisoners, which were immediately sent to Eyeo, according to a treaty which had been previously entered into with that Prince."[70]

"There were still several obstacles to prevent the execution of the design which the King of Dahomy had formed against Ardrah; the most important of which was the friendship of the King of Eyeo with the latter, and the alliance of Wemey."[71] However "Wemey became obnoxious to the King of Eyeo, on account of some of his trading-men having been way-laid and robbed, by a party belonging to that state. Upon this occasion, the King of Eyeo begged that Adahoonzou might chastise them, as it was too far for him to send an army for that purpose."[72] After capturing Wemey in 1786

Dahomey raided Porto Novo, the port of Ardrah, holding fourteen Frenchmen and other prisoners for ransom.

> The King of Ardrah was highly irritated at this infraction of the alliance which had lately subsisted between the two kingdoms. He immediately dispatched ambassadors to the King of Eyeo, complaining of this unprovoked breach of friendship, which was followed by a message from that Prince, reprehending the conduct of Adahoonzou, in terms the most menacing and offensive, forbidding him ever to think of a hostile visit to Ardrah in future, and telling him, "That Ardrah was Eyeo's callabash, out of which nobody should be permitted to eat but himself." [73]

Dalzel continues:

> The King of Dahomy was thunderstruck at this message, which, however, he durst not resent, but was obliged to appease his irritated master, by dividing with him his late ill-gotten spoil. Nor was this all: for so great was his dread of Eyeo's resentment, that for many months afterwards, whenever any warlike preparations were made by that monarch, Adahoonzou was under the greatest apprehensions that the kingdom of Dahomy would feel the effects of his vengeance. This impression continued to disturb the Dahomans for a considerable time afterwards; so that on the following year, 1787, when the King of Eyeo made some movements towards the Mahee country, Adahoonzou was so much alarmed, that he set all his people to work, to barricade and secure the halls of his different palaces. [74]

In 1788 he kept his army at home until it was known that the Eyeo army was on its homeward march. [75]

About this time messengers from Eyeo bought coral in Dahomey, although "coral had formed no part of the tribute which had lately been paid by the King of Dahomy; upon the plea, that for a long while there had been none to be found in the country, as there had been no ships in Whydah road for a considerable time. The King of Eyeo sent a special messenger to the Dahoman Monarch, to reprehend him for the supposed subterfuge, and to shew him the coral which had been purchased in his country; informing him at the same time, that Adahoonzou knew he held his dominions no longer than whilst he regularly paid his tribute; and when he neglected that, Dahomy belonged to Eyeo." [76]

In 1789 Dahomey attacked the capital of the Yoruba kingdom of Ketu,

> Ketoo the country where the fine red cotton cloths are
> manufactured. The town of Ketoo being surrounded by a
> large moat and a double wall, the inhabitants at first bid
> defiance to the Agaow (the Dahomean general), telling him
> from the walls, that the large gate was open for his recep-
> tion. This bravado was disregarded by the general, who
> contented himself, for the present, to pillage the neigh-
> bouring plantations. In the mean time, his succours
> arriving, he collected all his force, and prepared for a
> general assault; but before he proceeded to storm the
> town, he made a feint of retreating, which drew the enemy
> without the walls, to engage; upon which he attacked them
> with dreadful carnage, killing or taking the greatest part
> of the besieged. Two thousand prisoners, and a great
> number of heads, were the first fruit of this victory.[77]

According to Dalzel, the Eyeo failed to win their independence
from the Tappah (Nupe) in about 1790. "Eyeo, powerful as we have
seen it, appears to be tributary to a neighbouring and more powerful
Prince, called Tappah, of whose history little is known. The King of
Eyeo, desirous, it seems, to throw off the yoke, had ordered the
buffalo's hide to be twice trodden, in order to give Tappah a hearty
drubbing. His army, however, numerous as it was, met with a complete overthrow, and was under the necessity of submitting to the
victor's own terms, having lost thirteen umbrellas in the action."[78]

M'Leod, who visited Whydah in 1803, places Eyeo to the north-
east of Dahomy,[79] and observes that "Dahomy, about a half century
ago, one of the most powerful and flourishing of the African nations,
and the richest from its commerce with Europeans, is now much
fallen; not only from the loss of its trade, but it has also been extremely humbled by unsuccessful wars with the Eyeos and Ashantees."[80]

John Adams' two books are based on ten voyages between 1786
and 1800. The second, dated 1823 and cited here, provides new
information while repeating all the pertinent passages of the first
book, substituting Hio (Oyo) for Eyeo. No other reference, except
those simply citing Adams, has been found of his report of the visit
to Hio by a French officer. Adams described Hio as

> a country of great extent, and inhabited by a powerful and
> warlike nation; the capital of which, according to the na-
> tives' account, lies about N.E.E. from Ardrah, at the
> distance of nine days' journey, or 180 miles, allowing a
> traveller to proceed at the rate of twenty miles a day.

To the King of Hio the Ardrah people pay tribute, as he protects them from the incursions of the Dahomians, whose king has always been very jealous of their rivalry in trade. . . .

The Hios are a fine race of people, and are well skilled both in agriculture and in manufacturing articles for domestic purposes. The country which they inhabit is of great extent, being bordered on the north-east by Housa (Hausa) on the southwest by Dahomy, and the influence of its government extends to the south as far as the sea by way of Ardrah.

If we are to believe the accounts of the natives, the king of Hio has an organized army amounting to 100,000 men, composed of infantry, and cavalry; but the natives of Africa are so prone to exaggerate every circumstance connected with the nation to which they individually belong, that it is very difficult to ascertain the truth, particularly as connected with the population of a town, the numerical force of an army, or the extent of a kingdom.

I have heard of but one white man, who had ever been at the capital of Hio, and he was a French officer belonging to a slave ship. He certainly stated the population to be considerable, but by no means equal to what he had been taught to expect; and the army, as an African army, as far as he could judge, he thought to be a tolerably efficient one. A part of it was marshalled before him, and he strongly suspected that several of the corps were passed in review more than once, as corps which he had not seen before. This was a political strategem that would hardly have been expected from an African savage; but the Frenchman had no doubt of the fact.

He was treated by the king while in Hio, with great distinction, although he thought himself closely watched. He was absent nearly a month, and described the country over which he had passed, as level, wild, uncultivated, and possessing but a scanty population.

The cloth manufactured in Hio is superior, both for variety of pattern, color and dimensions, to any made in the neighbouring states; and some of the articles wrought by them in iron exhibit much skill and ingenuity. It surprised me to find the Hio women as well as those of Housa acquainted with the taste of cheese, as well as with the mode of making it, which they described, and which left no doubt in my mind that it was an article of domestic consumption in these countries.

"The Hios are extremely black and muscular, and generally above middle size; in disposition they are mild, docile and submissive. Their country mark on the face consists of three short cuts, each about one and a half inch long, running obliquely on each side of the mouth. . . . [81]

"The population of the town of Lagos may amount to 5,000; but there are two or three populous villages on the north side of Cradoo lake (the Lagos lagoon), over which the caboceer of Lagos has jurisdiction."[82] Adams locates Cradoo (Ikorodu) and Kosi (Ikosi), which he identifies with Quassi,[83] on the north east margin of Cradoo lake.[84]

It has always been the policy of the Lagos people, like those of Bonny, to be themselves the traders and not brokers. They therefore go in their canoes to Ardrah and Badagry, and to towns situated at the N.E. extremity of Cradoo lake, where they purchase slaves, Jaboo ('Jebu) cloth, and such articles as are required for domestic consumption.

The necessaries of life are here extremely abundant and cheap, and are brought chiefly from the country or northern margin of Cradoo lake, which communicates with Jaboo, a very fertile kingdom, and inhabited by an agricultural and manufacturing people.

It is these people who send so much cloth to Lagos and Ardrah, which the Portuguese traders from the Brazils purchase for that market, and which is held there in much estimation by the black population; probably not only on account of its durability, but because it is manufactured in a country which gave many of them, or their parents, birth, as the Portuguese have always carried on an extremely active trade in slaves at Whydah, Ardrah, and Lagos. . . .

The Jaboos inhabit a country situated between Hio and Benin, and are a fine looking people, and always seem as if they came from a land of plenty, being stout, healthy and full of vigour. They are a very industrious people, and manufacture for sale an immense number of common Guinea cloths: besides raising cattle, sheep, poultry, corn, and calavancies, which they supply their neighbors.[85]

Adams' map places the Tapa (Nupe) to the northwest and the Mahee (Mahin) to the north of Abomey, with the Hio (Oyo) and its city to the northeast, due north of Ardrah. East of Ardrah and

Badagry along the lagoon are the towns of Lagos, Cradoo (Ikorodu), and Quassi (Ikosi), with Jaboo ('Jebu) inland to the north of Quassi; no rivers in this region are named. Bowdich's map dated 1817 and Hutton's dated 1821 locate Jaboo, Hio, and Yarriba inland from the Lagos river, but less accurately than do some earlier maps.

In 1822-24 Denham and Clapperton explored northern Nigeria after crossing the Sahara from Tripoli. Clapperton brought back an Arabic manuscript by "Sultan Mohammed Bello of Hoossa [Hausa]," which states:

> West of Kashnah [Katsina] and Ghoobér [Gobir near Sokoto] there are seven different provinces, extending into the territory of Howssa [Hausa], which are — Zanfarah [Zanfara], Kabi [Kebbi], Ya-ory [Yauri], Noofee [Nupe], Yarba [Yoruba], Barghoo [Borgu], and Ghoorma. To each of these there is a prince appointed as governor. . . .
>
> Yarba is an extensive province, containing rivers, forests, sands, and mountains, as also a great many wonderful and extraordinary things. In it the talking green bird, called babaga (parrot), is found.
>
> By the side of this province there is an anchorage or harbour for the ships of Christians, who used to go there and purchase slaves. These slaves were exported from our country, and sold to the people of Yarba, who resold them to the Christians.
>
> The inhabitants of this province [Yarba], it is supposed, originated from the remnants of the children of Canaan, who were of the tribe of Nimrod. The cause of their establishment in the west of Africa was, as it is stated, in consequence of their being driven by Yaa-rooba, son of Kahtan, out of Arabia, to the western coast between Egypt and Abyssinia. From that spot they advanced into the interior of Africa, till they reached Yarba, where they fixed their residence. On their way they left, in every place they stopped at, a tribe of their own people. Thus it is supposed that all the tribes of Soodan, who inhabit the mountains, are originated from them; as also are the inhabitants of Ya-ory.
>
> Upon the whole, the people of Yarba are nearly of the same description as those of Noofee.[86]

In 1824, in Sokoto, Clapperton met an Arab who "had been detained a prisoner three years, in a country called Yoriba, on the west side of the Quarra (Niger). . . . The inhabitants of Yoriba he represented to be extremely ill disposed."[87]

30

In 1825 Clapperton and Lander entered Yoruba territory by way of Badagry and Ipokia, marking the beginning of its recorded history and the long-delayed ending to the period when it was known only through secondhand accounts. When they first entered Katunga (Old Oyo) in 1826, Clapperton recorded that Dahomey and Alladah were among its tributaries,[88] but that Ketto (Ketu) and Jaboo (Jebu) were independent.

A final event that belongs to this period, even though it probably occurred after 1825, is that King Gezo "freed Dahomey from the onerous tribute to Oyo." Burton, writing in 1864, says "Early in the present century, King Gezo (who came to the throne in 1818) seized his opportunity, and after hard fighting, finally drove out the warlike Oyos, who were sinking before the Fula (Fulani) or Moslem movement in the north, and distributed the tribute amongst his people,—one of his proudest achievements."[89] To commemorate this victory Gezo instituted an annual sacrifice at Kana (or Calmina), where tribute had been collected in which "the victims are made to personate in dress and avocation Oyos, a pastoral and agricultural people."[90] Dunglas dates this event about 1820-22, which is probably too early,[91] while Herskovits dates it as 1827, seven years after the beginning of Gezo's reign,[92] as does Parrinder.[93]

CONCLUSION

From the time of their first visit to Benin in 1485, the Portuguese heard of two powerful kings in the interior who Talbot believes were the Alafin of Oyo and the Oni of Ife. While there is little to support the former identification, it is probable that Ogene, as the Oni is known to the people of Benin, is the Ogane or Hooguanee to whom Barros and Pacheco Pereira refer; it thus seems likely that reports of the Oni of Ife, whom the Portuguese took to be Prester John, spurred their exploration of Africa.

References to the Ijebu people and their city of Ijebu-Ode recur repeatedly in the literature, from its first mention on a Portuguese map (c. 1500, cited by Talbot) until it was finally entered by European missionaries in the nineteenth century. It is mentioned by Pacheco Pereira (1507-1508), "D. R." (1604), Ruyters (1623), Alonso de Sandoval (1627), Dapper (1668), Ogilby (1670), Barbot (1682 published 1732), de la Croix (1688), a Portuguese map (c. 1700, cited by Talbot), d'Anville's map (1729; in Labat, 1731), d'Anville's map (1743; in Foa, 1895), Norris (1772, published 1789), Dalzel (1793), and Adams (1786-1800, published in 1821 and 1823). In the nineteenth century Ijebu-Ode is mentioned by Clapperton (1826, published 1829), Crowther (1843), and d'Avezac (1845), before it was first visited in 1854 by

Hinderer and Irving. There can be no question that it is Ijebu or
'Jebu to which Geebuu, Iubu, Iabu, Jubu, Jabo, Jaboe, Jabu, Jaboo,
Jabou, and Jebou refer.

Other dates may be found in the literature and on maps, but
these only substantiate the fact that this kingdom and its capital city
have been known for the past 460 years. It is clear that the city of
Ijebu-Ode antedates the slave wars that developed with the slave
trade to the New World, but since the earliest account mentions a
moat and a trade in slaves, it is not possible to say whether or not
it developed as a result of warfare.

Yoruba cities clearly antedated the nineteenth-century invasions
by Dahomey from the west and Fulani from the north, which depopu-
lated or destroyed many cities that had been large and important.
Others were swelled with refugees, and new cities such as Ibadan
and Abeokuta were founded as a result of these wars. But according
to Yoruba tradition, which the early documents confirm in part, Old
Oyo, Ketu, Ijebu-Ode, Ondo, Shabe, Ilesha, and other cities were
founded by the "sons of Odudua" in the same epoch as Benin; i.e.,
before the Portuguese explorers reached Nigeria. Ife was established
even earlier.

Ondo, possibly, is mentioned from 1668 through 1729 as Oedobo,
Odobo, Oedebo, Oedoba, Oudobo, or Udobe, though the basis for this
identification is mainly its location on d'Anville's maps. Lucumies,
Ulkami, Ulkamy, Ulkuma, Ulcuma, Ulcama, Ulcami, Ulcumi, Oulcoumi,
Alkomijs, Alkomysh, Alkomy, Alcomische, and Lucamee, mentioned
repeatedly from 1627 to 1743, may refer to Oyo (as Talbot suggests),
to some other Yoruba group, or to the Nupe, who are mentioned in
the subsequent literature by their Yoruba name, Tapa.

The earliest certain references to Oyo are in d'Anville's map
(1729); Labat's account (1731) of the visit of 1725; Barbot's comments
(1732) on the invasion of Ardra in 1698, based on visits in 1678 and
1682; and Snelgrave's account (1734) of his visit in 1727. From this
period on, they are frequently referred to as Ayoes, Ayeots, Ayois,
Eyeos, Eyoes, Eyos, Oyeos, Oyos, J-oes, I:oes, Hios, and Ohio.

In 1724, having captured Allada, the Dahomean armies were
called home to defend their country against the Oyo cavalry, who
were defeated by means of a ruse and because their horses were
unaccustomed to firearms. To ward off further attacks the king of
Dahomey sent presents to the king of Oyo, but in 1728 Oyo cavalry
again invaded Dahomey because of the execution of the king of Weme.
Though the Oyo forces had to return home in 1729 without a decisive
engagement with the Dahomeans, who burned their homes and retreated
into the forest, the king of Dahomey sent more presents to Oyo,
including one of his handsomest daughters, and peace was established.
In 1738 Oyo invaded Dahomey because gifts and tribute had not been

received for some time; from 1738 to 1747 Oyo raided Dahomey at will, the Dahomeans again hiding in the forests to avoid a meeting in strength. In 1747 Dahomey resumed payment of annual tribute to Oyo, and a period of peaceful relations between the two kingdoms ensued, though the Dahomeans may have continued to try to evade paying tribute.

In about 1774 the king of Dahomey sent congratulations to the king of Oyo for having put down a palace revolt. In 1778 Dahomey refrained from attacking Weme, which had given refuge to an enemy, because it feared Oyo. In 1781 Oyo increased the amount of Dahomey's tribute, demanding the widows of an important Dahomean chief. In 1784 Nago auxiliaries, Lagos troops, and guides provided by the king of Oyo assisted the Dahomeans in conquering Badagry, in return for which some of the captives taken were sent to Oyo. At the request of the king of Oyo, Dahomey captured Weme in 1786; but when the Dahomeans went on to raid Allada they were warned that it was Oyo's "callabash." Dahomey was also warned that it would be taken by Oyo unless it paid tribute regularly. In 1787 and 1788 Oyo raided in Mahin country while the Dahomean armies remained home, fearing an attack. In 1789 Dahomey defeated the Yoruba city of Ketu, taking 2,000 captives alive.

In about 1790 Oyo was defeated by the Nupe. Thereafter Oyo became absorbed with the wars against Ilorin and its Fulani rulers, which dominated Yoruba history in the nineteenth century and led to the evacuation of Old Oyo. King Gezo of Dahomey seized his opportunity to end the annual payment of tribute, which for more than a century Oyo had been able to collect from Dahomey, itself a powerful and greatly feared kingdom.

NOTES

See the following bibliography for full references to publications cited in this section.

1. This chapter was previously published in a French translation: W. Bascom, "Les premiers fondement historiques de l'urbanisme yoruba," Présence Africaine, New Series, No. 23 (1959), pp. 22-40. However the 1959 version lacked several additions and revisions that are included here.

2. João de Barros, pp. 124-28. This portion was published in 1552, with further reports following in 1553, 1563, and 1613.

Lok in 1554 cited Gemma Phrysius as authority for his statement that toward the west of Nubia "is a great nation of Aphricerones, whose region (as far as may be gathered by conjecture) is the same as is now called Regnum Orguena, confining upon the East parts of Guinea."

3. F. Alvarez, pp. 266-67.

4. Duarte Pacheco Pereira, p. 126. These two kings are also mentioned as Miosaque and Agare by Figueiredo (p. 71) in 1614, and as Miosaco and Agare by Ruiters in 1623 (see S. P. L'Honore Naber, Toortse der Zee-Vaert door Dierick Ruiters [1623], pp. 78-79) and by Alonso de Sandoval (p. 17) in 1627.

5. P. A. Talbot, Vol. I, p. 282.

6. Talbot, Vol. I, p. 156.

7. Talbot, Vol. I, p. 218.

8. Pacheco Pereira, pp. 123-25.

9. Talbot, Vol. I, p. 219.

10. Naber, op. cit., p. 76.

11. Sandoval, p. 78.

12. Ibid.

13. Talbot, Vol. I, p. 162; W. Bascom, "The Yoruba in Cuba," p. 19.

14. O. Dapper, p. 404.

15. Ibid., p. 491.

16. Ibid., p. 492.

17. Ibid., pp. 494-95.

18. Ibid., p. 495.

19. Ibid., p. 505.

20. Talbot, Vol. I, p. 162.

21. Dapper, p. 506.

22. Talbot, Vol. I, pp. 162,324.

23. Dapper, p. 506.

24. W. Bosman, pp. 396-98.

25. R. F. Burton, Wanderings in West Africa, Vol. II, p. 201 fn.; M. J. Herskovits, Vol. I, p. 15; Talbot, Vol. I, p. 283; B. G. Parrinder, p. 26; W. Snelgrave, pp. 56-57; A. Dalzel, p. 14.

26. Dalzel, p. 13.

27. J. Barbot, p. 381.

28. Ibid., pp. 351-52.

29. Ibid., p. 348.

30. Ibid., p. 327.

31. Ibid., p. 346.

32. Ibid., p. 327.

33. Ibid., p. 356.

34. Ibid., p. 376.

35. Ibid., p. 375.

36. Ibid., p. 354.

37. Talbot, Vol. I, p. 219.

38. J. B. Labat, Vol. I, p. x; Vol. II, pp. 226-27.

39. Ibid., Vol. II, pp. 101-4.

40. Ibid., Vol. I, p. 1.

41. B. Foa, p. 10.
42. Snelgrave, p. 56–57.
43. Ibid., pp. 58–59.
44. P. B. Isert, pp. 142–43.
45. Snelgrave, pp. 55–56.
46. Ibid., p. 89.
47. Ibid., p. 120.
48. Ibid., p. 121
49. Ibid., pp. 122–23.
50. Ibid., p. 135.
51. B. Dunglas (p. 6) says that King Agadja (Trudo) agreed to pay the king of Oyo tribute in about 1715. Burton (A Mission to Gelele, King of Dahome, Vol. I, p. 130) also says it began in the rule of Agaja, 1708–30. Herskovits (Vol. I, p. 19) says that the tribute was paid annually after 1738. The statements of Norris and Snelgrave suggest that the agreement was reached in 1729, although gifts had been sent earlier, in 1724.
52. Pruneau de Pommegorge, pp. 11–3.
53. R. Norris, pp. 11–13.
54. Ibid., pp. 13–15.
55. Ibid., pp. 15–16.
56. Ibid., p. 139.
57. Ibid., p. 137.
58. Ibid., p. 139.
59. Ibid., pp. 137,139.
60. Dapper, pp. 486, 495.
61. Barbot, p. 356.
62. Dalzel, p. 229.
63. Ibid., p. 6.
64. Snelgrave, pp. 12–13.
65. This may refer to King Abiodun's defeat of the notorious Bashorun, Gaha, as described by S. Johnson (pp. 182–86). Both Johnson (p. 184) and Snelgrave (p. 157) say that children in the womb were killed in the attempt to annihilate all the descendants of the king's opponent.
66. Dalzel, pp. 156–57.
67. Ibid., p. 170.
68. Ibid., p. 175.
69. Ibid., p. 176.
70. Ibid., pp. 182–83.
71. Ibid., p. 191.
72. Ibid., p. 192.
73. Ibid., pp. 195–96.
74. Ibid., p. 196.
75. Ibid., pp. 198–99.
76. Ibid., p. 209

77. Ibid., pp. 201-2.
78. Ibid., p. 229.
79. J. M'Leod, p. 15.
80. Ibid., p. 126.
81. J. Adams, Remarks on the Country Extending from Cape Palmas to the River Congo, pp. 78-79, 92-94.
82. Ibid., p. 100.
83. Ibid., p. 240.
84. Ibid., p. 107.
85. Ibid., pp. 96-97, 108.
86. H. Clapperton, Vol. 11, pp. 451, 454-55.
87. Ibid., p. 339.
88. Ibid., p. 87.
89. Burton, A Voyage to Gchele, King of Dahome, cited in H. Clapperton, Vol. II, p. 87.
90. Ibid., p. 131.
91. Dunglas, p. 6.
92. Herskovits, Vol. I, p. 21.
93. Parrinder, p. 41.

BIBLIOGRAPHY

Adams, J. Remarks on the Country Extending from Cape Palmas to the River Congo. London: G. & W. B. Whittaker, 1823.

_____ . Sketches Taken during Ten Voyages to Africa, between the Years 1786 and 1800. London: Hurst, Robinson & Company, 1821.

Alvarez, F. Narrative of the Portuguese Embassy to Abyssinia, during the Years 1520-1527. Translated and edited by Lord Standley. London: Hakluyt Society, Vol. LXIV, 1881.

Barbot, J. A Description of the Coasts of North and South Guinea. London, 1732.

Barros, João de. Ásia de João de Barros: Dos feitos que os portugueses fizeram no descobrimento e conquista dos mares et terras do Oriente. 4 vols. 6th ed., Lisboa: Ministerio das Colonias, 1945. [Citations used in this chapter are from extracts translated in G. R. Crone, The Voyages of Cadamosto and Other Documents on Western Africa in the Second Half of the Fifteenth Century. London: Hakluyt Society, Second Series, Vol. LXXX, 1937. First published in 1552.]

Bascom, W. "Lander's Routes through Yoruba Country," Nigerian Field, Vol. 25 (1960), pp. 12-22.

_____. "Les premiers fondements historiques de l'urbanisme yoruba," Présence Africaine, New Series, No. 23 (1959), pp. 22-40.

_____. "Urbanism as a Traditional African Pattern," The Sociological Review, Vol. 7, No. 1 (1959), pp. 29-43.

_____. "The Yoruba in Cuba," Nigeria, No. 37 (1951), pp. 14-20.

_____. "Urbanization among the Yoruba," The American Journal of Sociology, Vol. 60, No. 5 (1955), pp. 446-54.

Bosman, W. A New and Accurate Description of Guinea. London: J. Knapton and D. Midwinter, 1705. [First published in 1704.]

Bowdich, T. E. Mission from Cape Coast Castle to Ashantee. London: John Murray, 1819.

Bradbury, R. E. The Benin Kingdom and the Edo-Speaking Peoples of South-Western Nigeria. Ethnographic Survey of Africa (Daryll Forde, ed.) Western Africa: Part 13. London: International African Institute, 1957.

Burton, R. F. Wanderings in West Africa, 2 vols. London: Tinsley Brothers, 1863.

Burton, R. F. A Mission to Gelele, King of Dahome, 2 vols. London: Tylston & Edwards, 1893. [First published in 1864.]

Clapperton, H. Journal of a Second Expedition into the Interior of Africa, vol. II, Philadelphia: Carey, Lea and Carey, 1829.

Croix, de la. Relation Universelle de l'Afrique, Ancienne et Moderne. 4 vols. Lyon: Thomas Amaulry, 1688.

Dalzel, A. The History of Dahomy, an Inland Kingdom of Africa. London: For the author, by T. Spilsbury, 1793.

Dapper, O. Naukeurige Beschrijvinge der Afrikaensche Gewesten. Amsterdam: Jacob von Meurs, 1668.

Denham, D., and H. Clapperton. Narrative of Travels and Discoveries in Northern and Central Africa, in the Years 1822, 1823, and 1824. 2 vols. 3rd ed. London: John Murray, 1828. [First published in 1826.]

Dunglas, E. "La première attaque des Dahoméens contre Abéokuta (3 mars 1851)," Études dahoméennes, Vol. I (1948), pp. 7-19.

Figueiredo, Manuel de. Manuel de Figueiredo. Lisboa: Vincente Alvares, 1625. [Quoted in Naber, Toortse der Zee-Vaert door Dierick Ruiters (1623), p. 78, fn. 1. [First published in 1614.]

Foa, E. Le Dahomey. Paris: A Hennuyer, 1895.

Herskovits, M. J. Dahomey: An Ancient West African Kingdom. 2 vols. New York: J. J. Augustin, 1938.

Hutton, W. A Voyage to Africa. London: Longman, Hurst, Rees, Orme, and Brown, 1821.

Isert, P. E. Voyage en Guinée et dans les isles Caraibes en Amerique. Paris: Maradan, 1793.

Johnson, S. The History of the Yorubas. London: George Routledge & Sons, 1921.

Labat, J. B. Voyage du Chevalier des Marchais en Guinée, isles voisines, et à Cayenne, fait en 1725, 1726 & 1727. 4 vols. Amsterdam: La Compagnie, 1731.

M'Leod, J. A Voyage to Africa, with Some Account of the Manners and Customs of the Dahomian People London: John Murray, 1820.

Naber, S. P. L'Honore, ed. Beschryvinghe ende Historische verhael van het Gout Koninckrijc van Gunea, anders de Gout-Custe de Mina genaemt, liggende in het deel van Africa, door P. de Marees. Werken Uitgegeven door de Linschoten-Vereeniging, Vol. 5. 'S-Gravenhage: Martinus Nijhoff, 1912. [First published in 1602.]

_____. Toortse der Zee-Vaert door Dierick Ruiters (1623). Werken Uitgegeven door de Linschoten-Vereeniging, Vol. VI. 'S-Gravenhage: Martinus Nijhoff, 1913. [First published in 1623.]

Norris, R. Mémoirs of the Reign of Bossa Ahadee, King of Dahomy.
London: W. Lowndes, 1789.

Ogilby, J. Africa. London: The Author, 1670.

Pacheco Pereira, Duarte. Esmeraldo de situ orbis. Translated and
edited by G. H. T. Kimble. London: Hakluyt Society, Second
Series, vol. LXXIX, 1937. Written in 1505-1508; [first published
in 1892.]

Parrinder, E. G. The Story of Ketu. An Ancient Yoruba Kingdom.
Ibadan: Ibadan University Press, 1956.

Pruneau de Pommegorge Description de la Nigritie. Paris, 1789.
[Extract published in Études Dahoméenes, Vol. 18 (1957).]

Sandoval, Alonso de De Instauranda Aethiopum Salute. Bogota:
Biblioteca de la Presidencia de Colombia, 1956. [First published
in 1627.]

Snelgrave, W. A New Account of Some Parts of Guinea, and the Slave
Trade. London: James, John & Paul Knapton, 1734.

Talbot, P. A. The Peoples of Southern Nigeria. 4 vols. London:
Oxford University Press, 1926.

3

THE WESTERN NIGERIAN
COOPERATIVE ADMINISTRATION:
AN OBSTACLE
TO DEVELOPMENT
Michael Koll

As defined by sociologists, and allowing for differences evolving out of the various national conceptions of law, a cooperative is "a joint partnership, all partners having equal rights and being united in their aim for lasting commercial cooperation."[1] Seen in this light there is no need at all for state administration in this sphere; cooperatives come into existence spontaneously and regulate themselves. This applies to the origins of the cooperative system in Western Europe but allegedly not to Nigeria or any other part of Africa, where cooperatives have been introduced by colonial administrations as part of their program of development from above. It has been believed that Africans had to "learn" cooperation.[2] This, however, is pure myth. In pre-colonial times there existed in Nigeria, as elsewhere in the world, cooperatives of all kinds, and at the beginning of the colonial era changes in the structure of commerce and society gave rise spontaneously to new cooperatives (as defined sociologically). Maybe this was the only time in recent Nigerian history when one could legitimately speak of a cooperative "movement": Yoruba cocoa farmers founded marketing societies,[3] Ibos and Calabaris founded rotating credit societies in rising numbers, imitating and encouraging each other.[4]

This movement was taken up by the colonial administration, canalized and subjected to the interests of the metropolitan economy. The administrative structures resulting from this were consolidated legally and in terms of bureaucratic procedures; subsequently these laws and procedures were taken over by the governments of independent Nigeria without question. These structures stifle spontaneity and self-control and thus hamper development. The following examples illustrate this.

THE BEGINNINGS OF THE NIGERIAN
COOPERATIVE SYSTEM

Indigenous Cooperatives

If we start with the definition quoted at the beginning of this chapter we can find numerous examples of economic cooperatives in the ethnological literature on Nigerian tribes. In their structure they are comparable to the West European pattern, with its emphasis on autonomy of the individual; cooperative activities are strictly separated from private activities (the alternative—a high degree of integration of the individuum into the cooperative—is typical of traditional East European cooperatives).

Cooperators as described in the ethnological literature (and such types of cooperatives can still be observed in Nigeria) do not hold common property, and they associate only temporarily and for definite, clearly stated purposes. The best example of an indigenous cooperative is represented by the esusu (the rotating credit associations of the Yoruba and Ibo, and generally found in West Africa). They unite members strictly on a commercial basis; contributions are levied periodically, and the sum total is given in rotation to one of the members. Quite contrary to the nineteenth-century European ideology of a cooperative being "an association of human beings," the esusu is "an association of financial members," membership being defined by one contribution unit. If a person pays two units, he holds two memberships and is entitled to receive the sum total twice in one cycle. Alternatively two or more persons may join to pay one contribution unit and consequently they receive jointly one sum total per cycle.

In agriculture and in house-building, work groups were common everywhere. Men teamed up to work in turns on their farms for clearing and harvesting, or to help one of their members to fulfill his obligations toward his future father-in-law. No free men would work individually for a co-villager for money, but work groups could be hired (labor cooperatives in the strict sense—the cooperative sale of one's labor).

Many more examples could be cited—for example joint building of canoes (a task too big for an individual fisherman), joint purchase of land, mutual insurance societies. All of these groups have in common that they cut across lineage affiliation and embrace people with identical economic interests for the pursuit of these interests.5

Cooperatives in Early Colonial Times

Without any guiding measures from Europeans the cooperatives of the tribes of present-day Nigeria adapted themselves to the changing economic conditions that arose from trade between Europe and West Africa. At the coast, canoe-house cooperatives were formed very early on; these were cooperatives prepared for fighting and trading, monopolizing the dangerous carrying trade.[6] The savings cooperatives changed from cowrie shell currency to English money.

After cocoa plantations had been introduced into West Nigeria by the English, marketing cooperatives were soon founded. We can find this noteworthy statement in a recently written Nigerian thesis: "In 1907 some farmers from Agege [in southwestern Nigeria] joined together to achieve an improvement in their economic status through cooperation. Their aims were: to provide members with loans, to circulate knowledge on methods of improving the quality of cocoa, to negotiate common tariffs for farm labourers, to build and improve roads and to export their products directly."[7] In the following years such enterprises multiplied until, in 1931, such development companies were to be found in the whole of the cocoa plantation area of West Nigeria.

The Introduction of State-Controlled Cooperatives[8]

In 1935 cooperatives were "introduced" by law into this country where traditional as well as modern economics had already produced so many forms of cooperative organization. The term "cooperative" was kept for those associations that were organized and registered according to this law. This law, however, had not originated as a result of a study of the Nigerian situation; it was not the codification of something already socially regulated. Rather it was based on imported European conceptions of law, which had no social equivalent in Nigeria.

On four points in particular this law and its application in practical politics was contrary to indigenous usage and the trend in development:

1. It forced on small, socially integrated groups an elaborate system of formal democracy and a system of bookkeeping by double entry that was just as elaborate.

2. It subjected the cooperatives to the central control of a registrar who was able to make the existence of each cooperative dependent upon the meticulous observation of all formal regulations.

3. It reduced the complex beginnings of existing development cooperatives (see the example quoted above) to the single function of marketing.

4. It took away from the cooperatives the chance of organizing the export of their products themselves, and it made them into mere suppliers of European business concerns.

The cooperatives were thus degraded. Once instruments of self-help, they had become an instrument of colonial economic policy.

THE STRUCTURE OF PRESENT-DAY ADMINISTRATION OF WESTERN NIGERIAN COOPERATIVES

When Western Nigeria achieved internal self-government in 1952 it retained the law and the administration of cooperatives as they were. A government declaration said "There is general agreement that the cooperative methods are the most suitable for satisfying the needs of the mass of the population."[9] There was no new reflection on this axiom; likewise there was no discussion as to the events that had led to the enactment of the cooperative law in 1935. Although it was always described as a "movement," the cooperative organization with its law and regulations had in fact become inflexible. It kept its registrar, who, as a state employee, understood his task more as that of checking that regulations were kept rather than stimulating a business policy or a drive to further development.

Structural Deficiencies in Administrative Staffing

In spite of the government's protestations that the cooperatives were receiving its whole-hearted support, the number of cooperative government officers stagnated, as the following table shows:

Category	Number in 1955	Number in 1967	Percent Increase
Cooperatives Officers	443	2,081	470
Registrars	1	1	
Principal assistant registrars	1	1	
Senior assistant registrars	24	20	
Assistant cooperative officers	10	11	
Inspectorate grades	117	139	
Total number of officers of the cooperative administration	153	172	

The reason for this is a lack of political planning. Conscious efforts to reduce government inspection in favor of greater self-administration were not made; nor were officers recruited to inspect effectively, as the law demanded, the increased number of cooperatives. Thus the system lapsed into inefficiency.

The burden of inspection that the government had assumed with the passing of the cooperative law has to be carried primarily by the 139 inspectors. However the inspectors are so badly paid that they soon move into private business as trained accountants. Thus new gaps in the staff are never properly filled. The twenty senior assistant registrars have no chance of advancement because there are only two places to be filled at the top, so the senior assistant registrars endeavor to be moved to other ministries. Thus the cooperative administration loses valuable staff members. Within the given framework of bureaucratic control, the success of the whole cooperative organization depends on the quality of the registrar and his deputy, for, in addition to their extensive legal authority, they wield practically unlimited social power. The men who hold these top posts worked themselves up over the decades, thus acquiring petty bureaucratic habits.

We must also remember that every detail of the inspectors' very detailed reports is read and a written comment added at various levels right up to the registrar. Usually months pass between the moment a report is written and the reception of the pertinent orders from above—months in which the inspector and the cooperative he looks after are unable to take any measures concerning the problem in question. The minute regulations of the cooperative law demand a detailed supervision—and this is carried out with bureaucratic precision but at a sluggish speed. The course of business is thus paralysed.

The Political Weakness of the Administration of the Cooperatives

The administration of the cooperatives developed no initiative itself. Also it could not count on the political support of the farmers organized in cooperatives for two reasons. First, the farmers were only a minority (only 20 percent of all cocoa is marketed through cooperatives). Second, the Cooperatives Union of Western Nigeria, which is claimed to be the political representation of the cooperative farmers, leads a phantom existence as a financially supported branch of the state cooperative administration. Consequently the cooperatives have never been able to enforce their demands on the government. Private cocoa businessmen, being skilled in politics and tactics, are able to secure the favor of the ruling politicians through bribery. The cooperatives are poorly represented on the board of directors of the state marketing board, which controls the exports of all cocoa and decides on the buying price and they cannot assert themselves against the interests of private rivals.

The cooperatives are also unable to assert their interests when dealing with other ministries. Compared with the 139 cooperative inspectors there are 1,838 agricultural advisors at the Ministry of Agriculture. For this reason there is a much more intense advisory service for production than for marketing. On the other hand other ministries saddle the cooperative administration with tasks without consulting them beforehand—as, for example, in the cooperative organization of farm settlements or weaving workshops.10 The cooperative administration puts up with this just as it did with the withdrawal of the tractors that were first set at its disposal by the government and then claimed by the Ministry of Agriculture.

To this we must add that at the time when political parties ruled in Western Nigeria the registrar had to register sham cooperatives, which had been founded with the one aim of receiving subsidies from the government to influence the vote. In spite of the lip service paid to the cooperative idea in public statements, cooperatives receive little attention when it comes to actual policy-making. This is so mainly because cooperatives are not sufficiently organized to exert political pressure.

AN EXAMPLE: CRAFTSMEN'S COOPERATIVES

State-Controlled Craftsmen's Cooperatives

As the government declared in 1952 and subsequently reaffirmed, its aim was to establish cooperatives everywhere. In every economic branch, small-scale, independent tradesmen were to join together in cooperatives. In reality, however, since the cooperative authorities need their staff to supervise the existing cooperatives (i.e., primarily in the cocoa-marketing sector), there was hardly any point in thinking of expansion in the spheres of agricultural production of food crops, loans, building trades, crafts etc.

All the more inconsequent it was then to stick to isolated projects in these spheres. For instance, in Ibadan, (a city of about 800,000 inhabitants who are mainly farmers and tradesmen—in 1964 there were only 3,803 employed in industry out of about 14,000 craftsmen[11]) only a few dozen craftsmen were organized into cooperatives—a group of tailors, one of goldsmiths, and one of artisans. The tailors' group alone had acquired a definite shape. From 1955 to 1967 a high degree of supervision, advice, and leadership was devoted to it, which would have been quite out of proportion even if the cooperative had been successful; but in the face of its complete failure this can only be explained by the fact that the cooperative administration lacked every faculty for putting its manpower into economic action. Whereas attention was focused on these ten tailors for twelve years (a fact that has filled fat files), no one was interested in the other approximately 4,900 other tailors and seamstresses in the city.

A similar disproportion can be noted in the state of the program for agricultural industrialization, which had to be taken over from the Ministry of Industry by the cooperative authorities. Groups of 25 boys and girls are trained to be weavers and equipped with a workshop and tools. Then they are supposed to run the business as a cooperative. They know nothing about marketing or business, and their goods are not saleable on the free market. But, since so much capital has already been invested in this cooperative project, the government carries on with it whereas many independent craftsmen receive nothing.[12]

Cooperatives of Independent Craftsmen

Cooperatives of independent craftsmen of the kind described at the beginning (i.e., cooperatives in the sociological sense of people actually working together) have continued to develop in Nigeria. Such informal cooperatives differ in almost all respects from the legally recognized ones: they have usually less than the legally required ten members; the members retain their individual independence, which they would never abandon in favor of the legally required full integration into a cooperative; the coming together for joint action is the result of a longstanding personal acquaintance, and social control therefore renders formal control less important; and the group dissolves easily when members find other pursuits more rewarding.

Such groups may be found, for example, among butchers, who buy a cow jointly because as individuals they cannot afford to buy their own; among tailors, who buy bundles of cloth, thus profiting from the wholesale price; and among mechanics, who share the rent of a piece of land at a main road. The savings made in these cooperatives may be small, but they are important when compared with the size of the business. A gain is a gain, even if it is too small for government officials to care about. And since these informal cooperatives cause no overhead cost, the gain is a real one. (I wonder how much net profit would remain if the real cost of administration of government-controlled cooperatives were calculated.)

Even more important than these cooperative groups is the development potential of the associations of traders and craftsmen ("small enterprise" in the fashionable terminology). These associations came into being as a response to the diversification of the economy during the colonial period. Internally they regulate competition and business ethics; externally they were integrated into the political system as organs of tax collection. This latter function, however, was lost in 1952, when Western Nigeria became autonomous

46

and the associations disintergrated. The associations revived in the early 1960s due to economic progress of the urban trades, but all their efforts to regain government recognition failed. We will not deal here with the political role of these associations as potential pressure groups or as partners to local government in urban development, but only with their cooperative aspects.13

Craft associations have experimented during recent years in the fields of cooperative purchase, processing, and selling. Bakers have broken the monopoly of middlemen by buying flour directly from the mill in Lagos; butchers have tried (albeit unsuccessfully) to break the monopoly of Hausa traders in the shipment of cattle from the north; photographers have organized joint purchase of films in cooperation with a foreign enterprise. Cooperative processing and selling usually go together. Tailors have worked jointly on tenders for uniforms; butchers have planned the building of drying sheds for hides; and goldsmiths have obtained credit to buy gold, work it into jewelry, and organize sales exhibitions.

All of these efforts were undertaken upon the initiative of the associations; the authorities in charge of trade promotion took no notice, and in cases when they were approached for help, they sent a specimen statute for cooperative societies, sixty-seven paragraphs long, which did not fail to have an intimidating effect.

None of the cooperatives of craftsmen (as defined sociologically) has become a legal cooperative. But only the legal cooperatives are entitled to receive government loans and assistance. Development efforts by social groups and by government go on along different lines. Government expects the people to comply with the law that the colonial administration promulgated in 1935, but that law is impracticable. Who should adjust to whom—the craftsmen to the government, the government to the craftsmen? The answer will differ according to the type of political system—according to whether it is authoritarian or democratic.

CONCLUSIONS

With its law on cooperatives and the pertinent rules and specimen statutes, the government has created a complicated scheme that cannot be mastered by farmers and craftsmen, and thus perpetuates the compulsion for supervision created by the government itself. The cooperative authorities are fully taken up with supervision and find no time for new enterprises (unless these are forced upon them by other ministries). Law and statute are like a straitjacket which doom free enterprise and any experiment to failure. It was not without reason that the bakers' guild organized its purchasing cooperative into a limited company in order to be free of the supervision of the authorities that never fail to stifle business spirit.

A new thinking is required. In order to become an important instrument in the development policy, the state-controlled cooperatives have to give up their allotted role of protector in economic competition and take an active part in competition from a business point of view. Hundreds of small cocoa-marketing cooperatives are being kept alive artificially, as are the weavers' production cooperatives. The administrative costs, met by the government, are put to uneconomical use. If the unprofitable cooperatives were allowed to disappear, and in their place there was encouragement for amalgamating big cooperatives under a capable manager (for instance, as has been tried out in spite of resistance from the cooperative authorities in Ilesha, Western Nigeria,[14]) then the share in the cocoa market—which is still around 20 percent in spite of 35 years of state cooperative support—would certainly rise. The same is true of the unprofitable use of administrative means to preserve single craftsmen's cooperatives, whereas the experiments of craftsmen's associations remain unsupported.

Cooperative reform must become a political issue. The cooperatives themselves have to find ways and means of formulating and proclaiming political demands. Since they were put under state control in 1935, they have been patronized. The state economic policy dictates what the cooperatives are to do. This could be to plant cocoa for export and to provide it at state-determined prices, or to back social experiments (farm settlements and craftsmens' production cooperatives), or ease the chronic underfinancing of those cooperative banks that provide funds for marketing cocoa by founding savings cooperatives, or to imitate the pattern of English cooperative wholesale societies that is renowned in the world and therefore accepted as the standard in Nigeria. Cooperatives are employed for all these aims of state policy, but their members are never asked about their own aims.

The "self-administration" of the cooperatives within the framework of a cooperative central association is absurd, since this association depends on the government's favor; the cooperative conferences are dominated by the registrars of the state cooperative authorities who have to represent the government's interest and naturally do so because of long years of practice. In recent years, however, self-assurance and political will among the leaders of the agricultural cooperatives has grown (thus they showed determined resistance towards the leveling efforts of the Akintola government). Foreign advisors (e.g., the American Cooperative League) support these efforts to become independent because they doubt the ability of the cooperative authorities to reform internally without pressure from outside.

A more general conclusion can be added. Development aid provided by one government for another gives privileges to the administration that has to carry out the programs. Because of the technological backwardness of developing countries, Euro-Americans easily assume that the administration, as a "modern" structure, is perhaps best in furthering development. But this must be examined empirically in each case. The example cited here illustrates that the cooperative authorities are a "traditional" structure arising out of the beginnings of the colonial era, with certain functions that are no longer opportune today. Social energy shown here in the independent cooperative associations is not furthered by the official cooperative administration but rather hindered because the administration clings blindly to a set program.

Change will not come automatically; it will need much political pressure from below to force an established administration into a period of reform.

NOTES

1. P. Trappe, Warum Genossenschaften in Entwicklungsländern? (Neuwied: Hermann Luchterhand Verlag, 1966), p. 1.

2. J. C. deGraft-Johnson, African Experiment: Cooperative Agriculture and Banking in British West Africa (London, 1958); S. Gorst, Co-operative Organization in Tropical Countries: A Study of Co-operative Development in Non-self-governing Territories under United Kingdom Administration 1945-1955 (Oxford, 1959); A. Hanel, "Genossenschaften in Nigeria" (unpublished manuscript, University of Marburg, 1967).

3. S. O. Adeyeye, "The Forerunners of the Nigerian Cooperative Movement," (unpublished postgraduate seminar paper, University of Ibadan, Department of History, January 24, 1967). Adeyeye's thesis is still unpublished, and Nigerians continue to be taught that cooperatives were a gift from their colonial administration. Neither the Cooperative Division of the Western State's Ministry of Trade and Industry nor the Nigerian Institute of Social and Economic Research, which sponsored the research, have taken steps toward publication of the paper. There ought to be a new professional position, "Academic Journalist," to popularize research and to bring results to the attention of the persons and institutions concerned.

4. Hanel, Genossenschaften in Nigeria.

5. Hans Dieter Seibel and Michael Koll, Einheimische Genossenschaften in Afrika. Formen wirtschaftlicher Zusammenarbeit bei westafrikanischen Stämmen (Bielefeld: Bertelsmann Universitätsverlag, 1968).

6. G. Kenneth Oniverka Dike, Trade and Politics in the Niger Delta 1830 to 1885. An Introduction to the Economic and Political History of Nigeria (Oxford: Clarendon Press, 1956), pp. 34-7.

7. Adeyeye, op. cit., p. 1.

8. For further evidence see M. Koll, "Crafts and Cooperation in Western Nigeria. A Sociological Contribution to Indigenous Economics" (Düsseldorf: Bertelsmann Universitätsverlag, 1969).

9. Western Nigeria, "Cooperative Department Policy for the Western Region, Nigeria" (mimeo, Ibadan, 1955).

10. M. Koll, "Western Nigerian Integrated Rural Development Scheme—A Governmental Attempt to Solve the Employment Problem through Cooperatives," in Yearbook of Agricultural Cooperation 1969 (Oxford: Blackwell 1969), pp. 196-210.

11. Author's sample census, 1967.

12. M. Koll, "Western Nigerian Integrated Rural Development Scheme."

13. M. Koll, Das Entwicklungspotential der Interessenverbände am Beispiel westnigerianischer Handwerksverbände (Düsseldorf: Bertelsmann Universitatsverlag, 1971). See also M. Koll, ed., African Urban Development. Four Political Approaches (Düsseldorf: Bertelsmann Universitätsverlag, 1972).

14. W. D. Sorenson, "A Financial and Management Analysis of Ilesha Cooperative Produce Marketing Union, Ilesha, Nigeria" (mimeo., Ibadan, 1966).

4

SYSTEMS OF STATUS ALLOCATION AND RECEPTIVITY TO MODERNIZATION

H. Dieter Seibel

THE PROBLEM

The discussion of the process of modernization in developing countries has largely centered on exogenous agents of change as causal factors. This emphasis may be attributed to the influence of structural functionalism, which defined traditional societies as "extraordinarily conservative and resistant to change," tending "to reject traits that would create imbalance."[1] Societies were classified dichotomously into relatively modernized and relatively nonmodernized ones, and the former were described as achievement oriented and receptive to change while the latter were said to allocate social status on the basis of ascribed criteria and to be resistant to change. Hence change could be due only to exogenous factors.

However it has become apparent that some traditional societies modernize much faster than others. In many cases these differences cannot be explained in terms of differential activity of agents of change. Therefore one may postulate that there may be features inherent to societies that act as determinants of their differential receptivity to change. In this chapter the following five hypotheses will be tested in a number of societies in two African countries, Nigeria and Liberia:

1. There is a relationship between certain structural features and receptivity to change.

2. There is a relationship between structural complexity and receptivity to change.

3. There is a relationship between the system of stratification and receptivity to change.

4. There is a relationship between the amount of social mobility and receptivity to change.

5. There is a relationship between the system of status allocation (i.e., the qualitative aspect of the system of social mobility,

whether it is based on achieved or ascribed criteria) and receptivity to change.[2]

METHODOLOGY

The data have been collected from published sources and from five studies done by the author between 1963 and 1969. The published sources consulted are: anthropological literature, official statistics, and various other studies. The original studies are: an interview sample study of 509 workers in ten factories in Ibadan and Lagos (Nigeria), done in 1963-64[3]; an anthropological survey of the Krahn, a Kru tribe, done in 1967-68; an interview sample study of 383 workers in a Liberian mining enterprise; and two interview studies of the staff in two mining enterprises in Liberia, done in 1968-69.

Some remarks about the relationships between these studies are in order. The study in Nigeria was set up to test the first two hypotheses, which seemed to be the most plausible ones. They were rejected. During an anthropological survey among the Krahn, the author "discovered" a new set of hypotheses (hypotheses 3, 4, and 5 above). Their formulation led to a reevaluation of the Nigerian data. Hypotheses 3 and 4 were rejected, hypothesis 5 was corroborated. Since this was an ex post facto argumentation—i.e., the hypothesis to be tested was formulated after the data had been collected—it was felt a study should be set up specifically ex ante facto to test the hypothesis. This study was done in a Liberian enterprise; hypothesis 5 was again corroborated.

THE NIGERIAN CASE

Hypothesis 1: There is a Relationship between Certain Structural Features and Receptivity to Change

The following reasoning led to the formulation of hypothesis 1:
1. All industrial societies have certain structural features in common, in particular:
   a. centralization of political functions;
   b. high degree of urbanization;
   c. existence of a market system; and
   d. large-scale organization of a technologically highly developed system of production.[4]
2. All industrial societies are highly receptive to change.

3. Thus a relationship between these structural features and receptivity to change is hypothesized.

4. There are societies in Africa where some of the structural features of industrial societies are found, while in others they are either absent or formulated in a different way; some African societies are more similar to industrial societies than others in terms of certain structural features.

5. Thus it is predicted that African societies with structural features of industrial societies are more receptive to change than those without.

The Societies Tested

The Hausa. The main areas of settlement are the provinces of Sokoto, Katsina, Kano, Zaria, and Bauchi in Northern Nigeria. Seven states were founded to which later on an eighth was added. During the 13th century, the Islamic faith was adopted by the Hausa and exerted a strong influence on their social, political, and religious life. A new form of government came into existence with a well-organized system of taxation and a highly qualified judiciary. Around 1500 the Fulani, a nomadic tribe, started to immigrate peacefully into Hausaland. Some of them settled in the Hausa towns, adopted Islam, and inter-married with the Hausa. The others, so-called cow-Fulani, retained their nomadic style of life and their beliefs. In 1802 Othman dan Fodio, a Fulani sheikh, led a holy war (jihad) against the Hausa and overthrew their government; from then on, Fulani emirs were the rulers, and they have retained their feudal system of government until today. All of the structural features mentioned above are found in the Hausa social system: The Hausas have a central government; the degree of urbanization is high, seen against the African background; there is a rather elaborate marketing structure; crafts are well-developed and organized into guilds; and the system of occupational roles is highly differentiated.[5]

The Yoruba. The Yoruba comprise a number of closely related kingdoms with a history of about a thousand years. Under the Oyo Empire, they dominated a large part of the West African coast. Its influence started to decrease around 1700. After a long period of fighting against the kingdom of Dahomey during the eighteenth century, civil war led to internal disintegration during the nineteenth century. This made it possible for the Fulani to penetrate Yoruba territory and to Islamize its northern part. The Yoruba emerged from this divided into largely independent kingdoms. The Yoruba are the tribe with the highest rate of traditional urbanization in Africa. The government of the king is centered in a usually large city and administers to the city as well as to the whole kingdom. The kingdom is subdivided into chiefdoms, which depend on the king in military and extrapolitical affairs, in taxation, and in certain kinds of trials. Administration is performed by officials. The structural features mentioned above are found among the Yoruba in a similar way as they are among the Hausa.[6]

The Ibo. Before the arrival of Europeans, the Ibo had no common name, nor did they have a common tradition of origin. They also were never politically united. In many cases the village group is the largest recognized political unit. In regard to the fact that they speak a related group of dialects, inhabit a coherent tract of land, and have many cultural features in common that distinguish them from neighboring groups, they may be called a people or tribe. There is no central political authority, neither over the whole of Iboland nor over parts of it. Authority is, in principle, never vested in one individual. In each community, political functions are served by a council of elders. And even they are not fully authorized to make political decisions, which have to be presented to the community that ratifies them by acclamation or refuses acceptance respectively. All structural features listed above are absent: there is no centralization of political functions; there are no towns, and villages are split in hamlets consisting typically of dispersed homesteads; there is no elaborate market system (there are only small local markets); while the Hausa and Yoruba have specialized craftsmen organized in guilds, the Ibo have none—there is very little, if any, specialization; the technological level of craft production is very low, and there are no large production organizations, such as guilds.[7]

According to hypothesis 1, the following prediction can be made about the three societies' receptivity to change: the Hausa and Yoruba, who have many structural features in common with industrial societies, will be receptive to change; the Ibo, who do not have any of these structural features and come very close to what most people would call a truly primitive tribe, will be resistant to change.

Indicators of Receptivity to Change

Receptivity to change is measured as actual change when opportunities for change are offered. The following indicators will be used:
a. geographical mobility;
b. intergenerational occupational mobility;
c. intragenerational occupational mobility; and
d. adaptation to wage labor.
The data will be taken from three sources: official statistics, published studies, and a sample study of 509 workers in Ibadan and Lagos.

Measuring Receptivity to Change

Geographical Mobility. Interregional mobility may serve as a crude measure of geographical mobility. The distributions of the societies under consideration in regions other than their own shows that the Hausa (constituting 0.40 percent of the two southern regions) rank lowest and the Ibo (constituting 2.22 percent of the Northern and Western regions) rank highest, slightly above the Yoruba (constituting 2.20 percent of the Northern and Eastern regions). Comparing the proportions of each tribe residing in regions other than their own eliminates the bias introduced by the differences in size among the three societies and among the three regions. The Hausa again rank lowest, with 1.01 percent of the total population of the tribe residing in other regions. The Yoruba are most mobile, with 11.30 percent of the tribe residing in other regions. The Ibo rank somewhat lower, with 9.34 percent of the tribe residing in other regions (see Table 4.1).

Intergenerational Occupational Mobility. Since modernization is a rather recent phenomenon in Nigeria, the vast majority of people in modern jobs have parents in traditional jobs. Hence most people in modern jobs are intergenerationally mobile. In a sample of 509 factory workers in Ibadan and Lagos, 89 percent of the workers stated in fact that their father had a traditional job. According to hypothesis 1, the Hausa should represent a significantly larger proportion of the labor force than the Ibo.* No prediction can be made for the Yoruba, since they are the local tribe (Ibadan and Lagos both being large Yoruba cities), except that they are likely to supply the bulk of workers. A total of 63.3 percent of the workers were Yoruba. Contrary to expectation, 18.1 percent were Ibo, while only 0.8 percent were Hausa.
These results are validated by the findings of Wells and Warmington in Sapele, a city outside the native land of any of the three societies tested.[8] Most of the employees of African Timber and Plywood Ltd. (3,250 employees in 1959) were Ibo and Yoruba; Hausa did not appear in the labor force. In the Northern Region, the homeland of the Hausa, however, southerners (Ibo, Yoruba, and other tribes) were far overrepresented.[9] Intergenerational mobility is so high among Yoruba and

---

*The proportion of Hausa working in modern occupations in Southern Nigeria should be increased by the fact that modern employment opportunities are relatively scarce in Northern Nigeria. Since this may be balanced by the fact that the high population density in Eastern Nigeria tends to induce many Ibo to seek employment outside their own tribal territory, both factors will not be taken into consideration.

TABLE 4.1

Population of Major Tribes of Nigeria, by Region, 1952-53 Census

Tribe	Northern Region[a]	Number in Western Region[b]	Eastern Region[c]	Total Population of Tribe	Members of Tribe living in Regions other than Own	
					Percent of Total Population of Tribe	Percent of Total Population of Regions other than Own
Hausa	5,488,400	41,370	14,879	5,544,649	1.01	0.40
Yoruba	535,500	4,302,376	12,340	4,850,216	11.30	2.20
Ibo	166,900	342,335	4,942,530	5,451,765	9.34	2.22
Total population of region	16,879,200	6,085,065	7,967,975			

Sources: [a]Ministry of Economic Planning, Northern Nigeria Statistical Yearbook 1965 (Kaduna, 1966), p. 16.
[b]Ministry of Economic Planning, Statistical Division, Western Region Statistical Bulletin June 1959 (1959), p. 7.
[c]Census Superintendent, Population Census of the Eastern Region of Nigeria 1953 (Lagos, 1955).

Ibo that serious unemployment problems have arisen in recent years. In the Hausa-dominated north, intergenerational mobility is not nearly high enough to supply enough workers and clerks. In 1953, southerners held 82 percent of the clerical service jobs in the Northern Region.[10] In 1960, the year of independence, only 1 percent of the federal civil service was from the north, and of those most were in the lower grades despite NPC* control of many ministries at the top.[11]

Similarly industry in the north cannot rely on local supply of labor. A study in four groundnut-crushing firms in Kano has shown that 96 percent of the clerks, 60 percent of the artisans, and 20 percent of the laborers were southerners; half of the employees of a Kano shoe factory were found to be from the south.[12] Compared with the proportion of workers represented by Yoruba (63 percent) or southerners (99 percent) in the ten factories studied in Ibadan and Lagos, northerners reveal a very low propensity to leave the traditional sector. It should also be mentioned that for most Ibo and Yoruba, interregional geographical mobility means at the same time intergenerational occupational mobility. The Hausa who leave their own region, however, are frequently traders who do their business along the lines of traditional patterns.

Since Wells and Warmington do not distinguish between Yoruba and Ibo, only the studies in ten factories in Ibadan and Lagos are used for a comparison of intergenerational occupational mobility between the two societies. A total of 11.1 percent of the Yoruba and 11.1 percent of the Ibo stated that their fathers held modern jobs (corrected Chi square = 0.0326, df = 1; Gamma = 0.0018); the remaining 88.9 percent of both societies have moved from a traditional to a modern occupational setting.**

---

*Northern Peoples Congress—the party of the north, which had won the federal elections.

**To avoid possible misunderstandings, labor turnover must be discussed briefly in this context. In the initial stage of industrialization in Africa, labor turnover is extremely high. This is due to low labor commitment and a high degree of integration into traditional tribal society, which has not yet developed a place for modern employment. With increasing adaptation to wage labor and urban life, turnover decreases to a normal level and even below that later, when jobs become scarce due to an oversupply of labor. Among Ibo and Yoruba, labor turnover has reached a very low rate. In the north, labor turnover and absenteeism rates are still extremely high, and they would be even higher if there were no southerners to bring the rates down and if among the northerners the workers from the numerous small tribes were excluded (Wells and Warmington, Studies in Industrialization, pp. 43, 93).

Intragenerational Occupational Mobility. The data of Wells and Warmington and of Schwarz show that the Hausa do not move ahead in modern careers. This is not only true in comparison with Yoruba and Ibo but also with a number of northern tribes. Wells and Warmington found that in Kaduna Textile Mills, a large enterprise in Northern Nigeria that employs only northerners, Hausa were mainly found— as a matter of policy—in the lower strata of the hierarchy, while the upper positions were more often filled by people who came from some of the small middle-belt tribes.[13]

To compare the rate of intragenerational mobility between Yoruba and Ibo, the amount of social climbing between first and last job had been determined. No difference was found (chi square = 1.0468 df = 3; Gamma = 0.0043).*

Since, in both societies, nine out of ten workers come from a traditional environment, the appraisal of which tribe occupies the higher positions may also be used as an indicator of intragenerational occupational mobility. A very weak relationship between tribe and occupational position (Gamma = -0.07) was found to be significant at the .001 level of probability (chi square = 18.41 = df = 4), with the Yoruba occupying on the average slightly higher positions than the Ibo (see Table 4.2). The minute difference found may be due to the higher educational level of Yoruba in the sample. A moderate difference in educational attainment (Gamma = 0.35) was found to exist between Yoruba and Ibo beyond the .001 level of significance (chi square = 24.24, df = 4) (Table 4.2). Surprisingly, then, the mean monthly wage of the Ibo (£12.0) was higher than the mean wage of the Yoruba (£11.3). Apparently the Ibo occupied higher positions within each skill category than the Yoruba. However the difference between Yoruba and Ibo by wage was not found to be significant (chi square = 5.68, df = f; Gamma = 0.04; t = 0.97) (Table 4.2).

---

*The workers were placed in five categories: very downwardly mobile; downwardly mobile; stable; upwardly mobile; very upwardly mobile. For the computations of chi square, the last two categories were combined because of small frequencies. Workers who moved from semiskilled to skilled were classified as mobile; those who moved from unskilled to skilled as very mobile. Workers who started their careers as clerks, civil servants, or teachers were classified as skilled workers. Since this is somewhat arbitrary, computations were repeated without this group; again, no difference was found (chi square = 2.27168, df = 3; Gamma = 0.0952).

The number of previous jobs (Yoruba, 1.53; Ibo, 1.58) and the age at first job (Yoruba, 19.9 years; Ibo, 19.8 years) were also found to be the same for Yoruba and Ibo.

Adaptation to Wage Labor. The previous data show that the number of Hausa entering modern jobs—i.e., the social field where adaptation to wage labor may take place—is very small. They also demonstrate that of those Hausa entering modern employment only a few make their way up; most stay where they have started. Wells and Warmington found in Northern Nigeria that Hausa are less interested than Yoruba and Ibo and workers from middle-belt tribes in getting a steady job, acquiring skill, being promoted, and raising their standard of living. The Yoruba and Ibo, in contrast, even seek promotion, not only for its money value but also for the social prestige that it confers.[14]

The indicators used to measure adaptation to wage labor and some of its social concomitants signify that the Ibo have slightly better adjusted to modern work and are generally somewhat more progressive than the Yoruba. While all the differences found point in the same direction, many are so small that they fail to be statistically significant. A brief summary may suffice.

The average monthly wage was £12 for the Ibo and £11.3 for the Yoruba. Absenteeism was 3.4 days a year among the Ibo and 4.6 days a year among the Yoruba. A total of 81 percent of the Ibo and 76 percent of the Yoruba felt recognized in the factory. A total of 66 percent of the Ibo and 39 percent of the Yoruba stated they had no difficulties in the factory. A total of 79 percent of the Ibo and 70 percent of the Yoruba were satisfied with the fact that their wages were paid monthly. There was no statistically significant difference between the proportions of Ibo (45 percent) and Yoruba (41 percent) taking courses for occupational advancement. The Ibo, however, tended more to technical courses (79 percent of the courses taken being technical courses) than the Yoruba (49 percent)—hence were adjusting better to the needs of an industrializing economy. Similarly 62 percent of the Ibo but only 41 percent of the Yoruba would like to get a technical job (of those who want to change their job). For their sons, 50 percent of the Ibo and 48 percent of the Yoruba preferred technical jobs. These data signify that the Ibo conformed slightly more to the recent shift in high occupational prestige from white-collar jobs toward technical jobs. Ibo workers also appeared to have adjusted fairly well to the economics of city life: while they had £21.15 savings on the average, as compared with £10.71 among the Yoruba, their mean debts were only £4.79, as compared with £6.59 among the Yoruba. Finally the Ibo were more in accordance with the general trend from polygyny to monogamy; 82 percent of the married Yoruba and 91 percent of the married Ibo were monogamous. This difference was more pronounced in their preferences: 64 percent of the Yoruba and 86 percent of the Ibo preferred monogamy over polygamy (Table 4.2).

TABLE 4.2

Relationship between Tribe and Twelve Variables among
Yoruba and Ibo workers in Ibadan and Lagos, Nigeria

Variable	Gamma*	Chi Square X^2	df	p	Means Yoruba	Ibo	Student's t t	p
Occupational position	-0.07	18.41	4	.001				
Education	-0.35	24.24	4	<.001				
Wage	0.04	5.68	5	<.50	£11.3 (£/month)	£12.0	0.97	<.20
Absenteeism	-0.05	0.49	2	<.80	4.6 (days/year)	3.4	2.32	.02
Difficulties at work place	-0.50	19.60	1	<.001				
Savings	0.31	15.94	7	<.05	£10.71	£21.15	2.91	<.01
Debts	-0.06	9.65	7	<.30	£6.59	£4.79	0.88	<.20
Course enrollment	0.07	0.22	1	<.70				
Technical course enrollment	0.58	3.21	1	<.10				
Preference for technical jobs	0.37	8.03	2	<.02				
Preference for technical jobs for sons	0.09	3.32	2	<.20				
Type of marriage (mono-/ polygamous)	0.39	2.88	1	<.10	1.18 (no. of wives)	1.12	2.93	<.01
Preferred type of marriage (mono-/ polygamous)	0.55	15.12	1	.001				

*Positive Gammas mean higher values for Ibo, negative Gammas
mean higher values for Yoruba (e.g., Yoruba have higher occupational
positions, higher educational standards, higher absenteeism rates).

In their Sapele study, Wells and Warmington came to similar conclusions: "It was generally agreed that the Ibos make the most satisfactory workers. . . . Yorubas . . . also had a good reputation."[15]

Conclusion

On all levels considered, the Hausa are by far the least receptive to change. Looking into Hausa history during the past two generations and analyzing the attitudes of Hausa leaders to change and their policies designed to keep any agents of change out of Hausa territory, one may even state that they have been highly resistant to change. The difference between Yoruba and Ibo appears to be slight, if it exists at all. The Yoruba were the first in modern Nigerian history to show high social mobility. Around 1920 the educated Nigerian elite was almost entirely Yoruba. In 1921 Yoruba formed 40 percent and Ibo 11 percent of those in towns in Southern Nigeria who had received Western education. From that time, the Ibo tried to catch up, a goal they reached around 1945.[16] There is some evidence that they continued to move up the ladder of socioeconomic success so that they might have achieved some advantage over the Yoruba before the outbreak of the civil war.

According to our outdated information about geographical mobility, the Yoruba are somewhat more mobile than the Ibo. On the other two dimensions, intergenerational and intragenerational occupational mobility, however, no difference was found. Only some of the data summarized under "adaptation to wage labor" suggest that the Ibo have advanced somewhat further toward the goal of modernity than the Yoruba. Since the data available do not permit a clear conclusion about the existence of a difference between Yoruba and Ibo, the null hypothesis of no difference is accepted.

The prediction of a high receptivity to change among Hausa and Yoruba and a low receptivity among Ibo proved to be wrong for Hausa and Ibo. Hence hypothesis 1 is rejected.

Hypothesis 2: There is a Relationship between Structural Complexity and Receptivity to Change

The data presented to test hypothesis 1 also rule out that there is an association between structural complexity and receptivity to change. Both Hausa and Yoruba society are structurally very complex, while Ibo society is of a much simpler structure. But it is Ibo and Yoruba society that are receptive to change and Hausa society that is not.

Hypothesis 3: There is a Relationship between the
System of Stratification and Receptivity to Change

Does the existence of a more-or-less elaborate system of
stratification make any difference in regard to receptivity to change?
To test this hypothesis, further data are needed on the traditional
systems of the three societies.

The Hausa

The Hausa system of stratification is so complex that any exact
statement about the number of strata must be rather artificial. The
main determinants of the masculine status order (the women have a
quite different order) are political rank and occupational class. Two
broad strata groups may be distinguished: on the one hand the chiefs
and officeholders, on the other hand the subjects and commoners—
i.e., the rulers and the ruled. Both strata groups are in themselves
highly differentiated again. An important distinction in officeholding
is whether it is inherited (karda) or freely selected (shigege). The
same distinction is found in crafts. As to evaluation of the distinction,
"Karda enjoys higher status than shigege as well as greater prestige."[17]
Karda, inherited position, is the prevalent system. It implies the
existence of a set of closed occupational groups recruited by agnatic
descent. All occupational groups are ranked, with the officials, the
Islamic teachers (mallams) and wealthy merchants at the top, and
the butchers, matweavers, drummers, praise-singers, and buglers at
the bottom.

The Yoruba

The upper layer of the Yoruba system of stratification is formed
by royal families from which the king is chosen. Beneath that is the
stratum of hereditary chiefs and representatives of major territorial
and associational groups in the town. Commoners without hereditary
claims to titles are a further layer, which may be considered as
consisting of two substrata, one of craftsmen and one of farmers.*

---

*Slaves are not mentioned here. The main reason is that it
is difficult to locate them in the stratification system. Although they
are usually at the bottom, they may also be found anywhere else in
the stratification system. Among the Hausa, for instance, royal
slaves could hold very high offices; around 1870-80, for example,
there were slave generals in Zaria.

The Ibo

Ibo society, a so-called segmentary system, is characterized
by a differentiated system of ranked statuses that are not ordered
in strata with more-or-less clearly drawn strata lines. There is
no stratum into which a person is born, and there are no hereditary
positions.* Although it could be of some practical advantage to have
a rich father, everyone is born equal, and birth or family (lineage)
affiliation does not determine one's position in life. There is no
intergenerational status stability; even intragenerationally, status is
highly unstable.

Conclusion

The data do not support the hypothesis that the more rigid the
system of stratification, the less receptive it will be to change. Hausa
and Yoruba society are rather rigidly stratified; Ibo society is not.
However it is Yoruba and Ibo society that are receptive to change, and
Hausa society that is not. Thus no pattern of association emerges.

Hypothesis 4: There is a Relationship between the
Amount of Social Mobility and Receptivity to Change

Hausa

Despite its emphasis on hereditary positions, the Hausa socio-
political system is highly competitive. Polygamy and concubinage
greatly increase the number of persons eligible for all hereditary
offices, and succession is not determined either on the basis of
primogeniture or through any other automatic provision. A central
feature of Hausa society is an institutionalized system of competition
called neman sarautu, or clientage system. A person may become
the client of an officeholder expecting to be rewarded for his loyalty
and obedience with an office. Thus, despite the existence of an elaborate system of stratification, strata lines are no absolute barrier to
mobility (as they are, for example, in the Indian caste system). Social
rise and fall are quite common among the Hausa.[18]

---

*An exception are the osu cult slaves. They form a separate
group, and membership is hereditary. However, since this is very
atypical for the structural type of segmentary societies to which the
Ibo belong, no further attention is paid to this group in this study.

Yoruba

There is a certain amount of interstratum mobility. A wealthy man, for example, may be appointed to council membership and even receive a chieftaincy title, which involves the crossing of strata boundaries. There is, however, a considerable amount of intrastratum mobility, each stratum being a differentiated system of ranked statuses. There are two alternative institutions a man of ambition may choose between for raising his social status. One is a clientage system similar to the Hausa's, but not as elaborate. It is limited to the royal court, where a man may gain the favor of the king and be promoted to an office. The other one is the Ogboni society, which every male can join, but whose higher ranks, however, are open only to those who can pay the rather high fees. This way, a man can translate his wealth into political power and high social status.

Outside the political system, a man has a number of alternatives of amassing wealth on the basis of which he can raise his status. In addition the Ogboni society provides ways of securing political recognition of the social raise based on nonpolitical activities. Especially during the wars of the nineteenth century, a number of other avenues were open to men of ambition: in the army; in crafts that produced weapons and other supplies for the armies; in agriculture, which had a permanent market among the fulltime craftsmen as well as in the armies. In each one of these fields, a man could improve his position on the basis of his personal efficiency.

Ibo

Social mobility is very high among the Ibo. Every position is, on principle, open to everyone. A person has alternative choices between various ways of gaining prestige and between various occupations; he need not automatically take his father's job. The opportunity for upward or downward mobility is almost unlimited. Mobility is not confined to the political, economic, or occupational spheres; a person may also improve his position by high performance in athletics, the arts, and more recently in literature and science.

Conclusion

Hence the mobility hypothesis is rejected. In all three societies there is social mobility to a considerable extent.

Hypothesis 5: There is a Relationship between the System of Status Allocation and Receptivity to Change

Hausa

In Hausa society, achievement, defined as striving for excellence where standards of excellence are applicable, is of no importance for the individual's social rise or fall. Smith points out that "The American stress on occupation in status placement makes individual achievement primary and defines social mobility in occupation terms. The Hausa system of occupational status is almost the exact reverse. It is almost wholly ascriptive in its orientation, since its units are closed descent groups between which all movement is disapproved. . . . [The] occupational status model . . . incorporates such ascriptive factors as descent and ethnicity."[19] The only chance for mobility is presented by the clientage system. For a man of ambition, there are no significant alternatives to clientage. The ubiquitous clientage system allows for mobility on the basis of obedience and servitude, and denies it on the basis of competence. Whitaker found that this bias "is very greatly responsible for two ostensibly contrasting sets of qualities in the system as a whole: on the one hand, political and administrative insecurity, uncertainty, instability, arbitrariness, domination, dogmatism, coercion, and restrictiveness; on the other hand, competitiveness, flexibility, mobility, calculation, inventiveness, and secular devotion to whatever the requirements and rewards of power might be."[20] It has to be strongly emphasized that achieved roles (understood as referring to those positions that an individual has acquired on the basis of his qualifications or accomplishments directly germane to the actions carried out in terms of the position) are largely irrelevant.[21] "Political offence, defined by the system as attachment to the king's political rival, was the principal ground for dismissal; and political solidarity with the king and opposition to his rivals was the principal ground for appointment."[22] An important aspect of any social system is the system of values incorporated in it and internalized by the incumbents of the positions in the status system. In a social system allocating status predominantly on the basis of achieved criteria, a major value orientation is toward achievement that, in the ideal or extreme case, is not sought for its material or other rewards but for its own intrinsic value, as described by Max Weber. While there are certainly individuals with an "acquisitive drive" or a "need for achievement" among the Hausa (for instance, among the merchants) achievement is not a generally recognized and sanctioned social value. In Hausa society important values are loyalty, obedience, servility, sensitivity to the demands of those in authority, and respect for tradition. In an achieving society, individuals are socialized through early training in habits of excelling; Hausa society trains its members in the habits of subordination, political intrigue, and opportunistic choice of patrons.[23]

Yoruba

Upon first examination, the Yoruba system of status allocation appears rather ascriptive, most important positions being hereditary. There are the royal lineages from which the kings are chosen; there are the chieftainly lineages in which chieftaincy titles are inherited; there are the commoners whose stratum affiliation is hereditary. Among the commoners, there are the crafts held by certain lineages and controlled by guilds that would allow for some occupational mobility only if the demand for apprentices could not be satisfied from within the craft. In the same way a blacksmith's son would normally become a blacksmith, a farmer's son would become a farmer, and so on. However there is also ample opportunity for personal achievement leading to a rise of one's social position. This has partly been institutionalized in the Ogboni society—a man may become wealthy by working hard, being a clever businessman, etc. No equality norms forbid this, and no negative sanctions are imposed on him. If he uses some of his wealth to pay his way into the higher ranks of the Ogboni society, he also rises on the political ladder, possibly as high as the chieftaincy title. There are alternative occupations through which a man may choose to achieve a higher position, and there are also alternative institutions for political advancement (clientage, Ogboni society). Even within a stratum of hereditary positions, achievement is not absent. A king, for example, is chosen from among the royal families, on the basis of his personal competence and merits. Should he not fulfill the expectations, the council may decide to send him a parrot's egg, which means the king must commit suicide. Thus the allocation of important positions is partly based on ascriptive and partly on achieved criteria. Every member of Yoruba society can be said to be affected by both achieved and ascribed status criteria.

Ibo

Societies whose members emphasize achieved roles always place a major emphasis on ascribed roles as well, and so does Ibo society. Beyond that universally shared emphasis on ascription, there is hardly any social position allocated by Ibo society to an individual without his personal competence, capability, aptitude, etc. being involved. In principle all positions labelled as important are achieved. Personal efforts and the use of one's abilities lead to a rise of status. War leadership goes to the one who proves to be most efficient.

Matters in dispute can be judged by a number of persons or councils; there is no office of the judge. One chooses whom one considers best in judging and on whom both parties agree. Authority is never formally vested in a single individual. Important decisions are made by a council wherein everyone has a word, and the one with the strongest arguments has the highest chance of contributing to the final decision. This is also true when the council is presided over by the eldest; the opinion of the men with the highest prestige and/or with the best arguments will lead to a decision. Wealth may be amassed by any member of the society; there are no social limitations to that. There is an institution that allows the translation of economic power (wealth) into political status—the title society. Every freeborn male member of society may buy his way into the title society, titles as well as the fees being ranked. Political status and prestige accrue to the title. Ibo society may be characterized as an open society wherein high status may be attained on the basis of occupational skill, enterprise, and initiative, with achievement being one of the highest values.

Conclusion

At last the data support the hypothesis that there is a relationship between the system of status allocation and receptivity to change, such. that a society that allocates status predominantly on the basis of achieved criteria shows a high degree of receptivity to change, while a society that attributes social position ascriptively is not receptive, or is even resistant, to change. It is only Hausa society in which achievement plays no role in the allocation of social status, and it is Hausa society that is resistant to change. Yoruba and Ibo, the change-receptive societies, allocate a considerable amount of statuses on the basis of achievement.

One could use hypothesis 5 to predict a difference between Yoruba and Ibo since traditional Ibo society is more exclusive than Yoruba society in placing emphasis on achievement. A few remarks are in order:

—Looking at the rate of change, one could argue that a remarkable difference between Yoruba and Ibo does in fact exist. It took the Ibo, who had a very late start, approximately half as long as the Yoruba to reach about the same level of modernization.

—If the trend of the last few decades is extrapolated, it is conceivable that the Ibo have surpassed the Yoruba by now.

—Alternatively it could be that the extent to which a society emphasizes achieved roles is relatively unimportant for its determination of receptivity to change as long as achieved roles and achievement do constitute an important part of the social structure and the value system respectively.

—A society's receptivity to change is an attribute of its particular
social structure. Whether this attribute is activated (hence effectuates
actual change) depends on other determinants, the source of which may
be endogenous or exogenous. In the African case, receptivity to modernization depends for its effectuation largely on exogenous agents
of change, such as colonialism, Christianity and the various missionary
activities it involves, modern formal education, commercial relations
with Europe, introduction of modern employment opportunities, introduction of modern technology, etc. Prolonged and intense contact of
a society with various agents of change may, in the long run, lead to
a relatively high degree of modernization, even if the receptivity to
change is relatively low, and ultimately also to a higher receptivity
to change, by way of changes in its system of status allocation.
Alternatively a society with a high receptivity to change may not
modernize at all because no agent of change might become active
in its boundaries. So Yoruba society might have approached the Ibo
level of receptivity to change closer than it would have under the ceteris
paribus clause, because Yoruba had earlier and more intense contact
with such agents of change as colonialism and Christianity. One cannot
argue that Hausa lack of modernization is due to a lack of activities
of agents of change, because they had the opportunity to allow a number
of agents of change to become active but their successful policy was
to keep them outside Hausaland or, as in the case of colonialism,
to get the guarantee that the agent of change abstained from effectuating
any change. Instead of introducing change, the British, generally
inclined toward absolute rulers, protected the status quo. As the
most powerful group and under the protection of the British, the
Hausa even managed to keep modernizing influences away from the
middle-belt tribes and the Tiv, who would have readily accepted
modernizing influences that in turn would have had repercussions on
Hausa society. When the Ibo migrated in ever-increasing numbers
to the north and filled more and more of the important positions, they
became a major agent of change in Northern Nigeria. Already during
the colonial days there was fear that the southerners' economic power
might be translated into political power, as a quotation from Gaskiya
Ta Fi Kwabo, a Hausa newspaper, shows: "Southerners will take the
place of Europeans in the North. What is there to stop them? . . .
There are Europeans but, undoubtedly, it is the Southerner who has
the power in the North."[24] As a last resort to keep out modernizing
influences and preserve traditional order, the traditional Hausa elite
instigated a massacre of the most pushing group, the Ibo, in which
thousands were killed. Ironically the following civil war has given
the northern minorities (especially the middle-belt tribes) for the
first time a large-scale opportunity to enter the modern world—
through the army. Gowon himself, the military head of state, comes

from one of the small middle-belt tribes (Angas), and many other officers are recruited from them. Thus it is eventually the army that becomes the agent of change, by making use of these tribes' receptivity to change.

Further Tests of Hypothesis

It should be noted that the argument has not rested on a differential individual "acquisitive drive" in the three societies, or in a differential individual need for achievement. The concern was only with the social system, not with the personality system. It is the social system within which status is either allocated ascriptively or according to achievement, no matter what the individual's need is. However, the social system and the personality system are not isolated. One may, in most cases, expect with some probability a certain amount of congruency between the two systems. Thus, in a status allocation system where achievement is a leading social value, this value would be internalized by most individuals in that society and should produce a relatively high need for achievement in a number of them. In an ascriptive system, where compliance, authority, and tradition are the highest values, these should be similarly internalized by the individuals, and a need for achievement should be found in them to a significantly lesser degree.[25] This assumption is confirmed by a study of LeVine's, analysing dream reports and essays among male secondary school students in Nigeria: "The frequency of achievement imagery in dream reports was greatest for the Ibo, followed by the Southern Yoruba, Northern Yoruba, and Hausa, in that order. . . . The frequency of obedience and social compliance value themes in essays on success written by the students was greatest for the Hausa, followed by the Southern Yoruba and Ibo, in that order."[26] The differences between Yoruba and Ibo, however, were statistically not significant. These results are validated by a nationwide public opinion survey of Nigerian adults done by Lloyd A. Free: "The proportion of persons mentioning improvement of standard of living or national prosperity through technological advance as a leading aspiration for Nigeria was greatest for the Ibo, followed by the Southern Yoruba and Fulani-Hausa, in that order."[27] "The proportion of persons mentioning self-development or improvement as a leading personal aspiration was greatest for the Ibo, followed by the Southern Yoruba and Fulani-Hausa, in that order."[28]

THE LIBERIAN CASE

The explanation for the differential receptivity to change among Hausa, Yoruba and Ibo was given ex post facto. Many methodological objections can be raised against ex post facto arguments. Therefore, in a further test, the hypothetical association between the two variables system of status allocation and receptivity to change was used ex ante facto to predict the differential receptivity to change for some other societies whose systems of status allocation were known.

The Societies Tested

The tribes chosen were the Kpelle (known through the work of Gibbs[29]) and a cluster of six tribes generally referred to as the Kru group.*

The Kpelle

Politically the Kpelle are organized into a "polycephalous associational state"[30] consisting of a series of autonomous paramount chiefdoms of the same level of authority. Kinship and age are the most important criteria of status allocation. The positions of chief, subchief, head of secret society, and all other traditional offices are filled by the core lineage that is in the most direct line of descent from the founding ancestor. The main institution through which the allocation of all important positions is channeled is Poro, a secret society for men, together with its sister organization, Sande, for women. Poro and Sande are everpresent—at birth, during childhood and adolescence, during adult life, and at death. They implement the maintenance of patrilineal principles of organization, which otherwise would rest only upon the ideological orientation of high-status lineage segments. According to d'Azevedo the leaders of Poro and Sande represent an ideal family in which all members are agnates, symbolically married to one another. Poro and Sande may be called a patrilineal gerontocracy. "As initiation, schooling, and life-long membership in these unisexual organizations are compulsory for all persons as a basis of citizenship, the degree of control centered in the upper echelons of leadership is little short of absolute."[31] They are inherently conservative, directed toward the preservation of the status quo; even in situations of acculturation or social flux, they

---

*The Kru proper represent only one tribe in that group. The other tribes are the Krahn (including Sapo), Grebo, Bassa, De, and Belle—the latter two having migrated west and adopted certain features of the neighboring tribes. Since no De and only two Belle were in the sample, no account is taken of the possible influence of their deviation from the general cultural pattern of the group.

attempt to maintain adherence to the traditional norms, not the competing intruding ones. The ascriptive system of status allocation is mirrored in the value system; the primary structural device through which it is effectively instilled and strongly maintained being Poro and Sande. The most important values are respect for tradition and unquestioning and unqualified acceptance of authority exercised by elders. Education is basically coercive. Children are punished when asking a "why" question or acting in a manner unsanctioned by tradition. Elders are to be obeyed with great respect, and neither peers nor aliens are sources of knowledge. Gay and Cole summarize the main features of Kpelle education as (1) the pragmatic is subordinated to the traditional, which implies that the innovator is frowned upon, and independence is stifled; (2) reasons need not be given for what is learned; (3) learning is largely nonverbal—by observation and imitation.[32]

The Kru Tribes

The four main Kru tribes (Krahn, Kru, Bassa, Grebo) on which the following discussion is based occupy a continuous tract of land and are closely related linguistically and culturally. The political system is decentralized, the village typically being the largest political unit. Positions are on principle open to everyone, the almost exclusive criterion being personal achievement. Achievement is relevant not only during the period of striving for higher status; since there are no institutions like the Ibo title societies, only permanent efforts allow the incumbent to keep a position. If someone else turns out to be a better warrior, war leader, judge, rich man, etc., this person will get the position.[33] The coastal Kru, who are generally seafaring men, have been in contact with the West for centuries.* The land of the Kru and the other Kru tribes, however, has remained one of the most isolated and poorly developed parts of Liberia.[34] Only a few years ago was a road built to link the area with the capital. Emigration has been their only chance for modernization—which in fact they took eagerly; the Kru are today overrepresented in the population of Monrovia. The Kru tribes may be particularly suitable for another test of hypothesis 5, because they combine a high degree of traditional achievement orientation with an almost total lack of local development.

---

*Of the 105 members of Kru tribes in the sample, only 21 are Kru. How many of them are coastal Kru and how many are so-called bush Kru from the hinterland is not known. In any case, their number is too small to have any significant effect on the results discussed here.

Testing Receptivity to Change

To test receptivity to change, a probability sample of 383 workers was drawn in a German mining company located in Kpelle territory in Liberia. A total of 115 workers in the sample were Kpelle, and 105 belonged to the Kru tribes. Adaptation to wage labor was chosen as an indicator of receptivity to change, the opportunities for change being equal for both Kpelle and Kru workers once they entered the company. It was measured by a composite index, consisting of six subindexes (see Table 3). A 49-point scale resulted, and each individual was scored on this scale. The results confirm hypothesis 5: the Kpelle scored among the lowest and the Kru tribes scored highest, with the Kpelle mean score of 22.90 being different from the Kru tribes mean score of 26.45 beyond the .001 level of significance ($t = 3.906$; $F = 15.25$) (see Table 4.4). It may be interesting to note that the Gola ($n = 14$), whose traditional system of status allocation is very similar to that of the Kpelle, also scored very low (mean score: 20.1).

An additional test was done on the basis of the wage lists of the company by comparing the mean wage of all 476 Kpelle workers of the company and all 405 workers of the Kru group of tribes. The Kpelle averaged 19.97 cents per hours and the Kru group averaged 23.59 cents per hour, with the difference being significant beyond the .001 level ($t = 6.80$; $F = 2.42$).

The expected difference between Kpelle and Kru tribes is even more marked when mobility into the higher echelon of the industrial hierarchy is taken as a measure. In the same German mining enterprise where the workers were studied, the Kru tribes represented 33 percent and the Kpelle only 6 percent of the African staff ($N = 87$). In one American mining company in Liberia, the Kru tribes represented 44 percent and the Kpelle only 3 percent of the African staff ($N = 85$). Even when taking into account that the Kpelle make up 21 percent and the Kru tribes a little less than 40 percent of the population of Liberia (1962 census), the difference between the two groups is still remarkable.

CONCLUSION

Societies that traditionally allocate social status predominately on the basis of achieved criteria are receptive to change; societies that traditionally allocate social status predominately on the basis of ascribed criteria are resistant to change. This result may have far-reaching consequences. First, those theories of social change built on the assumption that achievement orientation characterizes modern societies and ascription orientation characterizes traditional societies

TABLE 4.3

Scoring System, using Six Subindexes, for measuring Adaptation to Wage Labor among Kpelle and Kru Workers in Liberia

Score	Education	Wages (cents/hour)	Time in Wage Labor		Attitude to Job	Rating by Supervisor
			(in years)	(as Percent of time since 1st job)		
0	illiterate	15	less than 1	0–20	very negative	very bad
1	grade 1-2	17	1	21–40		
2	grade 3-4	19	2	41–60	negative	
3	grade 5-6	21–23	3	61–80		
4	grade 7-8	26–28	4	81–100	neutral	
5		30–33	5			(continuous between 0 and 9)
6	grade 9	35,38,40,43	6			
7	grade 10-11	45,48	7		positive	
8		51,53,58	8			
9	grade 12	61,65,73	over 8		very positive	excellent

TABLE 4.4

Moving Average of Scores of Adaptation to Wage
Labor among Kpelle and Kru Workers in Liberia
(Percentages)

Score	Kpelle	Kru	Score	Kpelle	Kru
5	0.00	0.00	27	3.83	4.76
6	0.17	0.00	28	3.65	4.76
7	0.17	0.00	29	3.48	4.38
8	0.17	0.00	30	3.13	4.19
9	0.17	0.00	31	2.61	2.86
10	0.52	0.00	32	1.91	3.24
11	0.70	0.00	33	1.39	3.62
12	1.22	0.19	34	0.70	2.86
13	1.22	0.57	35	0.52	2.29
14	2.26	0.95	36	0.35	2.29
15	3.30	1.71	37	0.35	1.90
16	4.35	1.90	38	0.00	1.33
17	5.04	2.67	39	0.00	1.14
18	5.91	3.62	40	0.00	0.95
19	6.26	4.38	41	0.17	0.57
20	6.26	5.14	42	0.17	0.95
21	6.43	6.86	43	0.17	0.76
22	7.00	6.29	44	0.35	0.76
23	7.13	5.33	45	0.52	0.57
24	6.61	5.52	46	0.35	0.57
25	5.74	5.14	47	0.35	0.00
26	4.87	4.95	48		
			49		

Note, Total number of workers: Kpelle, 115; Kru, 105.
Mean scores: Kpelle, 22.90; Kru, 26.45.
T = 3.906, p<.001; f = 15.25, p<.001

have to be revised. Second, those theories that attribute the failure to modernize (or the failure of development projects) on principle to an allegedly inherent conservatism of traditional structures have also to be revised. Third, in traditionally ascriptive societies that turn out to be resistant to change, the result of this study provides a new basis for programs of modernization. In change-receptive societies, society and its members are likely to respond vividly to opportunities for change, and modernization from below is likely to be the most suitable procedure. In change-resistant societies, however, modernization from above may be the only way to implement change. If the leaders of such a society can be persuaded to introduce change, their subjects—well socialized in the attitude of authoritarian submission—could prove responsive. If the leaders cannot be persuaded to modernize, more radical devices are likely to be the only effective ones.

NOTES

1. Julian H. Steward, "Perspectives on Modernization: Introduction to the Studies," in Julian H. Steward, ed., Contemporary Change in Traditional Societies, Volume I: Introduction and African Tribes (Urbana, Chicago, and London: University of Illinois Press, 1967), pp. 1-55.

2. The independent variables refer to the social structure in pre-modern times. They do not characterize those segments of the population that are in the process of modernizing. The dependent variables refer to the contemporary, not to the pre-modern, situation.

3. H. Dieter Seibel, Industriearbeit und Kulturwandel in Nigeria: Kulturelle Implikationen des Wandels von einer traditionellen Stammesgesellschaft zu einer modernen Industriegesellschaft (Köln and Opladen: Westdeutscher Verlag, 1968).

4. A. S. Feldman and W. E. Moore, "Industrialization and Industrialism: Convergence and Differentiation," Transactions of the Fifth World Congress of Sociology, Vol. II (Washington, D.C.: International Sociological Association, 1962).

5. M. G. Smith, "The Hausa System of Social Status," Africa, Vol. 29, No. 3 (1959), pp. 239-52; M. G. Smith, Government in Zazzau (London: Oxford University Press, 1960); M. G. Smith, "The Hausa of Northern Nigeria," Pp. 119-155 in J. L. Gibbs, ed., Peoples of Africa (New York: Holt, Rinehart and Winston, 1965).

6. J. F. A. Ajayi, and Robert Smith, Yoruba Warfare in the Nineteenth Century (Ibadan: Cambridge University Press, 1964); W. R. Bascom, "The Principle of Seniority in the Social Structure of the Yoruba," American Anthropologist, Vol. 44 (1942), pp. 44-46; W. R. Bascom, "Urbanization among the Yoruba," American Journal of Sociology, Vol. 60 (1955), pp. 446-54; S. O. Biobaku, The Egba and Their Neighbors 1842-1872 (London: Oxford University Press 1957); Daryll Forde, The Yoruba-Speaking Peoples of South-Western Nigeria. Ethnographic Survey of Africa, Western Africa Part IV (London: International African Institute, 1962); P. C. Lloyd, "The Traditional Political System of the Yoruba," Southwestern Journal of Anthropology, Vol. 10 (1954), pp. 366-84; P. C. Lloyd, "The Yoruba Lineage," Africa,

Vol. 25 (1955), pp. 235-51; P. C. Lloyd, "Sacred Kingship and Government among the Yoruba," Africa, Vol. 30 (1960), pp. 221-37; P. C. Lloyd, Yoruba Land Law (London: Oxford University Press, 1962); P. C. Lloyd, "The Yoruba of Nigeria," in J. L. Gibbs, ed., Peoples of Africa, pp. 547-82.

      7. Daryll Forde and G. I. Jones, The Ibo and Ibibio-Speaking Peoples of South-Eastern Nigeria. Ethnographic Survey of Africa, Western Africa Part III (London: International African Institute, 1962); M. M. Green, Igbo Village Affairs (London: Sidwick and Jackson, 1948); G. I. Jones, "Ibo Land Tenure," Africa Vol. 19 (1949), pp. 309-23; G. I. Jones, "Ibo Age Organization with Special Reference to the Cross River and Northeastern Ibo," Journal of the Royal Anthropological Institute, Vol. 92 (1962), pp. 191-211; Warren Morrill, 1962-63 "The Ibo in Twentieth Century Calaban," Comparative Studies in Society and History, Vol. 5 (1962-63), 424-48; Phoebe V. Ottenberg, "The Changing Economic Position of Women among the Afikpo Ibo," in William R. Bascom and Melville J. Herskovits, eds., Continuity and Change in African Cultures (Chicago, London, and Toronto: University of Chicago Press, 1959), pp. 205-23; Phoebe V. Ottenberg, "The Afikpo Ibo of Eastern Nigeria," in J. L. Gibbs, ed., Peoples of Africa, pp. 1-39; Simon Ottenberg, "Improvement Associations among the Afikpo Ibo," Africa, Vol. 25 (1955), pp. 1-28; Simon Ottenberg, "Double Descent in an Ibo Village-Group," Proceedings of the Fifth International Congress of Anthropological and Ethnological Sciences (1956), pp. 473-81; Simon Ottenberg, "Ibo Oracles and Intergroup Relations," Southwestern Journal of Anthropology, Vol. 14 (1958), pp. 295-317; Simon Ottenberg, "Ibo Receptivity to Change," in William R. Bascom and Melville J. Herskovits, eds., Continuity and Change in African Cultures, (1958), pp. 130-43.

      8. F. A. Wells and W. A. Warmington, Studies in Industrialization: Nigeria and the Cameroons (London: Oxford University Press, 1963), pp. 46, 52.

      9. Ibid., pp. 102, 105.

      10. Frederick A. O. Schwarz, Nigeria. The Tribes, the Nation, or the Race—The Politics of Independence (Cambridge, Mass. and London: M.I.T. Press, 1965), p. 71.

      11. Ibid., p. 115.

      12. Wells and Warmington, Studies in Industrialization, pp. 102, 105.

      13. Ibid., p. 104.

      14. Ibid., pp. 53, 93, 102-105.

      15. Ibid., p. 52.

      16. James S. Coleman, Nigeria: Background to Nationalism (Berkeley and Los Angeles: University of California Press, 1958), pp. 142, 333.

17. Smith, "The Hausa System of Social Status," p. 248.

18. C. S. Whitaker Jr., "A Dysrhythmic Process of Political Change," World Politics, Vol. 19 (1967), pp. 190-217; C. S. Whitaker Jr., The Politics of Tradition: Continuity and Change in Northern Nigeria 1946-1966 (Princeton: Princeton University Press, 1970).

19. Smith, "The Hausa System of Social Status," p. 251.

20. Whitaker, "A Dysrhythmic Process of Political Change," p. 204.

21. Marion J. Levy Jr., Modernization and the Structure of Societies (Princeton: Princeton University Press, 1966) p. 190-91.

22. Smith, Government in Zazzau, p. 106.

23. Robert A. LeVine, Dreams and Deeds: Achievement Motivation in Nigeria. (Chicago and London: University of Chicago Press, 1966).

24. Gaskiya Ta Fi Kwabo, February 18, 1950.

25. David C. McClelland, The Achieving Society (Princeton: Van Nostrand, 1961); David C. McClelland, and David G. Winter, Motivating Economic Achievement (New York: The Free Press, 1969); C. Bernard Rosen, Harry J. Crocket Jr., and Clyde Z. Nunn, eds., Achievement in American Society (Cambridge, Mass.: Schenkman, 1969).

26. LeVine, Dreams and Deeds, p. 78.

27. Lloyd A. Free, The Attitudes, Hopes, and Fears of Nigerians (Princeton: Institute for International Social Research, 1964).

28. LeVine, Dreams and Deeds, pp. 69-72, 78-79.

29. James L. Gibbs Jr., "Poro Values and Courtroom Procedures in a Kpelle Chiefdom," Southwestern Journal of Anthropology, Vol. 18 (1962), pp. 341-50; James L. Gibbs Jr., "The Kpelle of Liberia," in James L. Gibbs Jr., ed., Peoples of Africa, pp. 197-240.

30. Gibbs, "Poro Values," p. 342.

31. Warren L. d'Azevedo, "Common Principles of Variant Kinship Structures Among the Gola," American Anthropologist, Vol. 64 (1962), p. 514.

32. John Gay and Michael Cole, The New Mathematics and an Old Culture: A Study of Learning among the Kpelle of Liberia (New York: Holt, Rinehart and Winston, 1967), pp. 18-20.

33. William Siegmann, Report on the Bassa (Robertsport, Liberia: Tubman Center of African Culture, 1969); Kjell Zetterstrom, Preliminary Report on the Kru (Robertsport: Tubman Center of African Culture, 1969).

34. Merran Fraenkel, "Social Change on the Kru Coast of Liberia," Africa, Vol. 36 (1966), pp. 154-72.

MANPOWER, TRADE UNIONS, AND ECONOMIC DEVELOPMENT

5

**MANPOWER
IN NIGERIA**
Ukandi G. Damachi

As the civil war is over and Nigeria is desparately trying to take off economically, the utilization of human resources becomes more crucial than ever. In Nigeria, in my judgement, human capital (shortages of skills) is probably more critical than shortages of capital funds, whereas the reverse would be true of a country such as, say, India. According to such human resource planners as Frederick Harbison, "human capital is the wealth of nations."[1] In order to create and employ capital effectively, Nigeria needs entrepreneurs, managers, and technical and professional personnel of all kinds.

The major human resource problems in developing nations are (1) a rapidly growing population; (2) mounting unemployment in the modern sectors of the economy, as well as widespread underemployment in traditional agriculture (the precapitalistic sector, according to Arthur Lewis); (3) shortages of persons with the critical skills and knowledge required for effective national development; (4) inadequate or underdeveloped organizations and institutions for mobilizing human effort; and (5) lack of incentives for persons to engage in particular activities that are vitally important for national development. There are still other major human resource development problems, such as nutrition and health, but these lie in other technical fields and are factors that lie beyond the scope of this chapter.[2]

The most pronounced manpower problem in Nigeria is rising unemployment, particularly in the urban centers of the southern states, and underutilization of available labor. Although there was a fairly high rate of economic growth in 1965 (estimated at 5 percent of GNP), unemployment continues to rise; the most affected are school leavers who are unable to qualify for the limited available places in secondary schools. The northern states are also beginning to experience unemployment in their urban areas. Industrialization does not provide adequate jobs for the new entrants into the labor force, and the

81

TABLE 5.1

Pattern of Total Gainful Occupation, 1969-74
(projected figures)

Industry Group	Estimated Employment 1970 (millions)	Percent Share of Employment 1970	Gross Domestic Product (£ millions)	
			1969-70	1973-74
Agriculture	16.790	69.8	801.8	880.6
Mining	0.055	0.2	68.4	266.5
Manufacturing, crafts, etc.	2.930	12.2	153.9	262.2
Construction	0.136	0.6	76.3	99.9
Commerce	3.030	12.6	190.0	212.9
Transport and communication	0.167	0.7	58.5	70.4
Services	0.946	3.9	164.9	200.8
Total	24.054	100.0	1,513.8	1,993.3

possibility of its absorbing larger numbers of workers in the future is negligible (see Table 5.1). The total figures are negligible compared to the total labor force, which, according to Arthur Lewis' rule of thumb, constitute about 38-40 percent of the population.

A second manpower problem is the shortage of critical skills. In the senior categories there is a short supply of engineers, scientists, doctors, veterinarians, and agronomists. At the immediate level, there are even more severe shortages of nearly all technical, subprofessional, and certified teaching personnel. In addition there is a considerable shortage of senior craftsmen and technical foremen, as well as high-level secretarial and clerical personnel. The statistics published by the National Manpower Board indicate that the country needs at least three persons in the paraprofessional, technical, and teaching categories for every university graduate. But at best the output of qualified personnel is less than half that required to meet the identified needs.

Yet the number of university graduates being produced is ahead of target. As a matter of fact many of the graduates in the arts, humanities, social sciences, and in law are already facing the problem of finding appropriate jobs. The tendency now is for them to accept

GDP Percent Increase 1969-74	Estimated Percent Increase in GDP per worker 1969-74	Estimated Percent Increase in Employ-ment 1969-74	Estimated Employ-ment 1974 (millions)	Percent Share of Employ-ment 1974
9.8	3.7	6.5	17.881	65.5
289.6	262.3	27.3	0.070	0.3
70.4	16.0	54.4	4.524	16.6
30.9	5.0	25.9	0.171	0.6
12.1	2.0	10.1	3.336	12.2
20.3	3.0	17.3	0.196	0.7
21.8	1.5	20.3	1.138	4.1
31.7	20.3	11.4	27.316	100.0

Source: Second National Development Plan, 1970-74, p. 326.

starting positions in the lower "executive" rather than the "adminis-trative" level of government service. There is evidence that the production of nontechnical university graduates will continue to exceed the economy's capacity to absorb them productively, at least in the kinds of jobs they most prefer. Table 5.2 reflects the current pattern.[3]
A third manpower problem area is the rural sector—agriculture, animal husbandry, forestry, and related fields. Basically the solution of this manpower question lies in "a rural transformation"—i.e., the development of the intermediate industries and professions. Rural transformation is a prerequisite for industrial development, although there is no consensus on its scale and scope, on the resources re-quired to bring it about, or even on its relative priority in the overall development plans of the country.

THE LABOR FORCE

Nigeria's labor force (in 1970 figures) is about 26 million, of which 2 million are unemployed. Of the remaining 24 million in gainful occupation, 70 percent are employed in agriculture and 30 percent in nonagriculture (both rural and urban). Less than 6 percent of those in gainful occupation are employed in the wage sector (see Table 5.3).[4] It is likely that until 1980, the modern sector will barely hold its own in absorbing increments in the total labor force. Thus the proportion of the labor force employed in the modern sector in 1980 may be only slightly greater, if at all, than at present.

The Nigerian government spends more of its budget on education than on any other sector. It accounts for about a fourth of all recurrent expenditures by governments. Its total employment is more than half of all industry and commerce put together, and it utilizes the services of at least a third of the country's high-level manpower. Its main function is to satisfy the aspirations of Nigerians for a better way of life, to generate needed skills, and to develop and extend knowledge for nation-building. An activity of this kind, which consumes so large a share of the nation's resources, should be operated efficiently and economically, but a common criticism of the education industry in Nigeria is that "it is top heavy, structurally imbalanced, inadequately geared to the needs of the economy, at times unnecessarily costly."

Nevertheless Nigeria has made spectacular progress in building its systems of formal education. University enrollment tripled in the six-year period, 1960-66, far exceeding even the ambitious goals of the Ashby Commission. Secondary grammar school enrollment has expanded at almost equal pace. Primary education enrollment in the southern states is perhaps higher than in any other country in Middle Africa, although enrollment figures are still only 10 percent of the school age population in the north.

The expenditures for education have risen accordingly. In 1966, for example, Nigerian federal and regional governments allocated over £41 million ($123 million) for recurrent expenditures on formal education, in comparison with £5 million ($15 million) in 1952. Today public expenditures for education account for more than 3 percent of national income (see Table 5.4), and constitute over 21 percent of the recurrent budgets of the state and federal governments. Since independence, educational expenses have increased annually by about 15 percent; this is more than three times the average growth in national income.

The average annual costs per student from all sources are approximately £8 at primary schools, £100 at secondary grammar schools, £185 at technical and vocational schools, and £1,000 at universities (Table 5.5). Approximately 80 percent of the cost of primary education, 60 percent of the cost of secondary education, and 85 percent of the cost of university education is borne by the government.

TABLE 5.2

University Graduates (bachelor degrees) in 1966

Field	Number
Humanities	311
Education	600
Fine arts	109
Social sciences	1,228
Natural sciences	242
Engineering (incl. technology)	321
Agriculture	573
Languages	376
Law	161
Others	28

Source: National Register of High Level Manpower.

The tremendous resources being devoted to education are staggering. But they are more so if one considers that Nigeria's system of formal education is oriented predominately to the modern sector, which provides employment for only about 5 percent of the labor force. For example the combined annual output of Nigeria's formal education establishments is over 600,000 school leavers. Most of this output is from primary schools, and in turn most of the primary output consists of dropouts. Yet the aspirations of the vast majority of school leavers are to gain entry into the modern sector. The values, subject matter, and examination criteria at all levels of Nigeria education (as those of other developing nations) assume that school leavers will become government civil servants, teachers, and employees of relatively modern industrial and commercial establishments. But at present there are new employment opportunities each year for only about 40,000 persons in Nigeria's modern sector.

Except in a few categories, Nigeria's educational and training system will be capable of meeting most of the country's future needs for high-level manpower in the modern sector. And, if anything, the universities are expanding too rapidly in relation to other parts of the educational structure. The problem, therefore, is not under-investment of high-level professional and administrative manpower; on the contrary one can argue that too great a proportion of the country's resources are committed to modern sector development at the cost of

TABLE 5.3

The Labor Market, 1970-74
(projected figures)
in millions

Category	1970	1974	Change
Labor force	26.080	28.560	2.480
Unemployment gap	2.030	1.250	-0.780
Gainful occupation	24.054	27.316	3.262
Agriculture	16.790	17.881	1.091
Nonagriculture	7.264	9.435	2.171
Medium and large-scale	0.695	0.905	0.210
Small-scale	6.569	8.530	1.961
Wage employment	1.385	1.790	0.405
Nonagriculture	1.215	1.600	0.385
Agriculture	0.170	0.190	0.020
Medium and large-scale establishments	0.765	0.985	0.220
Small-scale establishments	0.620	0.805	0.185
Small-scale establishments (non-agriculture)	0.522	0.694	0.172
Self-account, Unpaid household workers, and unpaid apprentices	22.669	25.526	2.857
Agriculture	16.620	17.691	1.071
Nonagriculture	6.049	7.835	1.786

Source: Second National Development Plan, 1970-74, p. 327.

neglecting the needs of the economy's less productive sectors—those in which the vast majority of Nigerians must somehow earn a living. Even more significant is the average annual rate of increase in expenditures for education.

THE UNEMPLOYMENT TRAP

The most intractable manpower problems in Nigeria are rising unemployment and persistent underemployment. Despite planners' and government leaders' concern, there are still no appropriate solutions to these problems. Up to now there have been no comprehensive studies of unemployment in Nigeria, but there are ubiquitously held beliefs about its composition, causes, and consequences. Indeed

TABLE 5.4

Federal and State Capital Expenditures
on Education, 1970-74
(projected figures)
£ million

Level of Education	1970-71	1971-72	1972-73	1973-74	Total
Primary					
Federal	1.320	2.020	1.520	1.600	6.460
State	5.019	9.295	8.657	4.507	27.478
Total	6.339	11.315	10.177	6.107	33.938
Secondary					
Federal	1.500	1.800	1.800	1.900	7.000
State	4.689	6.428	6.186	4.097	21.400
Total	6.189	8.228	7.986	5.997	28.400
Technical					
Federal	0.620	0.860	0.560	0.600	2.640
State	1.994	2.842	2.808	2.007	9.651
Total	2.614	3.702	3.368	2.607	12.291
Teacher training					
Federal	0.600	0.600	0.600	0.200	2.000
State	1.969	3.427	3.252	2.547	11.195
Total	2.569	4.027	3.852	2.747	13.195
University					
Federal	5.000	6.000	7.000	7.500	25.500
State	4.611	4.152	3.995	2.760	15.518
Total	9.611	10.152	10.995	10.260	41.018
Others					
Federal	1.526	1.665	1.385	0.946	5.522
State	1.194	1.805	0.975	0.555	4.529
Total	2.720	3.470	2.360	1.501	10.051
Total of all levels	30.042	40.894	38.738	29.219	138.893

Source: Second National Development Plan, 1970-74, p. 246.

TABLE 5.5

Mean Annual Costs per Student
from all Sources

Level	Costs (£)	Index Number
Primary	8	1.00
Secondary grammar	100	12.50
Teacher training	110	13.75
Technical and vocational	185	23.25
Form VI	200	25.00
University	1,000	125.00

Source: A. Musone and Margaret Gentle, cited in Frederick H. Harbison, Nigerian Human Resource Development and Utilization (New York: United States Agency for International Development 1967), p. 110.

the causes of unemployment include high rates of population increase, excessive country-to-city migration, educational facilities being out of balance with the nation's manpower needs, high wages in the modern sector, and the slow rate of economic growth and industrialization.[5]

What are some possible solutions to these causes? The governments (federal and state alike) may decide to try some of the handy solutions that have but temporary effects. They may decide to restrain wages and prices, a policy that has a dual advantage—namely, it tends to reduce migration by decreasing the income gap between rural and modern sectors. Doing so would increase employment demand. Tanzania, Kenya, Ghana, and Sierra Leone recently reduced wages, which has resulted in a substantial increase in employment.[6] Application of this solution in Nigeria could meet resistance from organized labor. Maybe that is why the Adebo Commission recommended high wages as a measure of curbing inflation.* Another possible solution is the adoption of more labor-intensive technologies, which would emphasize creation of employment opportunities rather than rates of

---

*The Adebo Commission was set up by the Nigerian government to review the wages of public employees. It recommended an increase of wages as a measure of curbing inflation.

capital return. None of these approaches, however, is without drawbacks. Public works could help to unknot the unemployment trap as well as break of skill bottlenecks in both the intermediate and modern sectors. The assumption here is that jobs are available for high-level manpower if only the workers are prepared to work for the wages offered. The militaristic approach, under which the boys and girls are put in the army, is becoming increasingly popular. Exponents of this approach hope that wages could be relatively controlled or held at low levels. Besides, skills relevant to civilian employment could be developed, and respect for order and discipline would be encouraged. The Nigerian experience is the reverse of all this. The army is costing the federal government more than the government ever imagined. Its size has grown to almost uncontrollable proportion, the unruliness of the army is becoming a common experience despite great efforts at control and discipline. Besides, even if there was consensus among the commanders (who might resist using the military for skill-training purposes) to teach the soldiers skills relevant to civilian employment, there would still be the problem of finding the trained personnel to implement such a policy. The Nigerian army is not all that skilled, and the reason for this is understandable—the army was in a hurry, during the civil war. A further solution could be to keep the young in school longer and retire the older earlier. This would create an increase in employment opportunities. But it is unlikely that politicians will adopt this method, if only because of political considerations. A system for national service for all youth could create jobs during the period of service and thus temporarily restrict an influx into the labor force.

Whatever would be the success of any of the above solutions, the main solutions on a long-term basis are population control and increase of rural income, which will lead to the retention of surplus labor in the rural areas and which will generate skills.[7] Indeed "rural development involves much more than improvement in agriculture. It calls in addition for the modernization of rural communities and villages, the development of small industries and crafts, the improvement of communications, and the extensions of education and health services to rural areas. It requires massive investment, extensive training of human resources and determination on the part of government to give priority to rural development."[8] The "educative services" required include agricultural extension, adult education, community development, youth organizations, and in-service training, as well as formal education.

The most difficult problem that can result from implementing rural development plans is the lack of trained manpower and the need to set up efficient organizations.[9]

What human resource development is necessary for the rural transformation? The investment needed to carry forward a rural transformation will be very great indeed. But the limiting factor is more likely to be human rather than financial resources. It is important, therefore, to consider the problems of developing the human agents needed to lead, manage, and direct this transformation.

We assume that it may be relatively easy to estimate the numbers of persons required for agricultural extension and to determine the means for training them. The organization and staffing of research centers likewise should offer no serious problem. Today a great deal is known about the nature of institutions and techniques needed to train personnel for these activities.

When it comes to training community development workers, small-scale entrepreneurs, village leaders, and even rural school teachers, however, the requirements and needed programs are much less clear. Present knowledge about the processes of rural village development is sketchy. Even less is known about the forces that generate incentives for self-improvement in rural areas. And lastly, very few persons with much education and initiative are willing to commit themselves to service "in the bush." In this respect, for example, the experience of such countries as India with village development is probably the most underdeveloped and backward area of knowledge in the entire field of growth economics.

Let us elaborate by considering a few examples. In several African countries, proposals have been made to establish village polytechnics to develop among adults and children alike some of the essential but simple skills needed in rural areas, such as carpentry, latrine construction, canal digging, personal hygiene, use of fertilizers, seed selection, and weed control. The idea is basically sound, and expensive equipment would not be required. But can the organizing talent be found to initiate these institutions? What kinds of people could be selected as instructors, and how would they be trained?

A more imaginative idea, recently proposed by President Nyerere of Tanzania, is to turn rural schools into "economic and social communities." According to Nyerere, each school should have connected with it a farm or workshop to provide much of the food eaten by the students and teachers. In this way students would learn to cooperate in building self-reliant communities, and at the same time they would make a contribution to the national income. But the selection, training, and proper motivation of the "teacher-farmer" is likely to be a very difficult task. Probably Nigeria's present teacher-training institutions would be less than enthusiastic about this idea. And even if they could be induced to accept it, who would train the teachers to operate a successful farm in addition to teaching reading, writing, and arithmetic?

Most planners agree that it is important to encourage the development of small industrial enterprises, cooperatives, repair shops, commercial establishments, and cottage industries in the rural villages. But this requires a good deal of competent technical assistance. What will be required to select, train, employ, and motivate the human agents to provide this kind of assistance? How many activists would be required, and in how many different areas would they need specialized knowledge or training?

Finally many economists argue that a good deal of capital formation can result from mobilizing the efforts of the underemployed to build houses, community centers, local access roads, and other public works. In this way output can be increased by employing, for very little pay, underutilized human energies. But here the critical factor is to find and develop the organizing talent to energize and direct such an effort.

We could give a great many more examples to demonstrate the problems to be overcome in developing the human resources required to press forward a rural transformation. They would all show the importance of developing innovators and organization builders. But innovators and organization builders are perhaps the scarcest of resources in all sectors of a newly developing country. It is probably easier to develop talent to organize a large industrial enterprise than it is to select, train, and motivate leadership for rural development projects. In most modernizing societies it is becoming clear that the really perplexing problems of organization and human resource development lie in the traditional and intermediate, rather than in the modern, sectors of the economy.

Manpower surveys, almost without exception, have completely ignored the problems of low-productivity sectors. They have concentrated on the high-manpower requirements of the modern sector. Although we would not deny their usefulness in this respect, they have tended to give a very distorted picture of the fundamental dimensions of the problems of human resource development and utilization. Therefore it is not possible at this time to estimate precisely the numbers of persons with strategic skills needed to achieve a rural transformation. But here again, orders of magnitude matter.

Manpower planners think that, for every person required in agricultural extension activities, another two or three trained persons would be needed to provide the other necessary and related productive services. These would include new educational instructors, organizers and supervisors of rural public works programs, small enterprise experts, community development workers, credit supervisors and marketing specialists, and public health agents. The task of developing such personnel is larger and much more complicated than that of generating skilled manpower for the modern sector, for, as stressed above, in the modern sector the techniques are already known; expatriate personnel can be imported to fill temporary shortages of high-level skills; and a tremendous investment has already been made in education and training, especially in Nigeria. In the rural areas, on the contrary, effective techniques of manpower development are yet to be discovered; expatriates cannot be easily recruited or utilized; and very few investments of human and financial resources have yet been made.

We come now to the role of rural schools in promoting a rural transformation. They can and do make a contribution by turning out some literate children who may remain in the area. But they also tend to drain the more talented and ambitious young people from the countryside to the cities. It is questionable, therefore, whether rural primary education, as presently organized, is on balance a positive or a negative force in building Nigeria's rural economy.

The content and method of education in the rural primary schools, as in other schools in the country, is academically oriented. The emphasis is on preparation for higher levels of formal schooling. Thus the school environment is quite different from that of the rural community. Parents send their children to school, not to make them better farmers, but rather to provide for them an escape from traditional society. An educated child, therefore, has aspirations to move to "greener pastures"; he is no longer willing to accept a life sentence to traditional agriculture. Under these circumstances it is foolish to think that a solution can be found by "vocationalizing" the curriculum; i.e., teaching farming, handicrafts, etc.

In conclusion, experts recommend that, in rural transformation, other productive devices must be developed simultaneously with the spread of education. Unless conditions in the rural areas are improving and unless there are attractive job opportunities for local people in the rural areas, investment in formal education will bring dis-appointingly low returns. Thus it is important to decide first to make massive investments of human and financial resources for improve-ments in agriculture, in rural public works, and in community develop-ment of all kinds. In this way, leadership opportunity will be created for local inhabitants; the prospects for a better life will be brightened; and the hold of rural communities on their more ambitious and talented manpower resources will be strengthened.

If this reasoning is correct, then these policy decisions follow: insofar as possible, the new jobs in agricultural extension and village polytechnics, as well as organization of community activities, should be a by-product of fundamental training of local inhabitants to organize and lead such "productive services." Thus priority should be now given to building these productive services rather than to expansion of formal primary education. As the rural communities become transformed, greater resources can be generated for formal education and more opportunities will be provided for those able to obtain it. In short, we should not jump before we hop and leap. In economies with limited resources, every penny spent on education may be money taken away from other vitally needed productive services. But if these productive services can lead to higher productivity and earnings, the resources available for education will soon be increased, and the ultimate goal of universal primary education will be more easily and speedily attained.

POLICY CONSIDERATIONS

Nigeria is faced with two basic manpower problems—the under-utilization and mounting unemployment of primary school leavers, and the shortage of high-level manpower, which is perhaps the principal limiting factor in future economic growth. In addition to these man-power questions, there are the problems of substantially increasing the rate of material capital formation and of improving the productive-ness of investment of scarce funds.

Nigerian leaders and the Nigerian people as a whole therefore have a number of thorny issues confronting them. First, for the next twenty-to-thirty years, at least, Nigeria's economic growth will depend primarily on improvements in agriculture and animal husbandry. Most developing countries, including Nigeria, tend to downgrade in-vestment in these areas and to overemphasize the building of factories, ultramodern government and office buildings, or international airlines that always operate at a loss. The highest priority manpower needs in Nigeria are agricultural officers, agricultural assistants, and veterinarians. But educated Nigerians are not interested in agriculture or animal husbandry. especially if they have to go back to live in the bush. How then can more high-level manpower be found to bring about modernization of agriculture?

Second, as Arthur Lewis has pointed out, the current fashion of African nations, including Nigeria, is to spend lavishly on university education and on attaining the good of universal primary education, while neglecting secondary education and particularly secondary technical education. Logically Nigeria should not increase, and preferably should decrease, expenditures on primary education until the numbers of students in secondary education has increased about fivefold. But the feasibility of this is in doubt in a country where the popular pressure for education is so strong.

Nigeria now has five full-fledged universities and is planning several more. Should these be built on the lavish scale of the existing ones, where every student is a boarder? Or should the new institutions be nonresidential city universities? These questions involve more than economics. It will be difficult to avoid unnecessary and uneconomical duplication of expensive courses. What measures then can be taken to develop higher education on a more economical basis?

Third, in terms of numbers, the greater need for high-level manpower in Nigeria is school teachers at the secondary level and above. At the same time, though, most of the more ambitious young teachers look upon teaching not as a profession but as a avenue to politics or to jobs in the higher civil service. How then will it be possible for Nigeria to find, train, and retain the 15,000 new post-primary teachers that will be required in the next ten years?

Fourth, Nigeria desperately needs foreign capital, both public and private, for economic development. But other countries need it just as desperately. What particular measures can be taken to attract private foreign capital to this country? And how can Nigeria best present her case for public grants or loans to finance river development, dams, roads, and land-use improvement schemes?

Fifth, if a rapid rate of growth is to be achieved, personal consumption must be restricted in order to provide funds for the development of essential public services and for capital formation. Under normal circumstances this requires a high rate of savings, as well as rising taxes. How can Nigeria best increase taxes and promote savings?

Sixth, economic development in the modern era requires organization and effective planning. What measures can be taken to formulate effective organizational machinery within the context of Nigeria's federal system of government?

These and many other crucial issues are worth discussing. The Second National Development Plan 1970-74 addresses itself to some of these problems. But some of its criticisms spell pessimism rather than optimism. For example, Frank Method in his unpublished paper "Education and Manpower Development in the Nigeria Second National Development Plan 1970-1974" concludes thus:

(1) Capital expenditure estimates badly confuse capital and recurrent expenditure and contain much double counting of Federal and State estimates. They do not properly consider private contribution to education. (2) The enrolment estimates are generally unrealistically high and the prose sections selfservingly optimistic. Little attention is paid to manpower needs and expansion at all levels is given first priority. (3) The manpower planning sections are more conservative in their projections, critical in their comments and detailed in their analysis. (4) Problems of the educated unemployed will

94

continue to be serious, and will probably increase,
including secondary level and possibly university by the
end of the decade. (5) The size of educational investment
must be justified mainly on "social good" criteria. (6)
Private and local authority financial support will be
critical. (7) Teacher shortages will be the main constraint on expansion. (8) Technical education will expand,
but will continue to be inadequate for manpower needs
through the plan period. (9) More emphasis should be
given to qualitative improvements, structural and administrative reform, applied research and in-service, on-the-
job and non-formal training.[10]

Despite all the criticism of the 1970-74 development plan, one
thing is certain and encouraging: Nigeria now realizes that the problems
of development and utilization of human resources for a rural transformation are paramount and deserve preferential treatment. Yet
experts on the problem are only now beginning to understand the tasks
involved. The time has come for deeper thinking; for greater efforts
at measurement, and for a systematic examination of available
alternatives and priorities.
    The attack upon these problems is, of course, the sole responsi-
bility of the governments concerned, universities, and research
institutions. Help from the United States and other wealthy nations
is needed, for they can make resources available—both human and
financial. And above all they can show sympathetic understanding of
these problems, and willingness to help if requested to do so by the
planners, educators, and statesmen of Nigeria.

NOTES

1. Frederick H. Harbison, "Human Resources As the Wealth
of Nations," Proceedings of the American Philosophical Society,
Vol. 115, No. 6 (December 1971).
    2. Ibid., pp. 427-31.
    3. Nigeria, The Federal Ministry of Labour, The Nigerian
Labour Market (Lagos: The Nigerian National Press, 1968).
    4. Nigeria, The Federal Ministry of Economic Development,
Second National Development Plan, 1970-74.
    5. Ukandi G. Damachi, "The Manpower Crisis: Education is
out of steps with Needs," Africa Report (May 1972).
    6. Charles R. Frank Jr., "The Problem of Urban Unemployment
in Africa" (discussion paper no. 16, Research Program in Economic
Development, Woodrow Wilson School, Princeton University, 1970).

7. Ukandi G. Damachi, "The Manpower Crisis," pp. 14-15.
8. Frederick H. Harbison.
9. J. I. Roper, <u>Labour Problems in West Africa</u> (London: Penguin Books, 1958), pp. 82-87.
10. Frank Method, "Education and Manpower Development in the Nigeria Second National Development Plan 1970-1974" (unpublished paper).

BIBLIOGRAPHY

Bereday, George, ed. <u>Essays on World Education</u>. London: Oxford University Press, 1969.

Callaway, Archibald. "Nigeria's Indigenous Education: The Apprenticeship System," <u>Odu</u>, Vol. 1, No. 1 (July 1964).

Coombs, Phillip H. <u>The World Education Crisis: A Systems Analysis</u>. New York: Oxford University Press, 1968.

Damachi, Ukandi G. <u>Nigerian Modernization: The Colonial Legacy</u>. New York, The Third Press, 1972.

_____. "The Manpower Crisis: Education is Out of Step with Needs," <u>Africa Report</u> (May 1972).

Diejomah, Victor P. <u>Economic Development in Nigeria: HS Problems, Challenges, and Prospects</u>,. Princeton: Princeton University Press, 1965.

Harbison, Frederick H. "Educational Planning and Human Resources Development," in <u>Fundamentals of Educational Planning</u>. Paris, UNESCO-IIEP, 1967.

_____. "Human Resources as the Wealth of Nations," <u>Proceedings of the American Philosophical Society</u>, Vol. 115, No. 6 (December 1971).

Harbison, F. H., et al., <u>Indicators of Development and Modernization</u>,. Princeton: Princeton University Press, 1971.

Harbison, F. H., and J. D. Mooney. <u>Critical Issues in Employment Policy</u>,. Princeton: Princeton University Press, 1966.

Harbison, F. H., and C. A. Myers. Education, Manpower, and Economic. Growth: Strategies of Human Resource Development,. Princeton: Princeton University Press, 1964.

International Labour Organization. Human Resources for Industrial Development. Geneva, 1967.

_____. The World Employment Program. Geneva, 1969.

_____. Towards Full Employment—A Program for Colombia (Geneva, 1970).

King, Hugh. "The Contribution of Technical Education, Background." Paper No. 2, Plan-Indian Ocean Conference on Technical Education and Training, Perth, Australia, August 1966.

King, Jane. Planning Non-Formal Education in Tanzania. Paris: International Institute for Educational Planning, Report 16.

Lewis, Arthur. "Education and Economic Development," International Social Science Journal, Vol. XIV, No. 4 (1962).

Method, Frank. "Education and Manpower Development in the Nigeria Second National Development Plan, 1970-74." (New York: Ford Foundation, 1971) Unpublished paper.

Roper, J. I. Labour Programs in West Africa. London: Penguin Books, 1958.

Shaw, R. Employment Implications of the Green Revolution. Washington: Overseas Development Council, 1970.

Tobias, George. Human Resources in India. New Delhi: Menakshi Prakashan, 1971.

UNESCO, Final Report, World Conference of Ministers of Education on the Eradication of Illiteracy. Teheran, September 1965.

6

INDUSTRIAL RELATIONS IN
THE SAPELE TIMBER INDUSTRY:
THE DEVELOPMENT OF
COLLECTIVE BARGAINING
Ukandi G. Damachi

The location of the plywood plant at Sapele, which came into operation in 1948, was a major development in the Nigerian timber industry. It illustrates a typical development process in the economics of an underdeveloped country. In the first stage, raw material is exported in its crude form; later, elementary processing is undertaken; in the third, or present, stage, manufacture through which the raw material is converted into a refined product is in full swing.

There were several factors that appear to have favored this development at Sapele. Timber supplies were abundant. The location of the plant (Sapele is a port) was convenient both for receiving timber and for exporting the finished product. Much waste is involved in timber processing and this favors location near the source of supply. Further, the waste can be used as fuel for the plant.

The main problem at Sapele was to build up a labor force right from the inception of the industry in 1948, and adapt it to the conditions of factory work and the related bureaucratic organization. It is this problem, and the means by which it has been met, that concerns us in this chapter. Consequently the following areas will be probed: (1) The organizational structure of the timber industry, (2) labor-management relations, (3) union action in the industry, (4) the collective bargaining process, (5) some local disputes and solutions, and (6) A Comparison of the Nigerian situation with some aspects of labor-Management relations in the United States. As a conclusion, a kaleidoscopic view of the timber industry itself will be presented.

THE ORGANIZATIONAL STRUCTURE OF
THE TIMBER INDUSTRY

The two main divisions of the Sapele plant are the sawmill and the plywood mill. Timber to be shipped in the form of logs is cut to length by power saws in the forest, and the bark and soft outer layer are removed by hand tools. Massive equipment is used in the sawmill, and it is now manned entirely by Africans.

Maintenance is an important factor in the efficiency of the sawmill, especially the changing of the saws, for which the sawyer keeps a log showing reasons for the changes. The work is done by Africans but inspected by a European foreman. Conditioning of saws, or saw "doctoring," is skilled and responsible work. This again is now largely done by Africans, under European supervision.

Although the sawmill has the characteristics of a manufacturing plant, its output is processed raw material that is still in a relatively crude state. The plywood mill, however, turns out a refined manufactured product. The aim of the United Africa Company (UAC), the African Timber and Plywood Company's (AT&P) parent company, in setting up a plywood mill at Sapele was to produce hardwood plywood of the highest quality (by world standards) and suitable for exterior use.

The plywood plant, installed by a Czech expert, was planned on a large scale, and it is still essentially the same now as when it first came into operation. The production process begins with the peeling of logs. The whole operation is very mechanical.[1] Despite the high degree of mechanization, skill and judgment are required in certain of these operations, and vigilance is all-important. Mechanical breakdowns, personal injuries, and waste of valuable material can result from carelessness and inattention. The peeling process is one of the most exacting, and the speed attained is regarded as highly satisfactory.

In its management structure and methods, AT&P follows the general European practice for a firm of its size and range of activities. There are four main divisions: administration, engineering, forestry, and production (the last one being further divided into sawmill and plymill as noted above). Each division is under a European manager; with few exceptions, all subordinate managerial posts are also occupied by Europeans.[2] But most of the foremen and clerical workers, including some senior clerks, are Africans.

Great importance is given to the personnel function.[3] The office of personnel manager is a senior post in the administrative division, and includes responsibility for recruitment, personnel records, welfare services, disciplinary action in accordance with company rules, and advice on labor policy. The principles of the company's labor policy emanate from the parent concern (the British-based Unilever Brothers), and the rules and conditions of employment, including wage and salary scales, are clearly set out in a booklet issued to every employee.

A system of record cards is used giving information about each employee in considerable detail; such information concerns his career before joining the company, his medical history, and his progress in the firm. The cards are carefully maintained as a basis of management's relations with the individual worker. Attendance records are also used to produce a daily strength return. This shows the total nominally employed compared with the establishment of each section, the number of leaves of absence, the number sick, the number in hospital, and the total on duty.

Here then we have a highly organized firm equipped with all the devices of efficient management. Its personnel records are well adapted to the study of turnover and absenteeism.

LABOR-MANAGEMENT RELATIONS

To discuss adequately the relationship between management and labor, a birds-eye view has to be taken on how management reaches its decisions and under what conditions it makes those decisions. Decisions concerning budget, capital expenditure, and expansion are not made in Nigeria; they are made instead by the parent company in Britain. Nevertheless the parent company makes its decisions in light of recommendations coming up from management in the Nigerian branch.

On the other hand, decisions with regard to labor are made in Nigeria. The personnel department is exclusively responsible for such decisions. It does research into different aspects of labor and then submits reports and recommendations to the board of directors, which normally approves them without any modification. Leadership tends to be diffuse, as the board of directors places emphasis on a management process called "dilution of management."[4] This is to ensure more efficient supervision, and more economical use of supervisory and administrative skills. On the whole, however, it implies breaking down the general function, and reducing it whenever possible to a series of simple techniques that can be effectively used by lower-grade foremen. The same method is applicable to office work, in which, hitherto, members of higher management had wasted time supervising routine operations. In the opinion of the administration director this approach in the factory and office offers the most promising prospect for increased productivity under existing conditions. The work-study program that has been established would do much to facilitate the process. As a consequence of this management practice, the personnel department has become very important. It is exclusively responsible for labor relations. At this stage it performs two functions—personnel work and industrial relations.

The industrial relations department is of recent origin. We shall see how it has come into existence when discussing unionism in the industry. The personnel department has therefore to deal with problems concerning productivity, labor turnover, and wages.

Among the criticisms commonly leveled at African labor are lack of confidence and lack of initiative. It has been said that the saw doctoring department of AT&P requires four times as many men as a comparable Canadian plant. This is not due merely to deficiencies in the department, but is at least partly a reflection of the misuse of equipment in the sawmill.[5]

The test of efficiency in the sawmill is the conversion rate; that is, the quantities of the various grades of timber produced per hour from a given input of logs. In recent years productivity has been increased by improved organization of work by the operators. The machinery has been running at the same speed as when first installed. For productivity measurement the plant has been broken down into sections and targets have been set up. When possible the same device has been applied to individual operators in each section. In the opinion of the sawmill manager, the system works well. The workers appear to take pride in their performance and like to be assured that productivity is being maintained at the expected level. This system has been worked out by the personnel department.

In relation to its productivity, Nigerian labor is no longer cheap.[6] For instance many of the jobs in the Sapele plymill that demand little effort or skill and that are done by men are done by girls in comparable European plants. In the large clerical staff, too, there are hardly any girls. Moreover, intensive supervision is necessary to sustain the work flow, to maintain quality, to safeguard the machinery, and to prevent accidents. The degree of supervision required is one of the main factors contributing to high labor costs, compared with manufacturing establishments in more advanced countries.

In 1959 a new approach to the productivity problem was being made with the introduction of work-study. The production department analyzed the jobs in both the sawmill and the plymill with a view to determining the exact nature of the work performed, the knowledge and skill required, the degree of responsibility, the supervision received or given, and the environmental conditions.

These job descriptions were being used as the basis for job evaluation. An elaborate wage structure was already in existence; but no careful analysis of jobs had been undertaken, and in any case the classification was often out of date because of a change in methods. Thus it was found that certain jobs, though differently classified, were in fact similar in their demands, while others appearing to fall within one category were actually different in character. Some jobs needed to be upgraded and others downgraded if a rational structure was to be produced.

The further aim of work-study was the improvement of job methods, the better adaptation of the worker to the job, and the simplification of maintenance and supervision. Much emphasis was placed on the regular recording of performances by men and machines as a means of maintaining production standards.

A particularly interesting feature of the introduction of work-study at Sapele was in connection with personnel management. The task of determining job specification and evaluations was largely carried out as a cooperative effort by the work-study engineers and a job analyst responsible to the personnel manager. In this way personnel managers were brought into much closer touch with what the men were doing, and with actual working conditions in the factory. Thus the standards of personnel management, particularly as regards recruitment, placement, and training, improved appreciably.[7]

In the main, however, the organization of work was determined by the nature and layout of the plants, and the scope for improvement was largely in the better adaptation of labor to the requirements of existing processes. This was a matter of training. Although the firm was now training craftsmen in an apprentice school, the ordinary process workers had, for the most part, merely learned the job from seeing it done. Thus faults were handed on; much inefficiency was due to ignorance of the proper method and of the standard of performance expected.

Work-study was intended to remedy these conditions by devising a drill for all repetitive operations. There was a right and wrong way of making even the simplest movements, and instruction was needed to avoid waste of effort.[8] Skill was particularly important in the maintenance of equipment, and the work-study specialists were intending to produce manuals for this purpose with the help of the personnel department.

As a check of performance, records were being devised for each operation, and, where appropriate, points were given for quality. The records were kept by the personnel division.

Today the firm still operates on the same principles except that the personnel department has been relieved of its industrial relations function by the establishment of a separate department of industrial relations.

At the initial stage, two very crucial problems faced the management; they were the demand for the higher skills of management and the productivity of the forests. At that time higher skills of management were supplied entirely by Europeans, which made administration, including such related services as accounting, very costly. AT&P was hoping eventually to fill more of the higher management posts with Nigerians, but the supply of men suitable for training was extremely small then. The shortage of Africans with technical and managerial skills naturally inflates the value of those available.

This problem has been narrowed down by the great campaign for educated Nigerians to be trained in management by the personnel division. As a fact this problem is almost nonexistent today.

The productivity of the capital and labor directed by AT&P depended ultimately on the productivity of the forests:

> It was formerly believed that under the warm moist conditions of tropical forests, productivity would take care of itself and that the main problem was merely to extract timber. But it is now recognized that a program for maintaining and replenishing forests is indispensable to provide a satisfactory basis for their long-term exploitation. At the present rate of expansion there is a danger that the most valuable timber stands may be exhausted in a few decades. Provision must be made, therefore, for new plantations and the regeneration of forests.[9]

As regards regeneration, operations in the existing concessions were based on a working cycle of 100 years. AT&P claimed that this was far too long. The evidence from areas cutover some twenty years previously indicated a faster rate of growth than had been assumed. Further, natural regeneration could be assisted, and fertility, in the commercial sense, increased by protecting saplings of marketable species from the competition of other species. Much research and survey work was needed, and this was done under the guidance of the personnel department.

But a more fundamental question of policy arises; there is a conflict of interests between those who wish to conserve and increase the timber resources of the country, and those who want more land for agriculture. AT&P foresaw that supplies from existing forest concessions might be inadequate for the needs of the plant in the near future, and there was some concern about the prospects. The government understood the problem and made concessions accordingly. The survival of the enterprise can, however, only be ensured by a long-term policy that guarantees a continuing supply of raw material.

With regard to labor turnover the gross turnover rate is about 16 percent.[10] Many workers leave after a very short period of service; often they are discharged as unsuitable at the end of their three months' probation. But the figure of 16 percent, low as it is, overstates the seriousness of the problem that we usually have in mind when discussing labor turnover. For instance there is inevitably a loss of workers through retirement, infirmity, and death. Also, employees may be discharged as redundant and then reengaged or replaced later on; here the turnover is at the employer's convenience. What matters to the employer is remediable turnover or, as we may call it, net turnover, which, because of the cost involved, he seeks to reduce. The clearest instance of this is the resignation of established employees whom the employer would prefer to retain— though not necessarily on the employees' terms.

In any event, labor turnover is not a serious problem to AT&P. Neither is absenteeism, which is less than 2 percent.[11] Records of absenteeism are kept by the personnel division. Taking the experience of labor turnover and absenteeism together, it is clear that AT&P has established a high degree of stability in its labor force.

Wage rates are obviously an important factor in the attraction of labor. An elaborate grading system is in operation. There are four grades of clerical workers, three classes of foremen, and no fewer than fourteen occupational groups (as they are called), in which the great majority of workers in the engineering, production, and forestry divisions are to be found. These occupational groups repre- sent different categories of skill and responsibility, and they also take into account the arduousness of the job.

The scales of the categories illustrate the company's policy of offering attractive conditions to skilled men in responsible jobs. The maximum salary of a Grade I foreman is six times the highest wage of an unskilled laborer. But it may take the foreman ten years to get to the top of his grade. Increments within grades are, of course, a reward for loyalty. They are also undoubtedly popular with Africans, who tend to assume that promotion should be by seniority. This is not accepted by AT&P as a general principle, but extension of the salary scale within grades represents a partial concession. Another fact to be noted is the payment of higher grade manual workers on a salaried basis, which enhances their prestige. In the absence of adverse reports, increments within grades apply automatically to employees.

But still more important is the prospect of promotion to higher grade jobs. Most of the workers are interested in promotion; some have already achieved substantial promotion, others are striving for it, and some are disgruntled, or perhaps merely puzzled, at having been passed over.[12] Anyhow, an indication of each employee's prospect of promotion is given in the personnel records.

In addition to the prospect of promotion there is also the promise of a pension for higher grade employees who stay until the retirement age. The pension scheme is contributory, in proportion to salary, the firm's contribution being at a higher rate than the employee's. To qualify for the full pension an employee must have completed at least twenty years' service and have attained the age of fifty-five;

smaller amounts are payable to those with less service, on reaching the retirment age, and to those with twenty years' service who retire before fifty-five at the employer's request.

Annual leave at full pay is another benefit for which employees may qualify. This is granted to all after twelve months' service; it ranges from two or three weeks for pensionable staff members, according to grade, to six days for other employees. Leave rosters are prepared, and every effort is made to meet each employee's wishes in the allocation. With management's consent, leave may be accumulated to some extent; travelling time may be added and compassionate leave may be granted. The personnel department is the pivot between the workers and management in these arrangements.

Generally wages fail to keep up with the company's gains and with the standard of living.[13] This failure of wages to keep abreast with existing conditions brought about workers' consciousness in the late 1950s, and eventually a union to press management for benefits, better wages, and better conditions of work. With the formation of a union in the company a lot of things changed—for example, policies toward wages and working conditions.

UNION ACTION IN THE INDUSTRY

The first beginnings of trade unionism in Nigeria go back to approximately 1912. It came into full swing with the passage of the trade union's ordinance, in 1939, which gave the unions legal status and provided for freedom of organization. British colonial development grants contingent upon the existence of reasonable facilities for union organization proved an additional incentive. But the strongest stimuli came from the rapid rise in the cost of living in the early years of World War II, which aroused discontent in workers and made them receptive to organizers, and from the passage of the general defense regulations, which prohibited strikes and lockouts and were seen as an attempt to crush the emergent labor movement.[14]

Although a registered union of AT&P workers has been in existence since the plant's inception, it did not secure recognition from the management at the beginning. This situation was a legacy of events in the early 1950s, when the Amalgamated Union of UAC African Workers was active. Strikes had been threatened in various UAC enterprises in 1949, but agreement was reached (after intervention by the Ministry of Labour) on most of the issues in dispute, including wages. Later on, strikes did occur accompanied by violence and damage to property. The main demand was for a further rise in wages; when the matter was referred to arbitration, 12.5-percent increase was awarded.[15] Differences about the application of the award, in which the arbitrator upheld the company's interpretation, led to further strikes, which the firm met by threats of dismissal.[16] AT&P became involved in 1952, but the stoppage lasted only a few days and many of the strikers were dismissed. By this time the UAC union was disintegrating.

Despite the ease with which the strike at AT&P was broken, the experience did reveal serious weaknesses in management's relations with employees; in the following year management was clearly feeling its way to a more satisfactory relationship. This was in accordance with the general policy of UAC; the trade union was discredited in the eyes of UAC, and many of its employers shared the same view; but it seemed some form of representative action was called for whereby regular contact could be maintained between management and labor. This gave birth to the industrial relations department. Industrial relations problems were now detached from the personnel function.

Before we go to consider the industrial relations function, let us first analyze the nature of the trade union at AT&P. The AT&P union was indeed industrial in kind despite the fact that it was a branch of UAC's amalgamated union. All the workers belonged to the same trade union regardless of their trades. Union members insisted on full membership of all the workers, despite the fact that the law forbade closed shop and compulsory membership. They insisted on full membership because that would aid them fight the company for recognition. As a matter of fact every worker joined the union for fear of victimization by his fellow workers. The leaders were skilled workers who had many years of service with the company. Most of them were not well educated and thus had a problem in stating their case properly to management.

The situation has since changed. Young social science graduates and young lawyers graduating from colleges every year find no good jobs, so some of them turn their attention to organizing workers. As a result, the AT&P trade unions* now have adequate and effective leadership. This phenomenon heralds a new era—one of strong collective action against the management, and hence a new trend in industrial relations.

Government legislation helps to bring about the new trend in labor-management relations. A look at some of the legislation affecting labor-management relations will bear out this contention. General conditions of labor are governed by the Labour Code Ordinance, which establishes minimum standards for contracts and general

---

*There is no longer one industrial union; it has fragmented into separate trade unions.

conditions of employment, provides for the payment of cash wages
and for the setting of minimum wages; regulates the recruitment of
labor and apprenticeship; and provides for the registration of
employers and industrial workers. Other law acts are the Trades
Union Ordinance of 1939, which governs the condition of association
and labor relations; the Workmen's Compensation Ordinance of 1948,
which provides for the payment of compensation to the families of
workers injured or killed at work; the Employment of Ex-Servicemen
Ordinance of 1945, which gives exservicemen preference in employment; the Labour (Wage Fixing and Registration) Ordinance of 1943
and the Wages Boards Ordinance of 1957, establishing the machinery
for wage fixing; and the Eastern and Northern Regions' Fatal Accident
laws.[17]

THE COLLECTIVE BARGAINING PROCESS

The process of collective bargaining is a new phenomenon in
the timber industry. The settlement of disputes or grievances at the
company can be viewed in terms of three stages—the arbitrary stage,
when management had an overall say in all disputes and matters
involving labor and management; the second stage, which is the joint
consultation era; and the third stage, which is collective bargaining.
Let us now look at the last two stages.

With the wave of strikes and mounting restiveness in labor-
management relations, management realized for the first time its
unawareness of African reactions and the extent of its failure in
personnel administration. The experience was salutary; it led to the
overhaul of the company's personnel policy, and to an effort in genuine
joint consultation.

An early result was the issue to every employee of a handbook
setting out the principles of the firm's labor policy. These principles
were stated in terms of mutual obligations and rights, and among the
latter was "the free right to employees to form and join responsible
and truly representative trade unions."[18] At the same time, depart-
mental managers were firmly told that the responsibility of the
managerial staff was to be discharged in a manner compatible with
the company's personnel policy. The industrial relations officer (a
new post), who was responsible to the personnel manager, was to see
that this was done, and he was to be regarded as an expert adviser
on labor relations matters, not only to the board of joint consultation
but also to individual managers. This definition of the industrial
relations function aroused opposition from the workers at first, but
gradually it came to be accepted.[19]

The new scheme for joint consultation provided for two bodies: the Joint Consultative (Employment) Committee, and the Joint Consultative (Production) Committee. The former was to be concerned with "all matters arising from rates of pay, conditions of service, welfare and other allied subjects and provide a recognized means for a regular exchange of views between the employees and the management."[20] The latter was to deal with matters relative to production, work organization and other allied subjects, with the object of improving techniques and the general efficiency of the plant. Each committee was precluded from discussing matters falling within the terms of reference of the other.

Thus between them the two committees were intended to cover a wider range than is normally accorded joint consultation in British industry. For instance in industries where wages and conditions of service are settled by collective bargaining, such matters are usually excluded from consideration by joint consultative committees. It must, however, be understood that there was still no organized collective bargaining at AT&P. The joint consultative committees were therefore the only means of discussing wages and conditions of employment. Although discussion was undoubtedly valuable to both sides, it did not amount to negotiation; management still had the last word, although its decision might well be influenced by consultation with the employees' representatives.

In framing the constitutions of the two committees, great care was taken to make them as representative as possible. Owing to the widespread and varied character of the company's activities, zones of representation were defined. At Sapele, where about two-thirds of the 3,000 workers were employed, there were five zones, based mainly on the nature of employment—namely, sawmill, plymill, engineering, transport and security, and office staff; forest workers were represented on an area basis. Besides serving as units for the election of representatives on the main committees, the zones and areas had their own local committees for "dealing expeditiously with minor day-to-day problems and maintaining the closest possible contact between management representatives and their immediate subordinates and employees on the job." Contact between management and immediate subordinates was ensured by providing that a member of higher management who was also on the central committee should preside at zonal or area meetings.[21]

Management representatives on the committee were nominated. The chairman of the committee usually acted as chairman of the production committee, but the administrative director presided over the employment committee. The reason for this arrangement is particularly interesting. In delegating responsibility for the employment committee the head of the firm was able to reserve his authority for the more serious matters that might arise and to prevent its being diminished or prejudiced by commitments hastily or unguardedly entered into in the heat of the moment. Although at that time this decision was strongly criticized from the workers' side, its wisdom was proved in practice, and as confidence increased it came to be accepted.

On the whole the practice of joint consultation at AT&P had a twofold purpose. First, the zonal and area committees were intended to deal with problems peculiar to the section they represented, including grievances of individual workers, with a view to speedy settlement. Second, decentralization gave more people the opportunity to participate in joint consultation, and prevented the central committees being overwhelmed with minor matters of interest only to one or two members.

Some workers apparently expected joint consultation to be completely superseded by negotiation. But there is a clear distinction between the two processes, and both have their part to play in a satisfactory system of industrial relations. It must be recognized, moreover, that the two processes are complementary in the sense that genuine joint consultation improves the atmosphere for collective bargaining, and vice versa.

In British industry the development of joint consultation has usually followed that of collective bargaining; it has often been difficult for the parties, accustomed to meeting on issues that necessarily divide them, to acquire the habit of working together in the common interest—which joint consultation is intended to facilitate. In the United States, collective bargaining has been greatly accelerated by legislation—the Wagner Act, for example. At AT&P the British sequence has been reversed. Joint consultation was developed—with considerable success it is believed—before the workers were able to produce their own organization, one that management was prepared to meet in negotiations. It can hardly be doubted that both sides learned much from the experience of joint consultation, and that it was valuable in collective bargaining. The practice of holding regular meetings emphasizes the desirability of having a recognized procedure for dealing with grievances and disputes. Such meetings provide useful training for both sides in the presentation of a case, and in demonstrating the efficacy of reasoned argument supported by facts. Further, more knowledge of the facts relevant to negotiations—on, say, a wage claim—should be available as a result of joint consultation. But most important is the mutual confidence that is engendered by joint consultation. It is not, however, being suggested here that these ideal conditions were fully realized in the short experience of joint consultation at AT&P, but only that substantial progress had been made in that direction. This promised well for the next stage in industrial relations that was subsequently established—collective bargaining.

The company recognizes the African Timber and Plywood Workers' Union as representing their employees and having the power to negotiate on wages and working conditions. The agreement, which was signed in 1957 and took effect on December 1, 1959 provided for the establishment of a negotiating committee composed of not more than seven members appointed by each of the two sides.

Besides providing for collective bargaining, the agreement includes a procedure of dealing with grievances. If the union considers there is a breach of the agreement, the general secretary is entitled to make representation to the company; on the company's side the industrial relations officer is to deal with the complaint with the aid of the personnel manager. Individual employees also have the right to present grievances to their industrial relations officer, with the support of a union representative if desired. If this does not settle the matter, the employee may petition the general manager through the industrial relations officer; if he is still dissatisfied and chooses to refer the dispute to the union, it may be dealt with as a case of breach of agreement.[22]

In the case of strikes the two parties follow government regulations on industrial disputes and collective bargaining. Government conciliation after contractual procedures for solving disputes have been exhausted is provided through the Trades Disputes (Arbitration and Inquiry) Ordinance of 1941. Unsuccessful attempts at conciliation may be followed by arbitration, if both parties agree to it. The arbitration tribunals, appointed by the minister of labour, are composed of arbitrators nominated in equal numbers by the employers and workers, and an independent arbitrator or chairman. Government conciliation has been effective in settling disputes in Nigeria; between 1950 and 1955 approximately one-half of the issues submitted were settled without strikes through the good offices of the government labor official.[23]

With the signing of the 1957 agreement at AT&P, a distinction is drawn between negotiation and joint consultation. Matters which, by virtue of the agreement, have become the subject of negotiation are excluded from consideration by the joint consultative committees. It is agreed, however, that joint consultation shall continue, and the cooperation of the union is acknowledged by giving its president a seat on the central committee and by giving its secretary the right to attend meetings as an observer. Now that the right to negotiate is established, the joint consultative committees should find further opportunities for making their own distinctive contributions to the improvement of industrial relations and productivity.

SOME LOCAL DISPUTES AND SOLUTIONS

It is of value to examine the proceedings of a meeting of the
central committee. The topics discussed in such a meeting include
some that merely call for explanation or clarification of the company's
policy and management methods, or perhaps a modification of the
latter in the interests of both management and workers. Another
administrative matter on which there have been lengthy discussion
concerns the deduction of income tax. The company is required by
law to make the deduction, but apparently the onus of proof that tax
has been paid rests on the income receiver, who can be required by
the government to produce a tax receipt at any time. It has been
generally alleged that the revenue authorities are extremely dilatory
in distributing these receipts, and the consequences can be serious;
there have been many cases of company workers being arrested
because of their being unable to produce tax receipts. The company
deals with such matters by giving each worker a statement of tax
deduction, although legally such a statement is not a valid substitute
for the official receipt.

More controversial are those matters wherein the workers are
pressing for some concession while management resists the proposal
on the grounds of cost. The most important of such issues concerns
increased paid leave for the clerical staff according to period of
service. The chairman normally points out that this will necessitate
the employment of more men and that the company has to consider
the cost. When asked what the cost may be, his reply usually is that
management has no intention of discussing finance with members of
the workers' side, that the committee is not intended to run the
business side, which is management's job. The workers' representatives then revert to a more modest proposal: that permission
to accumulate leave should be given more freely. This, they insist,
will not cost the company anything—an attitude that normally leads
to a rebuke by the chairman.

From the proceedings cited above, one can immediately realize
that there is the problem of communication between management and
workers. This is further complicated by the fact that management
always plays the predominant role and also has a veto on whatever
decisions are reached. An easy solution to this problem is difficult
to find because of the voluntary nature of collective bargaining in the
country. Collective bargaining is not compulsory but voluntary, and
government can come between the two parties only if both are willing.
In this sense it is patterned on the British model and is slightly
different from the U.S. model for the reason that there are no government labor courts where labor disputes could be settled; such legal
backing of collective bargaining is still absent in Nigeria. Maybe if

the industrial relations scene continues to deteriorate at its present rate, the Nigerian government will see the need of compulsory intervention irrespective of whether the two parties are willing or not.

Another local problem that occurs quite often, particularly in the committee representing the office staff, is the question of promotion. Here, as in other sections, there is a grading scheme, but with an efficiency bar at a certain level, which can be crossed only by passing a written examination. So far very few clerks have passed this test. The matter is often brought up at meetings of the central committee; promotion questions have also been raised in the plymill committee, complaints being made that vacancies in senior posts have been filled by workers promoted from other sections. There is some feeling that, in principle, preference should be given to men who work in the section where the vacancy occurs, but the chairman keeps reminding the committee that on other occasions it has been contended that worthy candidates were denied promotion because opportunities for transfer were limited.[24]

A COMPARISON OF THE NIGERIAN SITUATION WITH SOME ASPECTS OF LABOR-MANAGEMENT RELATIONS IN THE UNITED STATES

In both Nigeria and the United States, government action in labor-management relations is pronounced. In the United States, for example, the National Labor Relations Act (Wagner Act) provided a series of deterrents against industry, for it gave labor the right to organize free from employer interference, and made collective bargaining a legal obligation.[25] In Nigeria the Labour Code Ordinance legalized union organization, but made collective bargaining a voluntary procedure.

If one considers the various acts passed in the two countries, one can distinguish a certain trend in the actions of both governments. In the United States, the Wagner Act was in favor of labor, but the Taft-Hartley Act was supposed to be against labor—as was the Landrum-Griffin Act. Government favorable action toward labor at the beginning could be explained by the fact that up to the passage of the Wagner Act, labor was persecuted by management; therefore certain legislative action was necessary to prop up labor. The Wagner Act took care of that. When labor became rather strong, certain legislative action was vital to curb its activities, and that was seen in the Taft-Hartley and Landrum-Griffin acts (the two complement each other, from the government's point of view). These acts have more-or-less formed a perfect circle as far as control is concerned. Each movement of industry and labor that once operated in a rugged individualistic atmosphere is now regulated and controlled. So too in Nigeria, where government legislation is gradually taking over the former rugged individualistic atmosphere and managerial veto. Another common aspect is that both governments realize the importance of industrial peace and both take steps to promote it or bring it about.

The Nigerian governmental trend of action toward labor is especially worthwhile noting. While U.S. legislation tilted first toward labor and then tilted away again to achieve a balance between labor and management, Nigerian legislation is still predominately in favor of labor, because labor is not strong enough to bargain with management as equals. Moreover the voluntarism in collective bargaining still gives a veto to management, so it becomes necessary for government to shield labor from management's buffeting with favorable legislation. When labor becomes strong, there is no doubt that there will be a shift in legislation to achieve a balance between labor and management as in the United States.

With regard to union leadership in both countries, there is a vast difference. U.S. union leadership is in the hands of the unionists themselves; that is, leaders have to come from the rank-and-file of the unions, as in the cases of Samuel Gompers of the American Federation of Labor and Walter Reuther of the United Automobile Workers. Professionals, such as industrial relations experts and people in allied fields, do not lead the unions; they only serve the unions. The reverse is the case in Nigeria, for professionals are the leaders of unions. This has some disadvantage, for most of them are not interested in the workers' welfare; rather they use union leadership as a stepping stone to politics. As a result there is a lot of strain in the leadership, and hence there are inevitable weaknesses among Nigerian unions.

In Nigeria the unions have come to realize that divisiveness will not aid their cause. The current trend is to amalgamate, for unity means strength. The result is the formation of an All Nigeria Trade Unions Federation (A.N.T.U.F.) to help them formulate and disseminate unanimous statements on the issues.[26] Nowadays unions tend to strike out of sympathy with others. This happened in 1964, during the first nationwide strike, which paralyzed the country for two weeks.*

---

*The strike was first organized by the Civil Service Union and others joined in sympathy. The reason for the strike was that senior service personnel and politicians were having the larger share of the national cake. The existing salary structure for junior service workers as against that for senior service personnel and ministers

The same tendency is going on in the United States. For example the dockworkers' strike on the East Coast in 1968-69 was unnecessarily extended because the dockworkers presented a united front. The New York dockworkers' union leaders refused to sign their contract, despite the fact that a compromise was reached. They wanted a unanimous compromise for all the unions involved in the strike. This attitude is beginning to resemble the "principle of extension"* practiced in France and Germany.[28]

CONCLUSION: A KALEIDOSCOPIC VIEW OF THE TIMBER INDUSTRY

The difficulties of adaptation, on the part of labor, do create obstacles to good labor-management relations as well as to the progress of industrialization in African communities. But they can easily be exaggerated. The case of AT&P at Sapele is very different, though. Here, stability has been carefully fostered from the beginning with the object of conserving acquired skills and in general ensuring an adequate supply of dependable labor. There is evidence too that management has succeeded in inspiring many of its workers with a sense of loyalty. Theirs is an enterprise in which stability of labor is a condition of survival; and while it is true that local circumstances have been favorable, the stability achieved is largely the result of enlightened personnel and labor policies, and the adaptation of well-known methods to an African industrial environment.

Assuming that management is concerned about stability, the choice of methods is clearly important. This calls to mind another common criticism of African workers: there is a tendency among expatriate employers to insist on the differences between African and European or American workers, and investigators of African industrial conditions are prepared to find that the study of such differences becomes a major part of their task. For instance an extensive study of labor turnover and absenteeism in various African countries was undertaken in the 1950s because these factors were thought to be an important cause of low productivity in industrial enterprises. But it was found that, apart from enterprises dependent on migrant labor, turnover and absenteeism were at quite a low level.

---

was often described by trade unions as "colonial," "immoral," and "unjust."[27]

*The "principle of extension" means, if sizable number of firms are represented and conclude an agreement, the labor minister may extend this agreement to all the employers in the same industry.

As one report put it, "the evidence is that the black industrial worker in the Union of South Africa, for example, does not differ very strikingly from the Australian, British, or American operative."[29]

One seemingly elementary point concerning incentives is the importance of ensuring that the incentives offered are fully understood by the workers. This is part of another problem concerning communications. Again it is not a problem peculiar to African industry, but there are obviously special difficulties where managers and workers may be of different ethnic origins and where, as it is often the case, the labor force is largely illiterate. Such additional difficulties are easing with the spread of education. It is not, however, merely a matter of schooling; there is need for continual effort in industry. Joint consultation, for example, is a valuable educational experience for management as well as for workers, and it can be a most important means of improving communications. Foremen too are a vital link in the chain of communication within the firm, and they need training in this aspect of their job as well as on the technical side. The trade unions also have an important part to play, not only in the formulation of claims and the conduct of negotiations but in informing their members as to the nature of agreements and how they are affected by the terms of such agreements. This is not, of course, to suggest that management should rely on the unions to undertake functions that are properly its own responsibility.

As may be expected, Britain's long association with Nigeria has affected the structure of industrial relations in certain respects. The progress of trade unionism in Nigeria, though, is in striking contrast with the early history of the movement in Britain. Legal recognition of the right to collective bargaining came early, and the unions received a good deal of guidance and encouragement from a department of labor modeled on British lines. Similarly the development of a statutory labor code and the means of enforcement has been a far more rapid process than in Britain or the United States. But the very lack of interest shown by British and U.S. governments in the past did serve to emphasize the responsibility of the parties in industry for working out orderly negotiating procedures. It would be unfortunate if in Nigeria the growth of a similar sense of responsibility should be cramped by government intervention, however well-intentioned.*

---

*Here we are concerned with industrial relations within the existing political framework (federalism). It is conceivable that trade unionism could seek to become a major political force with the civil war over (there were attempts before the war) in opposition to the established authority and so give rise to government intervention on political grounds.

115

There are, however, factors that militate more immediately against the development of an orderly structure of industrial relations based on voluntary agreements. Such a system presupposes some continuity in the personnel concerned with negotiations; but in many African unions the officials change with disturbing frequency. It requires also that the representatives of the two sides in the negotiations be fairly well matched as regards experience and skill in negotiation and in bargaining strength. Such requirements imply the need for more full-time trained officers on the union side, and for more willingness on management's side to consider those officers as accredited representatives. The AT&P management has come to realize this fact. Above all there must be some degree of mutual confidence, the lack of which has in the past been increased by the fact that the parties generally belonged to different ethnic groups. The habit of introducing new claims while negotiation on an agreed-upon basis are in progress necessarily weakens confidence. Refusal to negotiate on the part of management, or precipitate strike action by workers, can have a similar unfortunate effect. On the whole, labor-management relations at AT&P have been improving because both labor and management see the need and the advantages.

NOTES

1. F. A. Wells, and W. A. Warmington, Studies in Industrialization: Nigeria and the Cameroons (Oxford: Oxford University Press, 1962), p. 30.
2. Ibid., p. 41.
3. Mallory Weber, "Individualism, Home Life and Work Efficiency Among a Group of Nigerian Workers," Occupational Psychology Vol. 41 (1967), pp. 183-92.
4. Wells and Warmington, op. cit., p. 38.
5. Ibid., p. 29.
6. Ibid., p. 32.
7. Weber, op. cit., pp. 183-92.
8. Wells, op. cit., p. 34.
9. International Bank Mission Report of 1959.
10. Wells and Warmington, op. cit., pp. 42-46.
11. Ibid., p. 44.
12. Ibid., p. 49.
13. J. I. Roper, Labour Problems in West Africa (Penguin Books, 1959), pp. 52-53.
14. U.S. Army, Area Handbook for Nigeria (1964), p. 221; see also Roper, op. cit., pp. 61-62.
15. Wells and Warmington, op. cit., p. 55.

16. Annual Report of Department of Labour, 1950-1.

17. U.S. Army, op. cit., p. 215; see also Nigerian Labour Market, The Federal Ministry of Information (Lagos, 1968), pp. 15-16.

18. Wells and Warmington, op. cit., p. 56.

19. Ibid., p. 56.

20. Ibid., pp. 50-57.

21. Ibid., pp. 57-58.

22. See Nigerian Labour Market, pp. 12-16; see also Wells and Warmington, op. cit., p. 75.

23. U.S. Army, op. cit., p. 224.

24. Wells and Warmington, op. cit., p. 60.

25. Robert C. Kree, Days of Our Years with Labor (Cincinnati: The W. H. Anderson Company, 1966), pp. 29-33.

26. C. C. Onyemelukwe, Problems of Industrial Planning and Management in Nigeria (New York: Columbia University Press, 1966), pp. 250-52.

27. West Africa, No. 2649 (March 9, 1968), pp. 272-76.

28. A. F. Sturmthal, Unity and Diversity in European Labor (Glencoe, Ill.: The Free Press of Glencoe, 1953), pp. 151-67.

29. Y. Glass, "The Black Industrial Worker: A Social Psychological Study," (Johannesburg: National Institute for Personnel Research, 1959), p. 14; see also Wells and Warmington, op. cit., pp. 252-53.

BIBLIOGRAPHY

Glass, Y. The Black Industrial Worker: A Social Psychology Study. Johannesburg: National Institute for Personnel Research, 1959.

Knee, Robert C. Days of Our Years with Labor. Cincinnati: The W. H. Anderson Company, 1966.

Onyamchukwe, C. C., Problems of Industrial Planning and Management in Nigeria. New York: Columbia University Press, 1966.

Roper, J. I. Labour Problems in West Africa. London: Penguin Books, 1958.

The Federal Ministry of Information, The Nigerian Labour Market. Lagos: Nigerian National Press, Ltd., 1968.

U.S. Army. Area Handbook for Nigeria. Washington, D.C.: U.S. Government Printing Office, 1964.

Weber, Mallory. "Individualism, Home Life and Work Efficiency Among a Group of Nigerian Workers," <u>Occupational Psychology</u>, Vol. 41 (1967), pp. 183-92.

Wells, F. A. and W. A. Warmington. <u>Studies in Industrialization: Nigeria and the Cameroons</u>. Oxford: Oxford University Press, 1962.

7

**POLITICAL DILEMMAS
OF NIGERIAN LABOR**
Robert Melson

LABOR AND POLITICS IN NIGERIA

This chapter is concerned with relating the political dilemmas of Nigerian labor to changes in the Nigerian political system. It will be shown that whenever Nigerian labor became important enough to get the attention of politicians and parties, Nigerian labor leaders were confronted with political dilemmas. The nature of such dilemmas varied as a function of the nature of the political pressure and of the political ambitions and perceptions of the labor movement. To initiate the discussion, let us briefly sketch out the changing character of the Nigerian political system, and then turn to the labor movement and its perceptions of the political process.

Between 1945 and the present the Nigerian political system was at different points in time a unitarian, a federalist, a polarized, and a fragmented system. The adjectives used here refer not only to constitutional arrangements but more importantly to the makeup and distribution of political power.

Between 1945 and 1950 the Nigerian political system was unitarian, in the sense that real power rested almost exclusively in the center. No regions or states had as yet been created, and the struggle for power took place between a Congress-type party integrating various political interests and ethnic groups on the one hand and the imperial government on the other hand.[1] Between 1950 and the early 1960s Nigeria became a federation, divided into Northern, Eastern, and Western regions, and the federal territory of Lagos; government was decentralized. Political power devolved to regionally based parties or to factions in the national parties whose bases lay

in the regions.* The political game shifted from one in which a
retreating colonial government yielded to a victorious nationalist
party, to a game in which three players jockeyed suspiciously for
marginal advantage and for opportune coalitions.

By 1965 forces were in motion that destroyed the rules of
federation. First, Nigeria became polarized by forces centering on
the north and south, and then, by 1967, she became fragmented by the
secession of the east (which became Biafra). The unity of the labor
movement was fragmented accordingly.

Turning from the political system to the labor movement, one
should make a crucial distinction between politically active or
"activist" labor leaders and politically inactive, neutral, or "neutralist"
labor leaders. Broadly speaking this distinction coincides with that
made by Lenin and more recently by Selig Perlman, between political
unionism and bread-and-butter unionism.** It is of interest here
because, in the Nigerian political system and labor movements, it
is far from being merely an analytical distinction; it differentiates
two quite different sets of leaders, organizations, and points of view
on politics. Furthermore, in the Nigerian political system and labor
movement, the activist-neutralist division largely coincided with the
division between those who favored a socialist labor party and supported a unitarian constitution for Nigeria, and those who opposed
(or were indifferent to) such a party and supported (or were indifferent to) the federal system. Although other characteristics,
such as support for communist states, may have separated the two
groups, and although there may have been differences concerning
strategy and tactics within groups, commitment to party and to a type

---

*By 1950 two other major parties were active. These were
the Action Group (AG) in the west and the Northern Peoples Congress
(NPC) in the north.

**In Leninist terms, Nigerian labor was mainly divided into
"trade unionists" who had no political ambitions as such (our
neutralists) and "social democrats" whose main short-range ambition
was the successful launching of a socialist labor party (our activists).
In Nigeria very few of the latter group had enough time or money to
become, in Lenin's terms, "professional revolutionaries." Perlman's
analysis of the failure of political unionism in the United States is
particularly applicable to Nigeria in the regionalist phase, less
applicable in the unitary and polarized phases discussed below. For
Lenin, see especially his What is to be Done? For Perlman, see
Selig Perlman, A Theory of the Labor Movement (New York: Augustus
M. Kelley, 1949).

of constitutional arrangement basically separated the activists from
the neutralists.

In the time period under consideration, and especially after
independence, the neutralists and activists, with dissenting factions
in each camp, were grouped into four central labor bodies. Activists
largely ran the Nigerian Trade Union Congress (NTUC) and the Labour
Unity Front (LUF).* Neutralists ran the United Labour Congress
(ULC) and a breakaway neutralist group ran the Nigerian Workers
Council (NWC). Connected to the activist central labor bodies by
committees whose members served both industrial and political
functions were two socialist labor parties. For the most part the
group of activists running the NTUC also ran the Socialist Workers
and Farmers Party (SWAFP) while the activists running the Labour
Unity Front also ran the Nigerian Labour Party (NLP). These
organizations are of particular interest to this discussion for their
role after the general strike of June 1964.

Having briefly sketched the four phases of Nigerian political
development and having distinguished between the two main factions
of the labor movement, we can now go on to examine how the two
factions faced political dilemmas in each of the four stages. However,
since no serious conflicts existed either for activists in the unitary
phase or for neutralists in the federal phase, one is left with six
major dilemmas. These are the dilemmas of neutralists in the
unitary phase, of activists in the federal or regional phase, of
activists and neutralists in the polarized phase, and of activists and
neutralists in the fragmented phase. Table 7.1 lays out the six
dilemmas and the structure of what follows.

NEUTRALIST LABOR IN THE UNITARY PHASE
OF NIGERIAN NATIONALISM

For the neutralists the dilemma of the unitary phase was posed
by the powerful pull of a nationalist party that demanded that labor
join it in nationalist agitation. This dilemma can perhaps best be
illustrated by analyzing what happened to the Trades Union Congress
of Nigeria after the general strike of 1945.

------

*The reader should be warned perhaps not to take this classifica-
tion too literally. For example, although activists were most prominent
in the Labour Unity Front, many large unions, such as the Nigerian
Union of Teachers (which belonged to the Labour Unity Front) were
by no means run by activists.

TABLE 7.1

Six Political Dilemmas of Nigerian Labor

| Type of Labor | Political Phase | | | |
	Unitary (1945-50)	Regional (1950-62)	Polarized (1962-66)	Fragmented (1966-)
Neutralist	first dilemma	no dilemma	third dilemma	fifth dilemma
Activist	no dilemma	second dilemma	fourth dilemma	sixth dilemma

As a consequence of that strike, labor gained the attention of Dr. Azikiwe and the National Council of Nigeria and the Cameroons (NCNC). Great pressures were exerted on the Trades Union Congress to join the NCNC. The effects of such political pressures were to divide the Trades Union Congress into three factions. One faction, headed by Michael Imoudu, supported direct affiliation; another, headed by N. A. Cole and Alhaji H. P. Adebola, resisted direct affiliation; and a third faction supported affiliation to a weak rival of the NCNC.*

The case of N.A. Cole and Adebola, president and general secretary of the Trades Union Congress respectively, illustrates the problems facing neutralist labor leaders in a unitary political environment. Although both Cole and Adebola were members of the NCNC, they were not convinced that direct affiliation was the best path for the Trades Union Congress to take. Cole in particular wanted to give his executive committee time to consider the matter. And so, when asked whether the Trades Union Congress had affiliated with the NCNC, he made an equivocal statement. The West African Pilot, the newspaper of the NCNC, gathered from this that the Trades Union Congress was indeed a member of the NCNC. In fact, when the Trades Union Congress had been invited to participate in the founding of the NCNC in 1944, it had sent two observers (A. A. Adio-Moses and I. S. M. O. Shonekan). These two never formally affiliated with the NCNC, but

---

*Throughout the general strike of 1945 and for some years after, the Trades Union Congress was wooed not only by the NCNC but also by the elite Yoruba organization, the Nigerian Youth Movement. Once the Action Group was formed, the Nigerian Youth Movement declined in influence.

Dr. Azikiwe took the fact of attendance for a declaration of affiliation. Alhaji H. P. Adebola reported that "since then, the NCNC has been publishing the name of the Congress as a member-union."[2]

On November 29, 1947 a pro-NCNC faction of the general council, meeting before the conference of the Trades Union Congress, took the decision that, since the executive had kept silent up to now, the Trades Union Congress was bound to consider itself a member of the NCNC. When neutralists then threatened to split the congress, Cole appealed to the individual unions to put the question to a vote at the conference.

At the conference held on March 19, 1948, activists wanted the decision made by "block-voting," voting strength to be proportional to the numerical strength of the union. Had this measure been adopted the Trades Union Congress would have stayed in the NCNC, since most of the big unions were pro-NCNC. But the measure was defeated, the big unions, such as the Railway Workers Union, walked out, and the resolution to remain independent of the NCNC was taken by the smaller unions alone.

It is interesting to note that not all NCNC partisans necessarily wanted the Trades Union Congress to affiliate with the NCNC. Cole himself was NCNC, and already at this early date, H. P. Adebola, who was to play a role of ever-increasing importance on the side of the politically "neutral" wing of the Trades Union Congress, explained the decision not to affiliate to the NCNC in the following terms:

> It is necessary to request the Conference to consider what relationship should exist between workers and political parties. . . . Unwarranted association with non-labour political parties tends to diminish the enviable positions which workers should occupy in the scheme of things. Instead of political parties soliciting for support of workers, the workers are soliciting for support of political parties whose political ideologies are at variance with those of the labouring class. Instead of affiliation I recommend full collaboration . . . not to tie ourselves so that in the face of any disagreement we may be able to part company without embarrassment.[3]

This position of neutrality seemed apolitical when first propounded. However once the federation (or second phase) became institutionalized, it seemed tacitly to support the regime and openly to oppose the radical activists who wanted to use the labor movement to break the regime.

The pro-NCNC stand taken by the activists was to have a payoff the very next month, April 1948, at the annual convention of the NCNC at Kaduna. Out of twenty-one members of the NCNC cabinet, five were trade unionists or radical young men who called themselves Zikists. They were F. O. Coker, publicity secretary; Luke Emejulu, assistant federal secretary; Raji Abdalah, assistant field secretary; Nduka Eze, assistant publicity secretary; and M. A. O. Imoudu, assistant field secretary.[4] The leaders who walked out of the convention—Imoudu, F. O. Coker, Nduka Eze, and Emejulu—formed what they called the Committee of Trade Unions, which was supported by the NCNC and the Zikists. On March 17, 1949 the committee renamed itself the Nigerian National Federation of Labour (NNFL), with Imoudu as president and Nduka Eze as general secretary. In addition to the Railway Workers Union, of which Imoudu was president, and the UNAMAG (acronym for the Ammalgamated Union of UAC African Workers), twenty other unions affiliated with the Nigerian National Federation of Labour. In May 1950 the NNFL absorbed the old Trades Union Congress in a new organization called the Nigerian Labour Congress (NLC). From this experience the neutralists learned that, in a unitary state with only one popular political party, it is not possible to remain neutral in politics without suffering the consequences of splintering and loss of power. Soon after, the activists too were learning lessons in powerlessness.

The Nigerian Labour Congress proved to be the highpoint of labor's interaction with a political party, for within the year of its founding the Labor-NCNC alliance broke down. The militants of the labor movement, whose power was predicated on a nationalist and unitarian NCNC, were left out in the cold.*

ACTIVISTS IN THE REGIONALIST PHASE

In the second, federalist, or regionalist phase of Nigerian politics (1950-60), the activists faced the dilemma of working for a labor party in a political system that had become unresponsive to their unitarian appeals. No problem existed for the neutralists, however. Claiming that political activity would divide their membership, the neutralists eschewed mixing politics with labor.

To understand the causes of the sudden rise and fall of the NCNC-activist alliance, one must be aware of certain developments

---

*In 1949 there occurred the Enugu Colliery shooting, which, for a year, kept alive the idea of a unitary nationalist movement. In retrospect, however, this incident merely delayed the collapse by one year. See Sklar, op. cit., p. 83.

taking place in the regionalist system as a whole, in the NCNC, and in the labor movement. In the late 1940s and early 1950s, regionalism was founded by a series of constitutional reforms. The effect of constitutional regionalization was to create a market for regional politics, and consequently to pose a challenge to all political organizations to enter this arena. It followed that a nationalist party such as the NCNC, which until then had been unitarian in its outlook, had to take an interest in contesting elections on the regional level. This also meant that, within the NCNC, there was a rise in the fortunes of politicians and groups that were regionally well-connected via the tribal unions, while the fortunes of labor activists and Zikists fell.

Believing constitutional advances a subterfuge, opposed to regionalism, and convinced that independence would come only by way of revolution, the more radical wing of the unitarian nationalists responded to the dilemmas of regionalism with a call to direct action.[5] Revolution would put an end to constitutional subterfuge, weaken the hand of the regionalist party in the NCNC, and accelerate the pace of independence. In trying to start a revolution in Nigeria, labor activists and Zikists failed. Moreover, by not being able to carry Azikiwe with them, the Zikists isolated themselves from the NCNC. Then, in February of 1950, a common laborer claiming allegiance to the Zikists tried to assassinate Sir Hugh Foot, the chief secretary of the government, and the Zikists were proclaimed an unlawful society.[6]

Regionalism proved a disaster to the unitarians in the NCNC. But the unitarians, and especially the Zikists among them, still had prestige in the nationalist movement; this stemmed from their connection with the labor movement, their successful launching of the Nigerian National Federation of Labour, and their presumed control over the strike weapon. This too was to be taken away from them by 1950.

The UNAMAG Strike

Not taken in the police roundup of the Zikists in February 1950, Nduka Eze, the brilliant secretary of the Nigerian Labour Congress and general secretary of the Zikist movement, decided on a series of strikes. His first move was to call a strike of the Amalgamated Union of the UAC African Workers (UNAMAG).[7] He struck twice; the first time, in August 1950, the strike was a success and workers won an increase in wages. In December he struck again, but this time the workers were not prepared to follow. In ten days the strike was crushed and with it the credibility of Eze's influence over the workers. Ironically, because Eze and the Zikists had crossed Azikiwe, support among member unions vanished. Antiregionalism had not as yet become a popular issue.

For a while Eze and the Zikists carried on. In January 1951 Eze and a splinter group of Zikists and radical labor leaders formed the antiregionalist Freedom Movement. The movement was one of the first of many attempts to found a Marxist, antiregionalist labor party outside the framework of cultural organizations and ethnic pressure groups. When the Freedom Movement failed in its goals and Eze was being hounded by the colonial regime, he relinquished his post in the Nigerian Labour Congress, the Freedom Movement, and UNAMAG. Without Eze, the UNAMAG and Freedom Movement disappeared and no federation of UAC unions appeared again until 1956. The events of the 1950s turned the militants against Azikiwe and the NCNC. Many of them turned to Marxism, some out of conviction and some out of friendship for those who were convinced. For the activists the period of isolation from Nigerian politics had begun. It was to last for thirteen years. Not until the strike of 1964 did the activists think that their vigil had come to an end. From what they considered to be Azikiwe's betrayal and from their obvious decline in power during the regionalist phase, the activists learned to distrust the nationalist parties and their leaders and to be unalterably opposed to regionalism. Regionalism they considered to be the structural cause behind their decline in power.

Between independence in October 1960 and the federal elections of December 1964, the situation changed remarkably. The British were out and the party nationalists were in power. The neutralists in the trade union movement found it increasingly difficult not to turn against the regionalist system and the party nationalists. As an antiregionalist faction began to grow in the neutralist camp, a basis for unity developed between the neutralists and the activists. By September 1963 rapprochement between the two wings had gone so far as to lead to the formation of the Joint Action Committee and the joint prosecution of the general strike of June 1964. As a consequence of the success of the June general strike, activists and neutralists buried their differences and continued to cooperate in the Joint Action Committee, where the major central labor bodies were represented.

But the June strike was followed by the federal elections of 1964 five months later. These elections, the first since independence, were crucial for the unity of the Nigerian political system and had profound effects on the unity of the labor movement. To a rejuvenated labor movement, they posed the problem—whom to support?

DILEMMAS OF THE POLARIZED PHASE

It will be recalled that the federal election of December 1964 was scheduled to take place at a critical time in the evolution of the

Nigerian political system. The party system had started out as a coalition of the Northern Peoples Congress and the Southern NCNC against the Western Action Group. By 1964, however, the Northern Peoples Congress-NCNC coalition was dead. The action group had been split in the Western Region into a branch, the Nigerian National Democratic Party (NNDP), in collusion with the Northern Peoples Congress and another branch, still calling itself the Action Group, which out of necessity allied itself with its old rival, the NCNC. The end result of these crises and manoeuvers was to polarize Nigerian politics between a northern party alliance (the Nigerian National Alliance) and a southern party alliance (the United Progressive Grand Alliance).

The federal election took place under special circumstances. The United Progressive Grand Alliance (UPGA) decided to boycott the election, because it charged the Nigerian National Alliance (NNA) with fraud and with rigging the election. Neither the neutralists nor the activists were exempt from the effects of this polarization.

In the polarized phase of Nigerian politics, neutralists were faced with the dilemma of maintaining their neutrality while the rank and file had become politicized and for the most part supported the southern party alliance. The activists were confronted with the dilemma of either joining a united front and having their ideology diluted or remaining independent—and thereby irrelevant to the political issues of the day.

The Neutralists

The success of the June 1964 strike created problems for the neutralists facing the federal election. Politicians had forgotten the failure of the UNAMAG strike of 1950. They assumed that labor leaders had control over the strike weapon, and, as the election approached, they began to lobby labor for support. For the neutralists this created the problem of having either to choose neutrality and risk the alienation of United Progressive Grand Alliance supporters within the labor movement, or to choose the United Progressive Grand Alliance and scrap their belief in nonpolitical trade unionism.

Halfway through the election, for example, the Western branch of the United Labour Congress split over support of the United Progressive Grand Alliance. One branch led by the dynamic E. U. Ijeh, secretary of the Western branch of the United Labour Congress, came out foresquare behind the United Progressive Grand Alliance: "The voice of the entire workers in Western Nigeria demand that every worker, his family, dependents . . . should vote massively for the workers' friend—the UNITED PROGRESSIVE GRAND ALLIANCE.

It is your duty as well as the responsibility of all of us to make sure that the reactionary Nigerian National Alliance will not gain one electoral seat in Western Nigeria."[8] What made the dilemma even sharper after the election was the victory of the Nigerian National Alliance.*

The reaction of the neutralists to the dilemma of polarization was to remain neutral politically and not to come out in support of the United Progressive Grand Alliance.** The result of this choice was to place the neutralist leaders seriously on the defensive. This defensive tone could be heard at the conference of the United Labour Congress in Port Harcourt in July 1965. For example, in trying to shift the blame to the Nigerian Trades Union Congress for the disbanding of the Joint Action Committee, Adebola darkly alluded to "their ulterior motives." And in trying to placate his pro-United Progressive Grand Alliance audience, he challenged the notion that the Nigerian Trades Union Congress favored that alliance: "Let me reveal to our own brothers who were misled by the NTUC to believe that the NTUC was on the side of UPGA . . . information revealed that at a meeting of the NTUC it was decided that infiltration methods should be adopted to give the major parties the impression that NTUC boys were . . . friendly."[9] Adebola sounded wan. Rumor had it that one or none of the ULC secretaries was in support of the Nigerian National Alliance. A rift became apparent in the leadership of the United Labour Congress. J. Oduleye, long-time treasurer and ally of Adebola, was defeated for reelection. A number of unions, among them the prestigious Railway

---

*It is ironic and further illustrates the neutralists' dilemma that the United Labour Congress came under attack not only from its United Progressive Grand Alliance partisans—especially in the Western Region—but that it also came under attack from its few Northern members. Thus Malam Yakubu Kaile, self-styled "Director of Organizations of the Northern Federation of Labour" (a breakaway from the United Labour Congress, formed after the general strike of September 1963), sent a memorandum to the Northern house of assembly in which he denounced the United Labour Congress as a wing of the NCNC and thus of the United Progressive Grand Alliance. See "Memorandum Addressed to the Northern House of Assembly," March 11, 1964; United Labour Congress files, 1963-64.

**This became clear when, on December 27, the NCNC approached the labor movement in the hope of coordinating a general strike with the boycott of the election. The activists gave their support, as did many of the neutralists. The leadership of the United Labour Congress, however, refused to participate in the strike, and the strike fizzled.

Technical Staff Association, quit the United Labour Congress. Other differences were papered over (as became apparent to this author, who attended the conference). Disunited as they were, the neutralists could have drawn some comfort from the realization that the activists too had their political problems.

The Activists

The neutralists wanted to stay out of politics—the activists wanted to get into politics. One would have thought that the general strike of June 1964 and the opportunities offered by the December election would have favored the activists. This, however, was not the case. Far from being united, the activists disagreed profoundly among themselves on how to take advantage of the strike and the election. The growing polarization of the political system created dilemmas for the activists, and it exacerbated the differences among them.

The major problem facing the activists was whether to join the United Progressive Grand Alliance and risk the dilution of ideology and power, or whether to go it alone and risk remaining politically irrelevant. A majority faction of the Nigerian Trades Union Congress and the Socialist Workers and Farmers Party (SWAFP) chose the "United Front" strategy. A minority faction, however, rallied about Michael Imoudu, "Labor Leader Number One," broke with the Nigerian Trades Union Congress and the Socialist Workers and Farmers Party, formed the Nigerian Labour Party, and prepared to contest elections without allying with the United Progressive Grand Alliance. Nevertheless the polarization of Nigerian politics during the election affected both the strategy and the unity of the Nigerian Labour Party.

When it became apparent that the Nigerian National Alliance was going to win the election, the pressure on the Nigerian Labour Party to cooperate with the United Progressive Grand Alliance increased. It was rumored that, by the end of December, the national secretary of the NCNC approached Imoudu and other labor leaders with an appeal to launch a general strike to coincide with the planned United Progressive Grand Alliance boycott of the election. By this time, Imoudu and the Nigerian Labour Party had changed their minds and, like the Socialist Workers and Farmers Party, were in full support of the United Progressive Grand Alliance. Thus, for example, on the eve of the boycott, Imoudu said: "The rigging of the election by the Nigerian National Alliance has precipitated a national crisis."[10] At the United Progressive Grand Alliance rally in Lagos announcing the boycott of the election, Imoudu was present, as were representatives of the Socialist Workers and Farmers Party.[11] And then, on

December 29, Imoudu, speaking in the name of the Joint Action Committee, called for a general strike in support of the United Progressive Grand Alliance boycott.[12]

The General Strike of December 1964

For the Nigerian Labour Party and the other activists who had called it, the general strike of December 1964 was a failure. After the call on December 29, A. Ikoro and four other activists traveled to the Western and Eastern regions seeking support from local unions and local leaders. In Ibadan, for example, the secretary of the Western Region branch of the United Labour Congress (who did not consider himself a labor activist, but was a strong supporter of the NCNC) called on the general secretaries and presidents in the Ibadan area to come to a meeting where the issue of going on strike would be debated. From the beginning the meeting was divided into those who were pro-United Progressive Grand Alliance and those who were pro-Nigerian National Alliance. Depending on which faction one believes, two decisions were taken at that meeting; the first to go on strike and the second not to go on strike. The result was no strike in Ibadan. With some variations the story repeated itself in the east and north.*

There were various reasons why the strike failed. The activists claimed that it failed because Alhaji H. P. Adebola, president of the United Labour Congress, refused to support the strike. Others claimed that the workers were not ready to strike again so soon after the general strike of June. But whatever the causes, the failure of the strike converging with the electoral failure of the party had significant consequences for the solidarity of the Nigerian Labour Party and on the explanations given for the failures.

The Reaction of the Nigerian Labour Party

After the December election,** the Nigerian Labour Party fragmented into two factions. One, maintaining the name of the Nigerian Labour Party, rallied around President Imoudu and Secretary

---

*Most southern workers in the north were members of the United Labour Congress; when the Congress did not call its workers out on strike, the strike did not materialize.

**It was later agreed to postpone the December federal election until March 1965 in Lagos and in the Eastern Region; but by March the Nigerian Labour Party was not contesting in Lagos.

Eskor-Toyo and supported their interpretation of the events of December. The second, calling itself the Revolutionary Nigerian Labour Party (RNLP), rejected the Imoudu and Eskor-Toyo interpretation, denounced the United Progressive Grand Alliance, rifled the files the Nigerian Labour Party, and opened its own branch in Ibadan.

It is interesting to note, from our observations, that there were very few renunciations of activist ideology by formerly committed people. The majority of the Nigerian Labour Party stayed with Imoudu, but it is our impression that they did not perceive the importance of the events of December. One young man, for example, stopped talking about Nigerian politics because most of his attention had been taken up with the forthcoming World Youth Congress in Algeria. Those who did perceive the events of December as needing an explanation were satisfied in the belief that it was not the Nigerian Labour Party that had changed, but the United Progressive Grand Alliance that had become "progressive," and that, on the basis of this explanation, they were satisfied with the "United Front" strategy.

The group that split from the Nigerian Labour Party did not accept this explanation and did perceive the events of December simply as failures for the Nigerian Labour Party. But instead of reinterpreting events, the Revolutionary Labour Party reaffirmed in even stronger terms the necessity for non-cooperation with the "bourgeoisie." Ironically they seemed to take some pleasure in the failure of the Nigerian Labour Party. This failure meant that, as before, they as "mature Marxists" would have to endure powerlessness. They seemed to welcome failure and the stance of men outside and above politics "like Lenin in Switzerland." The failure proved that tactics, not ideology, were wrong, electoral outlets in Nigeria were of no use, revolution and coups were the roads to socialism.

THE ACTIVISTS, NEUTRALISTS, AND THE DILEMMAS FRAGMENTATION*

By way of conclusion we shall discuss the dilemmas created for labor by the Ironsi coup of January 1966, the Gowon coup of July 1966, and the pogroms of southerners, mostly Ibos, of September—October 1966.

---

*For the sake of some closure we are including a section on the coups, but the reader should be warned that it is based entirely on secondary sources and tends therefore to be conjectural.

The Ironsi Coup

The Ironsi coup was welcomed by the activists for putting an end to the regionalist regime and removing from power the political elite. Nevertheless the very unitarianism of the short-lived Ironsi regime demonstrated to the activists the limits on their power to influence events.

At first the activists took the coming of the Ironsi government as verification of their belief that revolution was inevitable in Nigeria and that they were in the forefront of that revolution. Four days after the coup the Nigerian Trades Union Congress made political demands on the regime and stressed the following points: "That the workers through their trade unions shall be given adequate representation in the policy and executive bodies of the interim military administration. . . . That all forms of regionalism shall be abolished in the future set-up of the Nigerian Republic. . . . That the basis of any new constitution shall be the unitary system with provincial administrative machinery. . . ."[13] Only Eskor-Toyo of the Nigerian Labour Party realized that the abolition of regionalism would not necessarily give political power to labor. So he stressed that representation to the constituent assembly (whose formation was expected in the near future) should be based on an organizational and functional, rather than a population basis: "How will the Constituent Assembly be constituted? Two principles are available: territorial representation . . . and organizational representation. The Nigerian Labour Party rejects territorial representation because certain vital interests, for instance the army itself, may not be represented, and because the factor of tribalism must be played down."[14]

It is to be recalled that since 1945, when they had been powerful in the Zikist movement and the Nigerian Federation of Labour, activists believed that the main reason for their exclusion from power lay in regionalism. From this it followed that a reversion to a unitarian framework would place the activists back in a nationally influential position. The Ironsi regime demonstrated the fallacy of this reasoning. In spite of the activists' willingness to join in "the policy and executive bodies of the interim military administration," it is clear that the Ironsi regime had little use for the activists. This became clear by May 1966, when the regime chose a faction of the neutralist wing of the labor movement to represent Nigerian labor at the impending meeting of the International Labour Organization (ILO) in Geneva.*

---

*On May 26, 1966 the Ministry of Labour chose neither the United Labour Congress nor the Nigerian Trades Union Congress

The Ironsi coup teaches that, in spite of what the activists believed, it was not constitutional arrangements that were keeping them from power. Rather it was the distribution of political loyalties wedded to national and ethnic groups. In fact it turns out that labor activists had political power under very special conditions. These were (1) a system in which peasants and other rural non-urban groups had not as yet become politicized, (2) a system in which the "masses" were commercial and industrial workers in the urban centers, and (3) a system in which labor leaders either doubled as political leaders or had the trust of political leaders. It is clear that all these conditions existed in the period following the 1945 general strike and preceding regionalism. But what regionalism did was to change the first two conditions. The urban workers were not the only "masses" under regionalism. In fact their relatively small numbers, as compared to those in rural areas, relegated industrial and commercial workers as a whole to a relatively unimportant role in that system. The Ironsi coup may have abolished regionalism, but it did not change the relative proportion of peasants and peasant leaders to workers and workers' leaders. The very fact that activists did not understand this point emphasizes their misunderstanding of their dilemma.

It is interesting to note that, although one may have expected the neutralists to fare badly during the Ironsi regime, they actually came off rather well.* It was the second coup, that of July 1966, which ultimately led to the breakup of Nigeria. In giving rise to sectional labor movements this coup goaded some neutralists and activists into coming out in favor of Nigerian unity. Nevertheless the voice of Nigerian labor was not strong enough to stop the disintegration of the movement and the country.

---

delegates. Instead it chose N. Chukwura, A. Anunobi, and J. Enigbokan of the Nigerian Workers Council. See West African Pilot, May 26, 1966.

*By joining with a dissident wing of the neutralists, the activists sought to isolate the powerful neutralist United Labour Congress. Thus, on February 16, 1966, there came into being the Nigerian Trade Union Federation, a grouping of the Nigerian Trades Union Congress, the Labour Unity Front, and the Nigerian Workers Council. By the time of the above-mentioned international Labour Congress issue, however, the Nigerian Trade Union Federation broke up in a quarrel over whom to send to the conference, and the United Labour Congress remained independent.

The Gowon Coup

For labor, the crucial thing about the second coup that brought Colonel Gowon to power was the fact that by July 1966 the army had split along tribal lines. By September this split led to the pogroms of Ibos in the north and the secession of the Eastern Region, subsequently called Biafra. This secession proved disastrous to the unity of the labor movement and brought non-Ibo neutralists into politics on the side of the central government. For better or for worse, therefore, the voice of labor in this period was a voice for unity. Thus, for example, the old activist Imoudu declared: "Anybody who was feeling that what was happening now is between Hausas and Ibos is deceiving himself because the concern of one worker is the concern of all."[15] And his old adversary, Alhaji H. P. Adebola, struck the same note when he declared: "The United Labour Congress of Nigeria has urged the head of the military government to do all in his power to keep Nigeria a single united country. . . . We make this appeal in the genuine conviction and belief that a united Nigerian nation alone offers the most effective and lasting basis of serving and safeguarding the best interest now and in the future of every Nigerian worker. . . ."[16]

But greater issues were involved than the unity of the labor movement. The killing of forty thousand Ibos in the north set the conditions for the secession of the Eastern Region and the civil war. Some months passed, though, before the final steps were taken. In this period, the Eastern Region trade unions broke with their national central labor bodies. Everyone was similarly affected—activists and neutralists, the Nigerian Trade Union Congress as well as the United Labour Congress.

Thus, on October 12, from Aba in the east, came the announcement that Eastern Region trade unions had broken with Lagos and had set up their own central labor body, to be called The Eastern Nigeria Council of Trade Unions (ENCTU). The ENCTU was designed to bring together all unions, independent of their previous central labor body affiliation. The reasons given for the break stemmed directly from the pogroms in the north: Bernard Udokporu, formerly Eastern Region secretary of the ULC, and now president of the ENCTU, declared that "neither the ULC nor the NTUC nor any other labour organisation had shown sympathy for their Eastern brothers since the troubles. . . ."*

---

*It should be noted that soon after the ENCTU's accusations, all central bodies came out in support of the many refugees fleeing

134

Under conditions of regional fragmentation and growing passion the neutralist, bread-and-butter unionism of the ULC could not keep Eastern Region unions in the fold.*

The Gowon coup and its consequences teaches once more the old lesson that trade unionism not mixed with political unionism is possible only in a situation in which the political system is relatively moderate and non-polarized. This was true for the neutralists in the early stages of the regionalist system—after independence, when the regionalist system began to break down, the neutralist solution seemed even more divorced from the needs of Nigerian labor and Nigerian politics.

The Lessons of the Political Dilemmas of
Nigerian Labor

This brief overview of Nigerian labor history and its relations to politics may have lessons of general interest for the problem of labor and politics. The dilemmas of activists in the regionalist phase shows that the direction of influence between labor and politics in the early stages of industrialization—Nigeria was then and still is predominately an agricultural country—flows mainly from the political sphere to the labor sphere. Once regionalism set in, labor leaders who wanted to exert influence on politics were for the most part irrelevant to the larger political issues. The importance of the Ironsi coup for our argument is its demonstrating that simply structural or constitutional changes could not and did not bring the labor activists to power. The unitary phase was a unique and perhaps unrepeatable experience for the activists.

The dilemma of neutralists in the unitary phase after 1945 and the polarized phase after 1965 shows how difficult it is to remain neutral from politics when political forces are recruiting support. The neutralist position was a solution to problems of trade union organization in a multi-ethnic and politically competitive environment. It is ironic therefore that the neutralist solution began to break down

---

the north. In fact both the NTUC and the ULC set up refugee relief committees. It is also significant that all bodies opposed the regime's warning to refugees—that if they did not return to their northern jobs by December 31, 1966, they would forefeit their jobs in the civil service.[17]

*Some months later the Mid-Western unions also declared themselves independent of Lagos.

135

at a time of unity between political parties, at least in the south. This unity under UPGA undercut the neutralist argument that by staying out of politics the union would survive. By playing on the fears of southern workers that the north would take over the country, UPGA assured that there would be trouble in the neutralist camp. For the neutralists the appeals of UPGA against the north in the polarized phase were equivalent to the appeals of the NCNC against the British in the unitary phase.

It is interesting to note that whenever neutralists were able to acquire national prestige and, therefore, political visibility—as after the strikes of 1945 and 1964—political attention would focus on them, and political demands would be made of them. In each case in the unitary phase and the polarized phase the net result was disunity in the neutralist camp. Finally the coups of 1966 and the resultant breakup of the federation seem to show that both activists and neutralists were among those who favored unity on the one hand and who favored secession on the other. That secession was favored mainly by Biafrans and unity by non-Biafrans would seem to show that the unity of the labor movement, like that of other groups in society, depends in large part on political forces outside the labor movement.

NOTES

1. We refer here to the early National Council of Nigeria and the Cameroons (NCNC).
2. H. P. Adebola, "Annual Report of General Secretary at Eighth Annual Conference of the Trades Union Congress" (March 19-23, 1948); Nigerian Railway Corporation files, Vol. 3.
3. Ibid.
4. Richard L. Sklar, Nigerian Political Parties (Princeton: Princeton University Press, 1963), pp. 63-64, 68.
5. Ibid., p. 79.
6. Ibid.
7. Ibid., p. 76.
8. Joint Action Committee of Western Nigeria, "Workers' View Point on the 1964 Federal Election," (1964).
9. Alhaji H. P. Adebola, presidential address, United Labour Congress conference; Port Harcourt, 1965.
10. Daily Times, Lagos: December 27, 1964.
11. Daily Express, Lagos: December 28, 1964.
12. West African Pilot, Lagos: December 30, 1964.
13. West African Pilot, January 19, 1966.
14. West African Pilot, January 21, 1966.

15. West African Pilot, October 25, 1966.
16. West African Pilot, August 26, 1966.
17. West African Pilot, October 12, 1966.

8

THE MANAGEMENT
OF TRADE UNION
FINANCES IN NIGERIA
M. O. Kayode

INTRODUCTION*

Two approaches to the analysis of financial management of
unions are possible. One approach is to examine financial management for all the unions lumped together as a type of organization,
and to treat business firms as another type. This is a macro-approach
in the sense that it aggregates financial management function over the
unions. With this approach two aspects of management function could
be examined:
1. The degree of success with which this type of organization
performs financial management function. Here the problem would
be examining the special features of unions responsible for the degree
of success attained in financial management (and, if the degree of
success is not different from that of business firms, explaining the
lack of difference in spite of the special features of unions).
2. How the unions as a type of organization perform the financial
function. (It could be argued that this second aspect—"how"—is an
attempt to explain the first—"the degree of success," and therefore
it is not, strictly speaking, a separate aspect. This would, however,
be assuming that the cause of the success difference is due to the
method of organization rather than to differences in features. Whether
the features are in fact responsible for the "how" is an empirical
question. Theoretically there could be a distinction.)

---

*This chapter is based in part on a paper presented at the
National Seminar on Trade Union Finance at the University of Ibadan,
September 5-7, 1969. A modified version has appeared in The
Nigerian Journal of Economic and Social Studies, 1971.

A second approach to analysing union finance is at the micro level. Here one would attempt to explain the performance of individual unions—i.e., explain differences in performance of different unions on the bases of such features as size, age, and services rendered.

The two approaches are combined in the present study, although with greater emphasis on the micro treatment. In other words, we analyze the factors responsible for the success differences in financial management of different unions by applying the criteria of business firms to the measurement of success.

METHODOLOGY

The analysis is based on the financial returns of 234 trade unions for 1962,* representing one-third of the total returns filed with the registrar. We selected the unions on a stratified basis, varying the proportion selected from each size class directly with size.

Size is weighted in selecting the sample for two reasons. The first and most obvious is because the distribution of the unions varies inversely with size, ranging from over 500 unions with memberships not greater than 500 to just three with memberships over 10,000. Second, the larger the union, the richer the analysis one could make. For example, small unions do not incur administrative expenses and have no fixed assets. All we could hope to achieve with this analysis of financial returns is to highlight problem areas that could be further explored. It could be suggested, for example, that the success with which the financial function is being rendered would depend to some extent on the quality of the leadership. Yet the quality of the leadership cannot be accurately assessed from financial returns. Administrative expenditure is the nearest measure of leadership quality that can be obtained from the returns. But even this, one must admit, may be a reflection of market imperfections and the degree of administrative inefficiencies rather than the quality of management. Thus, to test the leadership-degree-of-success hypothesis, the interview method has to be employed.

---

*1962 was selected because it was one of the peaceful prewar years!

FINDINGS

Degree of Success of Financial Management

The degree of success with which the financial functions of the unions are being rendered would be determined by (1) the degree of attainment of the union goals, and (2) the amount of fund spent in attaining the goals.

These conditions are essential once we accept that financial management is primarily concerned with gearing available fund to ensure attainment of predetermined goal(s). To measure the degree of management success, it is not sufficient to measure how much of the union goal(s) is attained. The cost of attaining the given goal(s) is not fixed but is dependent on management, particularly the way the money is spent.

Union Goals

A major thesis that could be used as justification for the first success condition is that a worker's willingness to sacrifice money, time, and energy for the union would depend on the extent to which he sees the union as being able to meet his needs.

Members' demands are many and varied. But one could say that essentially the members want a higher job satisfaction than is possible without the unions. The two most important factors in this respect are pay and job security. To influence these variables, workers bargain together as a group and occasionally use strike action as a weapon for increasing their bargaining power. These factors, though, are not necessarily the variables used for evaluating the performance of union officials in assessing the desirability of the unions. For one thing the contribution of the union officials in achieving an increased value of any of these two variables is not always obvious.

As a result of the rather low frequency of occurrence of events that increase the workers' awareness and appreciation of the officials' work, more emphasis is placed on "friendly benefits" to assess the desirability of union membership. Under the circumstances, one would expect these benefits to be rendered frequently. Yet 72 percent of the unions in our sample rendered no benefits at all to their members, while 20 percent rendered not more than a total of £50 in benefits to their members. In short, only 8 percent of the unions rendered benefits worth more than £50 each to all their members in one year!

With a correlation coefficient (r) of 0.16 between size of union and members' benefits, one can infer that the size of a union has little to do with the benefits rendered. This is unexpected. With a high correlation between size of union and total income (r = 0.84), one would expect a high correlation too between size of union and size of benefit rendered.

The relationship between size of income and size of members' benefits shows a clearer picture than that between size of union and members' benefits. There is an inverse relationship between the proportion of unions in each income class rendering no benefits and the size of total income of the unions.

Other Uses of Union Funds

Administrative expenses were found to consume a substantial proportion of the unions' income. In fact, more than 50 percent of the unions do not have more than ₱100 each after paying administrative expenses. Seven unions could not even meet their administrative expenses.

A union's fund is spent not only on paying the salaries of officials but also on rent, stationery, and other running expenses. It is out of the balance left after salaries of officials and the other running expenses have been deducted from income that the benefits to members are financed. Unfortunately 14 percent (43) of the unions cannot meet these expenses out of their incomes. In fact the deficit incurred by one of the unions is over £700. Surprisingly this is a very big union with a membership of over 50,000 but with over 300 branches spread over the federation. It is probably this scattering of the branches over the country that has led to the entire swallowing up of total income by management salaries.

The explanation for the rather low balance of union funds after the total running costs have been deducted from income should be sought in bad planning and lack of clear objectives. With proper planning or budgeting expenses could be cut down such that at least a breakeven point is reached. One wonders how the unions could ever hope to render some friendly benefits to members if they cannot cover running expenses. It is interesting to note that, whereas about 20 percent of the unions did not incur any management salary, many could still not balance up. What is probably more interesting is that even unions with up to 1,000 members could not afford to pay management salaries. It should be added, however, that the two unions in question had very small incomes—of £63 and £108. It could be argued that they were perhaps forced to avoid incurring management expenses because of their poor financial positions. The distribution of management salary by size of income of the unions does not seem to support the last conclusion, since two unions in the income group of £500-1,000 were able to avoid paying management salaries.

Capital Expenditure Assets of the Unions

For a long time, financial management emphasized only the procurement function. Concern for the use of funds was limited to ensuring that the money spent was not more than the amount collected. It is not unlikely that this emphasis in financial management was influenced by the old advice: "Income, £20; expenditure, £19.19s. 11d.; result, happiness. But expenditure, £20. 0s. 1d.; result, unhappiness!" The result of this advice is that the degree of success of financial management is measured by the gap that exists between income and expenditure. Using this measure the financial management of 38 percent of the unions can still be regarded as unsuccessful, while the degree of success for two-thirds of the remaining 62 percent be regarded as low since they have very low surplus—of not more than £50.

Financial success as we have defined it bears very little relationship to size—the correlation coefficient being only 0.11. It is most interesting that each of the eight unions with the poorest degree of performance has more than 1,000 members. In fact the union with the poorest degree of performance is from the largest size group, of over 10,000 members.

So far we have used the difference between income and expenditure as the yardstick for measuring the degree of financial success. The appropriateness of this yardstick is questionable, however, and emphasis now is on how the money is spent. Thus, depending on the use of which the money is put, a deficit budget could reflect a higher degree of financial success than a balanced budget. The popular advice of spending £19. 19s. 11d. if one earns £20 and wants happiness is really too simple, and it is most appropriate for the individuals or associations interested in keeping their happiness at a given level. To increase happiness or ensure maintenance of the degree of happiness for a long time requires more than just balancing the budget. It requires (1) maintaining at least one "source" that will ensure an everlasting flow of funds at a constant, or preferably an increasing, rate of flow, and (2) multiple sources of income to the extent that no one source could promise the constant flow for long; the diversification would ensure supplementary sources when the main source dries up or decreases its rate of flow.

The question therefore is to what extent does the management of union funds ensure that these two requirements are met?

Sources of Union Funds

The financial management of the unions is not such that ensures that either of the two conditions above is met. At present there is heavy reliance on one source of fund—members' contributions. Over 33 percent of the unions derive up to 95 percent of their income from members' contributions.

The danger of this great reliance on members' contributions is that the flow of fund from this source could easily be influenced by the member's conception of the usefulness of union membership. It is therefore not a source on which unions should put all of their hopes. It is essential to pump out more funds from other sources.

The other sources open to unions include fines; entrance fees; levies; emblems, rules, cards, etc. sold; and interest secured or accrued on funds invested. These sources have obviously not yielded much to the unions. There are several ways of ensuring greater flow from these sources, but the one that is directly connected with financial management is flow of interest. The flow of interest depends on the uses to which the funds are put. We found that 50 percent of the unions had assets worth less than £51. This and the rather low value of benefits rendered to the members point to the financial management problems of the unions; these problems are essentially a lack of clear understanding of the objectives of the unions and the absence of planning to ensure the attainment of these objectives.

CONCLUSION

In concluding we should take a look at Professor Yesufu's diagnosis and prescription for improving the poor financial position of the unions.[1] The factors he has suggested as being the causes of the poor financial position include size of financial members, leadership and quality of administration, and poor accounting procedure. Comparing the financial position of the trade union with tribal association, he concludes that "Trade unions are financially weak, not merely because their members are too poorly paid, but primarily because the trade unions have so far failed to provide the services which are essential to sustain a loyal, regular, and militant following; and also because the rank and file owing to their ignorance as to the true functions of trade unions, do not seem to be aware of the necessity to pay regular dues."

Professor Yesufu then follows his diagnosis with this prescription: "One of the most important steps which the trade unions could take to improve their finances is to provide the friendly benefits, so much extolled by their constitutions; for experience in other countries amply demonstrates that the provision of these benefits constitutes the life-blood which sustains the unions between periodic bouts with employers for higher wages, or for improved conditions of service."

Professor Yesufu's diagnosis and prescription are certainly not wrong. But it would appear that his diagnosis merely scratches the surface of the problem, and this probably explains why his prescription is also weak. Our diagnosis and prescription are pinned on our thesis that the willingness of a member to pay his contribution depends on the benefits he thinks he could enjoy as a result of his membership in the union. We are treating friendly benefits as just one of the sets of benefits. It is doubtful if the friendly benefits represent the most important element in the benefit packet that could be made available to the members.

We are suggesting that more money be spent on capital projects and less on recurrent items. Capital expenditures however, should be in service-generating as well as income-generating programs. The effects of such programs are obvious. More funds would be generated, thereby reducing the union's exclusive reliance for income on members' contribution. This would thus ensure the satisfaction of the conditions specified above as being necessary for successful management of trade union funds—multiple sources of income and at least one source maintaining an everlasting flow of funds at least at a constant rate but preferably at an increasing rate. Also the services that would be generated by such programs would help meet some of the needs of the members and therefore help raise the benefits that union membership could provide. In turn this would not only increase the size of financial members of any given union but would also increase the willingness of members to sacrifice more money, energy, and time for the union. This would undoubtedly uplift the unions from the plane of the vicious circle of poverty to that of a continuous and reinforcing chain of success.

While accepting the above analysis, the cynic would likely ask for the source of the extra fund for the income- and service-generating programs when the unions are still very poor. We can dismiss right away the possibility of asking members to pay more money now that they do not seem to be getting much from the unions. The solution would therefore have to be in terms of making the best use of the present level of income and hoping that their use on behalf of the members would encourage more sacrifice. The real problem therefore is the management of the union funds—this diagnosis is fully supported by our thesis. Certainly the present position in which the bulk of a union's income is swallowed by administrative expenses is certainly not a healthy one.

Accepting for a start that the amount of money that would be available would be limited because of the poor financial status of the unions, the problem would be selecting the programs that would not require a lot of money, but at the same time with enough benefits thrown off to convince the workers of the advantages of being union members. For a start the unions could take over the running of cafeterias, for example, which means only operating costs where canteens are already built. Where there are no cafeterias, unions should be satisfied with modest shelters toward which management would be too happy to contribute in realization of the effects of such a program on good industrial relations.* The success of such modest programs would enable larger programs to be undertaken. This approach to solving the financial problems of the unions is very similar to the "bootstrap" approach often suggested for developing nations with low capital.

Another approach that if taken could remove the initial financial barrier to union development is a reorganization of the structure of the unions. At present we have a two-tier structure, with the individual unions at the lower level and the national unions at the upper level. A third level should be built in between the present two levels for the purpose of program development. It should be organized on a geographical basis and would therefore eliminate the disadvantages of smallness. Less than 20 percent of the Nigerian unions have more than 500 members. At present it would not be possible for all the unions in a town to come together to undertake a program, since they may belong to different national unions. Member unions of a national union in a town, however, could come together for the purpose of program development.** This approach need not be made an alternative to the bootstrap approach, but rather combined where the "town" unions can afford only modest projects.

One of the greatest advantages of this union involvement in income- and service-generating programs is that it enables the unions

----

*This really touches on management of union funds and industrial relations. It is true to say that because the union officials must justify their "existence" and because there is not much to be done between one crisis period and another, they tend to engage as the politicians of old in blindfolding the masses, propaganda campaign, corruption, thuggery, ruthless provocation, and victimization—to put it in the words of Effiong Udoh (Morning Post, September 28, 1968). The assumption here is that constructive programs would probably occupy the time of the officials and there would not be time to engage in noise-making just to justify the existence of the officials.

**The ideal structure would be one national union at the top, branches of the national unions on a geographical basis only (preferably on a town basis) in the middle, and company/house unions below.

to cutoff reliance on foreign sources. Foreign funds have brought
more troubles to the unions than the comfort such funds might have
enabled the leaders of the unions to enjoy.

In closing it should be pointed out that for the unions to be able
to takeoff from the poverty plane using the approaches suggested in
this chapter, leaders must have a good grounding in financial management. It would therefore be necessary for the government to help
by providing the necessary facilities for such courses or for the
various bodies running trade union courses to include financial
management in their programs.

NOTE

1. T. M. Yesufu, "An Introduction to Industrial Relations in
Nigeria" (London: Oxford University Press, 1962), pp. 66-74.

PART

III

**EDUCATION AND
ECONOMIC DEVELOPMENT**

9

**SOCIAL CHANGE IN
NORTHERN NIGERIA:
THE ACCEPTANCE OF
WESTERN EDUCATION**
Alan Peshkin

INTRODUCTION*

Islam predominates in Bornu emirate of Northern Nigeria,**
and historically its Muslim population has favored religious schools.
Only recently has political authority actively promoted Western-type
schooling—that is, the type of education introduced by the colonial
authorities and developed from urban models. Thus increasingly
since independence in 1960 two alternative and competing types of
school have coexisted: the primary school, which receives substantial
official support because of its hoped-for contribution to national development, and the Koranic school, which is rooted in centuries of
religious tradition. The Koranic school is a primary level religious
institution that stresses memorizing the Koran and learning proper
forms for religious observance. In Bornu such schools are mostly
single-teacher institutions operated by a <u>mallam</u>. (Not all <u>mallams</u>
teach, but the name "<u>mallam</u>," in its traditional usage, refers to one
who has acquired Islamic scholarship to some degree.)

Under the conditions described above, an investigation of adult
perceptions of Islamic and Western education may illuminate the

*This study was funded by the Northern Nigeria Teacher Edu-
cation Project. I was employed by this project at the time the data
were collected. Maryann, Nancy, and David Peshkin made a major
contribution to the organization of the data.

**Although Nigeria's political structure has been reorganized,
I will use the preorganization terminology, since it fits the circumstances under which I collected the data and does not detract from
the outcomes of the study.

process of accommodation to social change that occurs as a society passes through a transition period in which older respected forms of institutions are challenged by newer, more promising forms. In this study I analyze such perceptions as expressed by adult Muslims who have lived through the final phase of the independence movement and have experienced sovereign Nigeria's political and economic development.

We can observe the transition in education by means of enrollment statistics for Bornu and for Northern Nigeria. With an average of 11 percent of the school-aged cohort in school in all the former provinces of Northern Nigeria, and perhaps a lesser percentage in Bornu (the site of this study), the scope for growth is immense.[1] According to the Northern Nigeria Ministry of Economic Planning, the intention of the administrations governing the former region of Northern Nigeria, now decentralized into states, is to achieve universal primary education. If the present magnitude of educational growth in Bornu is viewed in terms of its population of several million, the aforementioned transition must be in its incipiency. Yet the enrollment statistics clearly indicate that a shift toward Western education, unquestionably irreversible in direction, is underway.

Limited data are available on Koranic schools. One government source estimates that there are 27,500 such schools in the north; it does not provide enrollment statistics.[2] For comparative purposes we may assume that each Koranic school has 10-15 students for an estimated range of 275,000 to 412,500 students—fewer than the primary schools and by all impressions (and government intentions) not expanding appreciably, if at all. At the time of this study, the government of Northern Nigeria, for several years, had compulsory religious instruction in all primary and secondary schools. In curricular terms this generally meant one daily period of religious teaching that included Arabic, theology, and history. Religious institutions remained viable, having received government aid for teacher training and for building advanced-level schools, although such support was substantially less than that given to primary education.

If the government assisted both types of schools, the comparatively larger investment in secular schools clearly demonstrated where the government placed its hopes for the future. Government hopes, however, are not necessarily shared by parents. For children to enter school, and barring compulsory education, parents must perceive primary schooling as conducive to attractive opportunities. In addition, if the people are Muslims, they must somehow rationalize their preference for Western over Islamic education, because Muslims throughout the world have tended to resist Western education.[3] They prefer Islamic schools; moreover they do not see other types of education as relevant to their "cultural needs," as Ammar noted in an

TABLE 9.1

Primary School Enrollment in Bornu, by Sex and Year

| Year | Sex | | Total |
	Male	Female	
1961	7,380	2,871	10,251
1962	9,754	4,127	13,881
1963	12,752	5,604	18,356
1966	18,791	8,822	27,613

Sources: Northern Nigeria Ministry of Education, School Statistics of Northern Nigeria (Kaduna: Government Printer, 1962, 1963, 1964), passim; Classes Enrollments and Teachers in the Primary Schools of Nigeria in 1966 (Kaduna: Government Printer, 1966), p. 13.

TABLE 9.2

Primary School Enrollment in Northern Nigeria,
for Selected Years

Year	Enrollment
1952	122,055
1957	205,769
1962	359,934
1966	518,846

Sources: Northern Nigeria Ministry of Education, Classes Enrollments and Teachers in the Primary Schools of Nigeria in 1966 (Kaduna: Government Printer, 1966), p. 12; Northern Nigeria Ministry of Economic Planning (1965), p. 114.

Egyptian village's rejection of Western education twenty years ago.[4] The fact is, however, that non-Islamic instruction not only can and does become acceptable but it becomes sought after. The preference of primary over Koranic school signifies a break with a time-honored tradition. Consequently, if we know how Muslim adults account for their reactions to both types of schools, we will have contributed to understanding the process whereby people come to terms with social change relating to educational institutions.

PROCEDURE

In 1966 I prepared a questionnaire to investigate reactions to primary level schooling in Bornu. This kingdom's dominant tribe, the Kanuri have been Muslims for 600 years.[5] The history of the Kanuri demonstrates that religious leaders have always played central roles in their society and that Bornu, as a center of Islamic scholarship, attracted students from beyond its boundaries. Even today Koranic education is accessible to virtually every village. Thus it is not the fact of formal education that is at issue when primary schools are introduced; the population is accustomed to formal education. What is at issue are the consequences of the two types of school as ascertained by the respondent's motives (defined below).

The questionnaire was administered to a sample of 158 adults — 116 males and 42 females, ranging in age from twenty to sixty. More than 90 percent are of the Kanuri tribe and all but one are Muslims living either in Maiduguri, Bornu's capital city of 100,000 population, or in a nearby village. One third of the respondents never attended any type of school; most of the educated two thirds had had a few years of Koranic education, while only a handful had attended primary school. In contrast, of the sample's children, 37 attended primary and 38 attended Koranic schools.

The questionnaire was administered in the vernacular by Kanuri-speaking research assistants, all of them students in a local teacher training college. Interviews were conducted in the respondent's home. Through open-ended questions, respondents were asked to describe why they did or did not send their children to the Koranic school and to the primary school; whether boys and girls ought to go to primary school and why; why people object to admitting children to the primary school; and if they had further comments to make regarding either Koranic or primary education.

The sample is not considered representative of the Kanuri since it was drawn on the basis of availability of subjects and their proximity to the homes of four children who had been studied for other purposes. Furthermore, since the respondent's are mostly urbanites, their awareness of opportunities associated with primary education most likely exceeds that of villagers. As Western education spreads, however, I should think that the villager's views of education will approximate those of the urbanite.

FINDINGS

When the item responses are sorted out, several fairly distinct positions emerge:
1. pro-primary education for girls;
2. pro-primary education for boys;
3. pro-primary education with reservations;
4. anti-primary education;
5. pro-primary and pro-Koranic education;
6. pro-Koranic education; and
7. anti-Koranic education.

Each position is presented separately below. The rationale, reasons, arguments, points, perceptions, or motives (these terms will be used interchangeably) listed under each position represent the views of 158 respondents; of this group, 130 thought that boys <u>ought</u> to attend primary school and 86 thought that girls <u>ought</u> to attend primary school. Thus the sample is biased toward the pro-primary position.

Pro-Primary Education for Girls

This position and the next one acknowledge unqualified support for enrolling children in primary school. We do not know whether the respondents oppose Koranic schooling so much as they place a higher value on primary schooling. Marital and economic motives dominate this position for girls, with educational parity and changing times receiving almost equal support.

Following are the reasons offered in support of primary schooling for girls. The quotations in this and all other sections are taken from the questionnaire responses.

Marital

Education improves a girl's chance of getting a mate. "[M]ost boys go to school. [This is not and will not be true for many years, but it may be true for those families whose sons would be considered acceptable to this respondent.] And when they get out of school they look for educated girls to marry. But in the years to come if your daughter doesn't go to school it will be difficult for her to get married."

It improves marital skills, including those relating to motherhood, health, housekeeping, and handling one's husband.

Economic

Since an educated girl is able to get a job, she can earn money to support herself, her family, and her parents. In addition, when she gets divorced, a common occurrence among the Kanuri, she will not have to become a prostitute or remain idle at home.

Educational Parity

If boys attend primary schools then so should girls, because girls require the same education to catch up and keep up with boys.

Changing Times

The terms "modern" or "Western" are often used to characterize the nature of change occurring in contemporary Bornu. Primary education allows a girl to get along in—to take advantage of—the new times.

Religious

In school, girls learn to pray and to make other religious observances that are enjoined by Islam.

Personal Behavior

Girls learn to be clean and to behave properly. "They turn out well-disciplined. For example, if a girl who attended Western school hands something to you, she does it very gracefully, even sitting on her knees before handing the thing to you."*

Family Honor

Educational achievement is a mark of distinction for the student's family. Moreover an educated girl can be addressed as "mallama," a title associated with academic success.

Pro-Primary Education for Boys

Economic arguments constitute the overwhelmingly major motive for primary education for boys. There are other explanations, and the full list is below.

---

*Kanuri female is expected to kneel, as a mark of respect, when handing an object to a male.

Economic

The following quotation from a retired, sixty year-old village man captures the several dimensions of the economic argument for schooling: "Yes, boys should go to English school. If my four children had been to English school they wouldn't have to trade in the market and farm to feed me. They'd work in an office and earn a big salary. Then they'd feed me without going in the hot sun every day."

In brief, the primary school leads to good jobs that are less physically demanding than most traditional jobs, especially farming.

Changing Times

Many respondents believe that what children learn in primary school is not only valuable for today's world but also cannot be learned elsewhere. They were far more cognizant of this fact for their boys than for their girls, acknowledging that primary education contributed to a needed accommodation with changing times.

"My children go to English school only to open their eyes, to know what is happening in the world, to learn the hardship of fending for one's self. . . ."

"[T]he children will be wise and learn many things that even their father does not know. When I am figuring the cost of something with my ready-reckoner my child shuts his eyes, looks up, and tells me the correct answer. They also learn about government, the people running the government, people's rights, and government laws and regulations."

Development

For the most part, the gains of education are couched in personal terms—for the individual, his parents, and, occasionally, his relatives. In this category we see one of the few examples of advocacy that goes beyond personal gain. Some reasoned that education was necessary to prevent the more educationally advanced southern Nigerians from getting their land and jobs. "We want progress. We can't progress without education. We want to catch up to southerners. With poor [educational] qualifications we can't catch them." And in more general terms a forty-three-year-old tailor stated, ". . . the boys learn about the wide world and they will help the older people develop the country."

The next four motives in each case were mentioned by fewer than ten respondents.

Family Tradition

Not many families in Bornu have a tradition of attending non-Islamic educational institutions. At best a very small minority have a son who went to the "white man's school," and today that son, now a father himself, wants to enroll his son.

Family Honor

Traditional occupations and honors continue to offer prestige and pecuniary gain, but since self-government and independence many new jobs have been created for which education is mandatory. The power and perquisites of these jobs makes their holders "big men" who do honor to themselves and their families.

Religious

It was noted that boys do learn about Islam in the primary school, although very few respondents made this point.

Personal Behavior

Schoolboys learn not to be idle. They are clean and their dress is attractive.

Pro-Primary Education with Reservations

At the same time that many people favor primary schooling and enroll their children, they have reservations, even fears, about its consequences. Since the motives for primary education have been presented, and those against primary education (the reservations) appear in the next position, no further discussion is presented here. Persons holding this position offered the following reservations: economic, marital, religious, and personal behavior.

Anti-Primary Education

Objections to primary education constitute a long and varied list, with marital reasons predominating for girls and the development of poor personal behavior for boys.

Marital

Most Kanuri believe that Islam requires a girl to be married at puberty. Consequently the majority of respondents, often including those who otherwise support primary education, would like their daughters to be released from school at "the right time." School authority, so it was expressed, does not agree to this release and the right time passes, thereby causing some parents to feel they have violated a religious injunction. Other parents feel that schooling may provide the occasion for premarital sex. Most teachers are male and schools are coeducational. Although secondary schools segregate the sexes, boys and girls as old as fourteen or fifteen sit side by side in the upper classes of the primary schools.

"If honest god-fearing girls stay in school, nothing bad will happen, but . . . sex matters are in the heart of youth. If they're also backward in study, that leads to complete failure—no marriage at the proper time and no good education. Or else a girl becomes pregnant and this means punishment of the parents by God for not marrying their daughter at the proper time. This brings shame to a community, especially the Kanuri. If an unmarried daughter has a child you can do nothing but leave town in shame."

Since respondents argued that their religion determines the proper time to marry and that they sin if they ignore this time, the marital argument is actually a subcase of the religious motive. Having been mentioned by the majority of respondents, it is seen as such a significant deterrent to the education of girls that it requires mention separate from both religious and personal behavior arguments.

Personal Behavior

For both girls and boys the primary school experience induces unsatisfactory behavior, including pride, disrespect, rudeness, lying, laziness, alcoholism, adultery, and sexual excess. There is abandonment of some characteristics that people feel distinguish them as Kanuris: "Once a person spends some years in English school they try to change their customs. See the clothes they wear now and their hair style. Unless they open their mouths [and hear them speak Kanuri] you wouldn't know they were Kanuris. Some girls also refuse to marry the person picked by their parents. That changes our tradition."

Schoolboys lose respect for authority and their taste in dress is expensive and troublesome:

—"One pair of trousers they wear is more costly than three pairs of their fathers."

—"A child in English school comes back to you with a nice big gown and trousers (which make it hard for him to sit comfortably), with a cap on his forehead, with high-heeled pointed shoes, and with his hair in different shapes, cut from here and there. . . . What can you do with such a child? You see him pass people sitting under a tree but he wouldn't take off his precious shoes."*

—"Some educated boys do not respect their elders. They follow the European way of living. They wear their shoes when they walk by. The Koran says that a boy who does not respect elders is one who does not believe in Allah."

Related to misbehavior, but assuming the form of a distinct evil, is the earning of a salary—a possibility open almost exclusively to the Western-educated. It is the products and the independence a salary affords that are actually objectionable: "[T]hey earn a salary which they spend in wrong ways—drinking is the worst of all."

But salary has come to be abstracted from the many concrete "evils" for which it is used and to be viewed as an evil in itself, a symbol of much that is undesirable in primary education.

Religious

In this domain the respondents find an all-embracing rationale for rejecting primary education. Its several facets are evident in the following excerpts (the "they" in each quotation refers to school-children):

—"They say incorrect things. That the sun doesn't move, but it does move. That rain is not made by God, but it is."

—"If a child goes to English school without going to Koranic school there is no doubt his father will go to hell."

—"They go to sleep so late at night they don't wake up early . . . to say their prayers."

—"Once you are educated in English school you will be dragged by angels on judgment day to join Europeans who go to hell."

Perhaps the strongest statement came from a forty-year-old village farmer who said:

—"School spoils children. . . . The Koran says 'God is one and is near everybody in the world.' One child asked me how can one thing be near everybody—it's logically impossible. Such thinking is due to too much Western education. Once a boy made me cry when he said he wouldn't believe there's a God just because the Koran says so. The boy said there is no proof, no one has seen God and talked

---

*When walking by his elders a young Kanuri shows respect by removing his shoes.

to him about his laws, so these laws may be just a belief, not proven facts. This is all due to too much Western education."

Economic

In this category, the case against primary education is straight-forward. First, children in school are unavailable to work as needed for their family: "[P]arents want their children to help them farm rather than sending them to school." Second, school-leavers often remain jobless. They cannot find "acceptable" jobs and they reject traditional jobs:

—"Children of poor people like me will hardly prosper from going to school. Because of our poor background they [the children] just study for some years and come out jobless. And with their feelings they reject our work—farming."

Family Disintegration

Parents are aware that education separates them from their children. Since as of 1967 there were about forty-five primary schools and only six post-primary schools (all located in one city), it was common for students to leave home to attend school. An extreme view is that the "schoolchild will go far away . . . and be lost in European lands." More serious than physical separation is the feeling that the educated rejects the uneducated: "So many of our boys nowadays . . . just because they are educated stay away from their parents." Finally, some parents, observing the accomplishments of the Western-educated, reject such schooling "because a father doesn't want his child to know more about people and the world than he knows himself."

General

Several of the negative reactions do not fit any but a miscellaneous category. For example one person stated that he was unaware that primary education had any value, another that he just didn't approve of the school, and a third that it "permitted too much beating."

Pro-Koranic and Pro-Primary Education

In this position the case for primary education is essentially economic, and that for Koranic education is essentially religious: "For making a living our children get a better education from English school. But this doesn't help them in the hereafter. . . . [A] Koranic education is useful right up to the hereafter."

For persons holding this position the most common pattern is to send a child first to a Koranic school for a year or two and then to a primary school. No respondent suggested the reverse pattern. Their reasons for Koranic school are religious, family honor, and personal behavior; for primary school their reasons are economic and changing times.

Pro-Koranic Education

As in the previous position, the dominant argument for Koranic education is religious; the others are almost incidental. Given the primacy of males both in Islam and in Kanuri society, these reasons apply more to boys than to girls. The particulars of the religious rationale are as broad as the role of Islam in the life of its adherents.

Religious

Koranic education satisfies religious obligations:
—"If I don't put my daughter in Koranic school, she won't learn to perform her prayers. Prayer is one of the five obligations. God would punish me if she didn't pray."
—"If my son studies Arabic he will save us from misfortune in the world hereafter by reading Koranic verses on our behalf."
—"[L]earn the Koran . . . to devote your life to God."
—"The Holy Koran says that every child must attend Koranic school to learn to read the Holy Koran; to know the history of Islam, the sayings of the Prophet, and his do's and don't's; and to become God-fearing. I want to give him a knowledge of the hereafter, not of the world of today."
Koranic education perpetuates Islam: "If we don't send our children to Koranic school, Islam will decline eventually. . . ."

Economic

Although Islam does not have a priesthood, certain occupations follow from mastery of one or another aspect of Islamic scholarship and tradition. The mallam is not supposed to charge his pupils for his services, but they do provide him with their labor. The mallam also offers many nonteaching remunerative services to his community, such as officiating at various ritual occasions and offering prayers for troubled persons:
"If you become a Koranic mallam people will come to you with their money, with their corn, or with anything they can give so that you'll ask God . . . to do something they want. If my children have education in Arabic, as I have now, they'll farm in the rainy season

and use their mallamship during the dry season, or even in both seasons."

Personal Behavior

Children in Koranic school learn to behave in proper traditional ways; they have good models for behavior in the mallams:
—"The best school is the Koranic school. You won't find a Koranic mallam doing bad things like carrying on with a prostitute or having hair on his head."
—"I do not want my children to be spoiled. Once I put them into English school they are beyond my control. They wouldn't come to see me often enough. They'd become drunkards."

Family Tradition

Some families in Bornu have a centuries-long history of attainment in Islamic scholarship. There are more families with a lesser tradition but nonetheless with a pronounced pride in their accomplishments, and a few others with an obligation to their community to maintain a certain religious posture. The following comment is made by a man from such a family:
"Learning in Koranic school is what we inherited from our fathers. All my brothers are Gonis [a person who has successfully demonstrated his memorization of the Koran] and my father too was a Goni. So is my eldest son who is now an Imam. He is married and has three children but still he is learning. Such is the custom of our house, and if we who the people imitate don't send our children as our fathers did, our followers would be led in an improper way."

Anti-Koranic Education

The case against Koranic education was not presented in direct terms. From the questionnaire responses we know why primary education is desired and therefore can infer why Koranic education is rejected. But those who indicated why their children did not receive Koranic education offered situational explanations—my children refuse to go, we live too far from a Koranic school, he will get religious training in the primary school. Of the clearly negative statements, the economic argument—that Koranic education does not lead to jobs—is the most serious one. Other arguments are that children are beaten and taught to steal.

DISCUSSION

In both locations from which the study sample was drawn, primary schools antedate 1960, and both locations offer considerable opportunities for Islamic instruction. Thus our respondents have been able to observe the consequences of children who were admitted to both types of school. Nonetheless when we consider the range of arguments for and against primary and Koranic education, and the varying emphases they receive, we are reminded of the blind men who describe an elephant in terms of the particular part of the animal they have grasped.

Since people vary in nature we should expect their perceptions of education to vary—and they do, with some focussing on the effects of schooling on males rather than on females, some on family honor rather than on the development of their country, and some on the needs of changing times rather than on requirements of the hereafter. No one appears to have examined the many possibilities of each type of school, weighing their several advantages and disadvantages, and basing a conclusion on such an evaluation. Decisions seldom are made in such a manner. Judging from their questionnaire answers, the respondents selected one or two points to justify their support of primary or Koranic education.*

For example, marital motives dominated in the pro-primary position for girls. This is not surprising given the salience of marriage in Kanuri culture. Young girls are socialized to think about marriage in general and their own marriage in particular. It is a topic of daily household conversation.[6]

There was no mention of such motives for boys, their parents overwhelmingly favoring the economic rationale. In fact the economic reasons preclude mentioning any relating to marriage: if a boy gets a salaried job he has thereby enhanced significantly his marriageability. Economic arguments occupied a strong second place in the case for girls. The Kanuri Muslim does not endorse the seclusion of women to the same degree as do Muslims in other parts of the Islamic world. Moreover their women often are small traders and farmers; as a result many women earn an income, and it is not unexpected that economic reasons rank high. Since marriage involves

---

*This impression could be no more than an artifact of poor interview techniques; if the interviewers had more successfully encouraged responses beyond the first or second one, then the interviewees' answers might have been more inclusive. In any event, from their answers, however limited, we do know what motives were most important to them.

substantial economic considerations, it is appropriate to consider the marital motives as at least partly a subset of the economic (as well as the religious) motives. Thus the economic arguments for female schooling have greater primacy than is suggested by the earlier list. In the analogy of the elephant and the blind men, most parents favoring primary education made their case in economic and/or marital terms for girls and in economic terms for boys.

In striking contrast, the religious argument prevails for the Koranic school. Economic opportunities, though available from Islamic education, have never been its basic attraction. Koranic schooling, moreover, is not noted for advancing a girl's marital prospects or happiness, even though its protagonists could claim that learning to be a good woman in accordance with Islam is to be acquiring the basis for marital success. Although this is reasonable, no respondent made the point, whereas the marital motive is the major one supporting primary education for girls.

The contribution of primary schooling to keeping up with changing times is acknowledged for both sexes, but the point is stressed somewhat more for boys. Changing times is of a different order than the marriage and economic motives. The latter clearly are drawn from traditional Kanuri values, and to posit them in relation to schooling is merely to accept new means to old and respected ends. Changing times, though, represents a break with the past in that it acknowledges new conditions in society that one may adapt to through Western-type, as opposed to Koranic, education. This motive, more than most others, signals a broad awareness of the consequences of primary schooling, of its linkage to social change—that is, to new societal requirements— rather than as a means to traditional ends. As a result it provides a very substantial basis for accepting the primary school. The majority of boys and girls get married, and all boys acquire an occupation; but given the direction of change in Nigeria, eventually no normal child will be able to "get along" without acquiring reading and number skills, anymore than his counterpart in the West.

Not surprisingly, adaptation to changing times is ignored as a motive for Koranic education. This is not a commentary on the future importance of Islam to the Muslims of Bornu—Islam certainly will remain central in their lives even as they attend government schools and depart from tradition in other ways. But Koranic education, at least as currently organized, is not perceived as germane to adapting to changes occurring in economic and political affairs.

For girls in primary school, development is not mentioned as a motive. Given the growing stress on female enrollments this is probably a temporary situation.[7] Perhaps educational parity is a forerunner of the development argument for girls, with its urging that girls should catch up with and stay equal to boys. For neither sex, however, do parents emphasize development reasons. This fact may reflect the relative lack of publicity relating education to national development. At the time of this study, the rhetoric for development was minimal. I doubt that many parents will ever see a connection between the education of their children and something as glorious and abstract as the progress of their nation. And I doubt that many of those who see a connection will give priority to development motives.

Reasons relating to religion, and family honor, though stated infrequently, should not be considered as unimportant points in the pro-primary position. Of the two the religious motive requires more attention here because, however much Koranic education surpasses primary education in providing an Islamic experience, the latter offers substantial religious instruction. While the primary school will never be valued primarily for its religious teaching, it cannot be faulted as a godless institution; it teaches girls as much or more about religion as people believe they should know, and no less to boys than is known by the average Muslim male in Bornu. Although a child is not sent to primary school for religious instruction, he receives it nonetheless, along with experiences that are valued for the many other reasons listed in the findings. Thus the parent favoring Western over religious education can, should he need to, point to this religious component to support his claim that Islam is respected, that children are not turned away from orthodoxy by the primary school.

But there can be no satisfactory answer to those who attack the school as not truly contributory to attaining the joys of the hereafter. Given the almost universal expectation for the hereafter, it requires some reconstruction of belief to accept the efficacy of primary school religious instruction as means to this end.

Concluding this comparison of the arguments in support of both types of education, we can note that both can claim to contribute to family honor and to be in accordance with family tradition. With respect to Koranic education, neither of these reasons is likely to be as significant for girls as for boys. While tradition is more important for Koranic than primary education, perhaps promoting family honor is a potentially stronger point for girls attending primary school. Female students are still relatively uncommon, and their success in primary school borders on the exotic (reading, writing, and speaking English!). And although people question how long girls should remain in school and for what jobs girls will become eligible, they do not view success in primary school as a male prerogative, nor do they define it in terms that favor males. On the contrary, opportunities associated with religious education are more circumscribed by role restrictions. In short, Koranic education is depicted as offering fewer advantages to girls than to boys (although the religionist could insist that Koranic education, despite its fewer advantages, offers more important ones).

164

By listing the full range of motives presented for sending children to either type of school, we obtain a fairly complete picture—with two exceptions—of the manifest functions of education from the individual family's point of view. The first exception is in the development argument for primary education; the second is in the concern to perpetuate Islam as found under the religious argument for Koranic education. Both cases transcend individual good. Only negligibly evident in this list of motives are consequences of schooling that relate to political socialization. For the present we may infer that the respondents tend not to associate the development of political attributes with either primary or Koranic education—a fact that reflects the lack of emphasis from controlling authorities at all levels to consciously conduct political education through schooling. In the pre-civil war period, political controversy precluded any heavy dosage of political content.

Conversely, in the respondents' list of motives for rejecting either school, we have respondent perceptions of the dysfunctions of education, again from the individual family's point of view. From available data it appears that they object to Koranic education in cautious terms that do not in sum necessarily constitute condemnation. For example there were complaints that it does not enhance economic opportunities; but then Koranic education, save for a small minority of boys, is not meant to have an economic payoff. In contrast, when a young man leaves primary school and fails either to continue to a secondary level school or to obtain employment (farming, of course, is rejected), his family is dismayed. The family's resistance to schooling based on economic failure is clearly justified. How incomprehensible it is to parents who hold essentially an instrumental view of education (and to whom non-Koranic education is still a novelty) that it should stop abruptly and eject a child who cannot find a job and has become unwilling to pursue his father's occupation! They are not placated by claims regarding the value of general education or of citizenship education. Indeed the other arguments advanced for providing boys with primary schooling become meaningless when there is no economic payoff.*

---

*This situation is unusually confusing to the many unwilling parents whose children were ordered to school as part of the government's campaign to increase enrollments. While we sympathize with the parent whose child was taken to school without his consent, this act appears no more cruel than our own compulsory education laws here in the United States. Perhaps the major difference is that our laws apply to all children, whereas compulsion in Bornu is selective,

That primary education is seen as a curse as well as a blessing is clear from the range of concerns expressed by the respondents. For girls the main objection to primary education is a justifiable fear that if they reach puberty—marriageable age—while in school the authorities will not release them for marriage. As long as it is believed that puberty is the time for marriage, primary education for females will be rejected or at best accepted with the qualification that they be released at the "right time." In addition, parents feel that girls may lose their virginity at school. This feeling, I believe, is merely their surmise based on the traditional Islamic notion of the separation of the sexes in order to prevent accidents that "must" occur should older boys and girls mix. Here is another example of a belief with religious sanction that undergoes modification when primary education for girls is accepted. This is evident from the primacy given to marital motives both in support of and in rejection of primary education for girls.

For both sexes there are several additional negative perceptions that are mentioned only for primary education. First, primary education evokes pride in girls, when they are expected to be modest and humble, and disobedience in both boys and girls, when obedience and respect for elders is the norm. The list of misbehaviors is long and constitutes the major reasons for rejecting primary education for boys, especially by the rural subjects. This is also true for the second point, that religious orthodoxy is jeopardized by schooling, and the third, that students become alienated from their parents. Rural adults were more prone to perceive the school as disruptive, whatever the category of objection. Not that urban adults are complacent or unconcerned; rather, what passes in the village as the evils of schooling may be viewed in the city as fairly common, albeit not prized, urban behavior.

Moreover the village father faces unique circumstances in that his son leaves home for the city and renounces farming, whereas the

_____

irregular, and therefore more unpredictable and difficult to comprehend. From an unwilling and often strongly negative beginning, parents do come to value primary education. One city mother said: "The first time my son was taken to school I quarreled with the ward head, his scribe, and also the teacher. I used to stop him from going. I even went to court. At last, I left the matter in the hands of God. The boy grew up and was transferred from this school to that. He attended three different schools and now is in Zaria [site of Ahmadu Bello University and the Advanced Teacher Training College]. I know that I was lucky they didn't listen to me and remove him from school."

urban father's son is already in the city and he is less likely to have an occupation that his son could, or, in his opinion, should, adopt. From the respondents' comments we judge that schooling creates a gap between village parent and child expressed in physical, psychological, and intellectual terms. Urban life better prepares a parent to adjust to the potential disruptions of primary education.

Notwithstanding the differential impact of primary education on rural and urban families, the changes associated with schooling are perceived by the anti-primary school group as a threat to traditional ways in marriage, work, religion, personal habits, and behavior with adults.[8] The parents of schoolchildren seldom are advocates of these changes, and few are participants in those aspects of society that are part of modern Nigeria. They see life as becoming more difficult to comprehend and their children in school as becoming more and more involved in what is incomprehensible in their society—and less obedient as well. We must recall, however, that the negative image of primary education comes from people who overwhelmingly favor it for boys and a majority of whom favor it for girls. Apparently they are willing to pay the potentially high price exacted for sending children to school, or perhaps they believe that the hazards of schooling will befall their neighbor's children and not their own.

Each of the major arguments against primary education requires further comment. When respondents criticize the marital prospects of schoolgirls and the behavior of schoolboys, they are not necessarily taking issue with any particular experience a child undergoes in school. They object to changes in traditional behavior (marriage, personal appearance, respect for adults) that somehow develop in schoolchildren—changes that are not taught by teachers nor learned from textbooks. It must be understood that Islam in Bornu is so entangled with Kanuri tradition that it is used invariably to sanction all behavior: whatever has been, has the endorsement of Islam. Therefore it is appropriate to join the marital and personal behavior motives to the religious, thereby making the religious motive predominant. Accordingly widespread acceptance of the primary school connotes the need for a modification of religious views—that is, a narrowing of its domain such that all of life is not explicitly and directly subject to religious dictate. Or, alternatively and perhaps more likely, given that in Islam there is no distinction between secular and sacred, a reinterpretation of Islam is required that will either sanction or ignore not primary education but those changes in behavior and institutional forms that are linked to Western-type education.

The family disintegration argument is similar to those grouped under religion in that the primary school does not intentionally encourage children to be alienated from their parents. So long as the

167

majority of Kanuri adults have not been to primary school, Western-type education will differentiate child from parents. It is to be expected, therefore, that parents will object to that which creates a gap between them and their children—a gap, moreover, that may never be bridged in the parents' lifetime. Even those who value primary schooling for its promise of financial gain realize that their children learn languages and acquire skills and knowledge that to them remain esoteric. Perhaps more important, the children acquire ambitions that can seriously attenuate parental authority. These ambitions may satisfy the economic aspiration of their parents at the same time that they support autonomy involving where to live, who to marry, and how to spend one's money.

When we juxtapose the motives for and against primary school, an interesting picture emerges. Almost every positive statement has its antithesis: girls improve their marital chances, but cannot leave school at the right time for marriage; earning power is improved, but jobless school-leavers are common; girls attain educational parity with males, but develop qualities unattractive to males; changing times are served by the more up-to-date primary school, but parents are uncomfortable with supposedly school-induced behaviors that are a response to changing times, but that, at the same time, differentiate them from their children; regular religious instruction is compulsory, but some schoolchildren come to doubt the tenets of Islam; personal behavior is improved in several respects, but students are accused of developing many highly undesirable qualities; and family honor is served by academic and occupational attainments, but, as in the previous illustration, poor personal behavior can shame the student's family.

The data do not provide such a counterpoint for the Koranic school. If there are many more objections, more forcibly stated, to primary than to Koranic education, there are conversely many more supporting arguments for primary education. In the personal calculus of any individual, the number of motives may not be as significant as the weight attached to any single one or set of them. Furthermore an abundance of motives can mean that many more chances to attract or repel an individual. If we acknowledge the compelling religious advantages of Koranic education, and add to them the negatives of primary education as plus factors of indeterminate magnitude, the result is still not especially encouraging for the perpetuation of religious schooling in its traditional form.

CONCLUSIONS

Though often contradictory, the respondents' views of primary and Koranic education square with reality either in an objective sense

(e.g., school-leavers both do and do not obtain jobs) or within a particular belief structure (e.g., attending Koranic school contributes to
attaining paradise). Which motives a parent focuses on determines
to what school, if any, his child is sent. Should he be that uncommon
person who tries to evaluate the pros and cons of both types of schools,
he could well be unable to make any decision.

Most Kanuri in Bornu are village farmers, tied to the money
economy through the products they sell and the taxes they pay, bene-
fitting from new tubewells and improved roads, but otherwise not integrally related to the evolving "modern" Bornu. Koranic education,
or no education, usually leads a child back to traditional society.
Western education, though, tends to project its students toward attractive new economic opportunities. Because Western education is
linked to a comparatively new world, acceptance of it is tantamount
to rejecting some aspects of the past. Koranic education is one aspect
of the past that is likely to be rejected. However much the primary
school appears to be a cultural intrusion (in terms of languages,
structure, and content), the respondents' answers signify that its
consequences contribute to accepted and valued goals. We conclude,
therefore, that many ordinary people in Bornu have moved from tra-
ditionalism to modernism, not so much in regard to ends as to means.
Traditional and modern people alike desire respect, status, and economic security. Can we doubt that the means to achieving these ends
have changed dramatically when the vehicle is Western education,
and all that it implies, in families where previously no child or adult
has ever experienced such education?

Williams has observed that in the early years of British occupation of Northern Nigeria, "The Emirs [the traditional rulers] were
frankly suspicious [of Western education]. They could see no necessity for the new education, which, to the old ways of life, was not only
unnecessary, but in their view dangerous."[9] The emirs were right,
but the threat that Western education poses "to the old ways of life"
must be risked if recent expectations for national development are
to be realized.[10] Given these expectations, Bornu will most likely
follow the path of other Islamic nations, such as Tunisia and Pakistan,
that wish to respect and support Islamic institutions while establishing
educational means conducive to development. After demonstrating
its affection for Islam, government in Bornu and elsewhere in Northern
Nigeria is more likely to heed the exigencies of the here-and-now
than the requirements of the hereafter. The sample's calculus of
motives for schooling already does, and increasingly will, reflect
this situation. Thus in time responses to the two types of schooling
will become polarized, with some people, the religious specialists
and the very orthodox, favoring the Koranic school, and a preponderance

favoring the primary school.* Sending a child first to Koranic school and then to primary school is not likely to continue once parents become reassured of the legitimacy of Islamic instruction in the primary school. And the alternative of not sending a child to either school will appear unwise as it penalizes the child's life-chances vis-à-vis his peers.

Meanwhile, under the transitional conditions of contemporary Nigeria, ample grounds exist for both approach to and avoidance of Western and Koranic institutions. First, each motive for primary school has its antithesis. Second, attending Koranic school to the exclusion of primary school bars a child from enjoying the potential opportunities of the latter. And, third, even success in the primary school may be marred by its lingering designation as a "godless" institution. For many families in the short run, a true dilemma exists in which they are as likely to err by admitting their child to either school or to no school at all. This we know from examining their conflicting and contradictory motives for schooling.

For the time being, Kanuri culture is ambivalent about the primary school because it is a new form of education that competes in some respects with an old form. It is still unfamiliar, and its consequences are most decidedly a mixed blessing. Although it is an alternative mode of formal education, it cannot presume to replace or compete with the unique religious and economic offerings of the Koranic school. But the Koranic school cannot begin to match the economic payoff of its competitor. In sum, although both schools offer formal education, they do not overlap in their basic raison d'étre, as far as their respective users are concerned—religious for one group and economic for the other. The economic superiority of the primary school and the transcendental superiority of the Koranic school represent indisputable facts for most Kanuri. But the system

---

*An unmentioned educational alternative is the Koranic school that introduces secular subjects. At present there are 300 such schools in Northern Nigeria. (I knew of none in Bornu.) Their religious origin and auspices may make them more palatable to some parents, although I doubt that such schools would survive unless their consequences prove to be as rewarding as those of the regular primary school. Experience with a similar type of school in the Indo-Pakistan educational past proved unrewarding in the long run. [See Abdul Haq, "Religion in Education," in Abdullah Sharafuddin, ed., Education in Progress (Dacca: The Star Press, 1969), pp. 57-58.] In the short run, though, these schools may offer a less threatening entree to modern education than does the primary school.

that offers access to both possibilities must survive the other: the primary school provides a full measure of Islamic instruction and is integrally linked to Nigeria's modern sectors. Thus in the long run the attractive opportunity structure associated with the primary school will make its arguments clearly dominant and the dilemma will be resolved.

NOTES

1. Northern Nigeria Ministry of Economic Planning, Planning for Prosperity (London: Brown, Knight and Truscott), p. 43. I would estimate the date of publication to be about 1962. The importance of the point holds up regardless of the datedness of the percentage—the overwhelming majority of school-aged children are not in school at this very moment.

2. Government of Northern Nigeria, Steps on the Path of Progress (Kaduna-Ministry of Education, 1965), p. 10.

3. Alan Peshkin, "Education, the Muslim Elite, and the Creation of Pakistan," Comparative Education Review (1962).

4. H. Ammar, Growing Up in an Egyptian Village (New York: Octagon Books, 1966), pp. 216-18.

5. See Ronald Cohen, The Kanuri of Bornu (New York: Holt, Rinehart and Winston, 1967).

6. Alan Peshkin, Kanuri Schoolchildren (New York: Holt, Rinehart and Winston, 1972).

7. New Nigerian, "Send the Girls to School," July 29, 1966, p. 6. The editorial in this issue observed that "[T]here is one aspect of education in the North which is disturbing and which must be overcome if all our children are to share in the benefits of education. This is the reluctance of a great many parents to send their daughters to school."

8. The great importance of this last point is underscored in Cohen's The Kanuri of Bornu. See, for example, pages 46-48, in which Cohen describes the discipline-respect relationship.

9. D. H. Williams, A Short Survey of Education in Northern Nigeria (Kaduna-Ministry of Education, 1959), p. 7.

10. See Government of Northern Nigeria, op. cit., which details the Northern Region's six-year development plan (1962-68) objectives.

BIBLIOGRAPHY

Ammar, H. Growing Up in an Egyptian Village. New York: Octagon Books, 1966.

Cohen, Ronald. The Kanuri of Bornu. New York: Holt, Rinehart and Winston, 1967.

Government of Northern Nigeria, Steps on the Path of Progress. Kaduna: Ministry of Education, 1965.

Haq, Abdul. "Religion in Education," in Abdullah Sharafuddin, ed. Education in Progress (pp. 51-64). Dacca: The Star Press, 1969.

Northern Nigeria Ministry of Economic Planning, Planning for Prosperity. London: Brown, Knight and Truscott, n.d.

_____. Statistical Yearbook 1964. Kaduna: Baraka Press, 1964.

Nothern Nigeria Ministry of Education, Classes Enrollments and Teachers in the Primary Schools of Nigeria in 1966. Kaduna: Government Printer, 1966.

_____. School Statistics of Northern Nigeria. Kaduna: Government Printer, 1962.

_____. School Statistics of Northern Nigeria. Kaduna: Government Printer, 1963.

_____. School Statistics of Northern Nigeria. Kaduna: Government Printer, 1964.

Peshkin, Alan. "Education, the Muslim Elite, and the Creation of Pakistan," Comparative Education Review, 1962.

_____. Kanuri Schoolchildren. New York: Holt, Rinehart and Winston, 1972.

_____. "Send the Girls to School," New Nigerian, July 29, 1966.

Williams, D. H. A Short Survey of Education in Northern Nigeria. Kaduna: Ministry of Education, 1959.

CHAPTER

10

**THE NIGERIAN
UNIVERSITY:
TOWARD MORE
RELEVANCE**
Akpan Esen

Nigeria's first university was opened in 1948 at Ibadan. At that
time Nigeria was still a colony of Britain. For twelve years Ibadan
remained the only institution of that status in the country. In 1960
Nigeria became an independent nation, and within two years four other
universities had been opened—at Nsukka, Lagos, Ife, and Zaria; in
addition Ibadan itself had shaken off its colonial ties with the University
of London. At the end of the civil war, when reconstruction enjoyed
a priority position in government policy, a sixth university was
opened, at Benin in 1971. No one sees this as by any means the end
of the chain.

With six universities serving an estimated population of 65-
million people, Nigeria's ratio of one university for every 11 million
inhabitants seems rather low on the face of it, even by African
standards. It is pointless comparing these figures with those of more
advanced countries, such as Britain or the United States (the ratio in
Britain is approximately one university for every million inhabitants;
in the United States it is even lower—about one per 200,000 people).
But confining the comparisons to Africa, one finds several cases of
apparently more attractive ratios. Ghana, for instance, has one
university for every three million inhabitants; Zaire, one per 5.3
million; and Egypt, one per 8 million. It does not improve Nigeria's
case to point to lower ratios elsewhere—for instance, Tanzania with
a 1: 12.5 ratio, or Sudan with a 1: 15 ration. Nigeria, however,
need not be apologetic nor plead its great size and greater complexity.
The fact is that it is in Nigeria that one finds the largest number of
university institutions of all countries in Black Africa, and Nigeria's
lead in this area is expected to increase in the future. Knowledgeable
people think that Nigeria will need several more universities in the
future to cope with the increasing pace of development.

In the face of the likelihood of further expansion, it seems in order to take a fresh look at the broad purposes of the university in the specific context of its Nigerian ecology. It is easy to lose sight of its basic purposes in the welter of activities incidental to such rapid development, especially in an environment of continuous change. With the goals clearly defined, the question of the university's faithfulness to them, and the larger issue of its relevance to the ever-changing social situation surrounding it, become a matter of practical concern rather than of merely academic interest.

THE HISTORICAL BACKGROUND

The decision to establish an institution of university status in Nigeria was taken by the British government following that government's acceptance of the recommendations of the Eliott and Asquith commissions of 1945. Before then, Nigeria's only post-secondary institution was Yaba Higher College at Lagos. To enter Yaba, students had to satisfy the same requirements as those entering the University of London and other British universities. After five years' study at Yaba, though, the students were not awarded degrees. The general dissatisfaction with Yaba, and the new awakening brought about by World War II, combined to start a trend that was to have a very profound effect on Nigerian higher education—a trend that culminated in the establishment of Ibadan University College in 1948.

Neither Cyril Asquith, nor Walter Eliott, nor their colleagues in the two commissions can be regarded as the foremost or earliest thinkers in terms of a university for West Africa. As early as 1868 a Nigerian resident in Sierra Leone named Dr. James Horton had called for the establishment of a university in that part of Africa. In time other strong African voices raised this same plea. These included Dr. Edward Blyden in about 1881, Casely Hayford in 1911, and the well-known Nigerian nationalist Herbert Macaulay in the 1920s. But it was Dr. Nnamdi Azikiwe who followed up the matter from the stage of advocacy and rhetoric to that of concrete plans and action. In 1937 Dr. Azikiwe's fiery words in Renascent Africa awoke the masses of the people to the need for universities in Africa. About two decades later, in 1960, he spoke again, but this time as the Chancellor of the then newly established University of Nigeria at Nsukka. Between 1937 and 1960 he had worked steadily to set up the political machinery and kindle the degree of public awareness necessary for transforming these old dreams into the type of tangible realities that, in his thinking, even Ibadan did not represent. The University of Nigeria at Nsukka is a worthy tribute to that effort.

174

The independence movement, too, was a great factor in the establishment of universities in Nigeria. As independence approached, the people became increasingly conscious of the need for the kind of manpower that would be required to cope with the obligations of self-government at all levels. The new commitments in international relations, economic and industrial development, education, and public health and other social services needed people with the specialized training that only universities can give, and it would have been impossible to train students abroad in sufficient numbers. The Ashby Commission was set up to examine Nigeria's needs in the area of post-secondary education and make recommendations. That commission recommended (1960) the establishment of more universities as a way out. Lagos and Ahmadu Bello universities were the direct result of those recommendations. The commission's report also endorsed the establishment of the University of Nigeria at Nsukka (but after the fact). The University of Ife, although not recommended by Ashby, was founded more or less in the spirit of that report.

Another factor that played a part in determining the pattern followed in the siting of universities was the political structure of the Nigerian federation. The Nigeria that became independent in 1960 was a group of three autonomous states, or regions—the Northern, Eastern, and Western regions—plus the Federal Territory of Lagos. Constitutionally any of the states could establish universities if they so desired. For its own part the federal government took responsibility only for the two federal universities of Ibadan and Lagos. As it turned out the states decided to exercise their option under the Constitution, and they established universities within their boundaries either to cater to local needs, interests, and sensibilities, as in the case of Ife, or to give expression to long-cherished ambitions or ideals, as in the case of Nsukka. Thus state universities emerged side by side with federal universities.

The Nigeria that surfaced in 1970, after the civil war, is a federation of twelve states. In spite of a much stronger federal image than ever before, each state shows signs of understandably sharp sensibility where local needs are concerned. And it is becoming increasingly clear that unless ways are found to make the existing universities serve not just the needs of the state in which they happen to be situated but also cater equitably to the interests of all the other states as well as those of the federation as a whole, each state will seek to establish its own university—and the prophecy about more universities may come true sooner than may be expected. The establishment of the Midwestern Institute of Technology at Benin in 1971 is an indication that this is not out of the question. To say the least such a proliferation would be at best a mixed blessing. The federal government seems to have a clear duty here to use its undisputed leverage with the

175

states to put curbs on this potentially undesirable situation before it gets out of hand, and at the same time to satisfy the legitimate desires of the nonuniversity states. The best such curb seems to be to bring the admission and other policies of the existing universities in line with federal policy in this regard, bearing in mind the feelings of the states adversely affected by the present arrangement. Other alternative measures are discussed below.

THE PURPOSES OF THE NIGERIAN UNIVERSITY

It is necessary at this point to make a distinction between a university situated in Nigeria and a Nigerian university. No one doubts that Oxford University is an English university. Its classical structure and curriculum designed to prepare a small gentleman-elite for leadership make it unmistakably so. Also the land-grant institution, with its wide range of unconventional offerings, is quite distinctively American. But the American University of Beirut, its location on the soil of Lebanon notwithstanding, can hardly be said to be a Lebanese university, any more than the old French University of Dakar could be said to be Senegalese.

Pre-independence Ibadan was the brainchild of the Asquith Commission, and in almost every conceivable way un-Nigerian. It was, properly speaking, the English University of Ibadan.

Cyril Asquith was uncommonly single-minded about his task on that commission, and clear about the purposes he wanted to see accomplished. He produced what Eric Ashby later (1964) called "Britain's blue-print for exporting universities to her people overseas." If Britain's influence was not to diminish (in spite of the sun setting on its empire), what could ensure its continuity better than British education? And if so, what better policy could there be than the exportation of "mini-Oxfords" and "immitation Cambridges," with strong practical and emotional ties to the mother country? On the side, these overseas institutions might, like the real Oxford, produce an elite capable of leadership and the preservation of "democracy" as defined by the metropolitan power.

From the beginning, therefore, Ibadan was an English university planted on the soil of Nigeria to serve the cause of an unequal partnership between Britain and Nigeria. True to colonial principles it was to undergo a long period of tutelage under the University of London. Its classical curriculum reflected no sensitivity to Nigeria's problems. Its highly selective and elitist residential setup was in direct contrast to the social practices of any Nigerian community. Its academic and administrative staff were mainly British. And its declared purpose of creating an elite received such overemphasis ("You are the leaders of tomorrow") that in the end it helped to distort the expectations of the earlier graduates—which did neither them nor the country any good.

A Nigerian university is conceived differently. It must of course be established on the soil of Nigeria. It should be run in the main by demonstrably capable Nigerians. Its curriculum and emphases must reflect the realities of the Nigerian cultural milieu. And its guiding philosophy, in the words of Dr. Azikiwe (1963) should be "based on the satisfying of the needs of Nigeria in the present stage of its development, with an objective of planning for a fuller and more abundant life for the many, instead of the few." In other words, a Nigerian university is a university dedicated to grappling with Nigeria's problems with a view to raising living standards for all Nigerians.

This definition rejects the concept of elitism. A Nigerian university has to be a people's university. It repudiates the goal of training leaders exclusively. It will of course educate the few who will turn out to be leaders in the various phases of national endeavor, but it will not be ashamed of educating the majority who will of necessity be followers. Above all this definition assumes a clear delineation and understanding of Nigeria's needs, and the readiness and ability of the institution to come to grips with them.

This shift in the stated purposes of higher education in Nigeria is an important matter. It is in line with the developing self-concept of the Nigerian people. Whether Ibadan, Nsukka, Lagos, Ife, Ahmadu Bello, and the Midwestern Institute of Technology at Benin are truly Nigerian Universities, or are still by and large universities built in Nigeria, is a moot issue. Most observers would be willing to concede some significant movement in the direction of Nigerian-ness since independence, but it is the view here that this has been sporadic and not geared to practical goals. New approaches to this problem are suggested below.

The Concept of Liberal Education

One factor that put the stamp of un-Nigerian-ness on Ibadan during the pre-independence years was the emphasis on "liberal education." Even since independence there seems to have been no hurry to reexamine the merits or other aspects of the liberal orientation. The act establishing the University of Ibadan as a successor to the University College of Ibadan in 1962 states as the main function of the new institution, "to hold out to all persons, without distinction of race, creed or sex, the opportunity for acquiring a liberal education." Surprisingly the University of Nigeria Law (1955) echoes the Ibadan aims almost verbatim. It says in part that the university shall

177

"hold forth to all classes and communities without any distinction whatever an encouragement for pursuing a regular and liberal course of education." It could be said for Nsukka that the intent of this clause may have been largely neutralized and negated by the more weighty pronouncements to the contrary of its founder, Dr. Azikiwe. No university in Nigeria that is committed to providing a liberal education can be a Nigerian university as defined here; the simple reason for this is that such an institution can never address itself to the needs of Nigeria.

The concept of liberal education is bound up with the broader controversies that have bedeviled the philosophy of education for as long as man can remember. Liberal education may be defined simply as education for culture and not as a preparation for a vocation, and the controversy is between the rationalist and the realist schools of educational thought.

The rationalists hold the view that what typifies man is his rationality, and the cultivation of reason is therefore the main aim of education—and indeed of life itself. Ideally, therefore, education should not concern itself with the physical or social (including the vocational) side of life, but with values and truths that are universal and timeless. Consequently, in the view of the rationalists, the university is a fixed and static institution concerned with eternal truths that cut across race, creed, or national boundaries. Mathematics, logic, the classics, literature, and philosophy are seen as basic to this type of education. Some of the best-known rationalists of this century include Robert Hutchins and Mark van Doren. It must of course be remembered that this was the philosophical position taken by Cardinal Henry Newman in the nineteenth century. To Newman, knowledge was indivisible; liberal education was the only real education. Whereas vocationalism was limiting, liberal education set a man free so that he could turn his hand to anything, and could communicate with other educated men in the true language of learning.

Opposing this view are the realists. They reject the concept of the static nature of knowledge. They see human beings as similar, but they see beyond the similarities to their differences in a variety of respects, including their needs. The content of education, according to the realists, should be inclusive of elements that reflect those differences, and that can be combined in various ways to satisfy the needs of the endless variety of human beings. James Bryant Conant and Sidney Hook may be regarded as the leading representative thinkers of this school.

As with individuals, so with nations. Education should not be static if it hopes to solve the problems of nations. In this sense, the realist philosophy of education is sympathetic to vocationalism, because the theory of vocations is based on a recognition of the differences between people.

In the pre-independence years, the leading departments at Ibadan reflected the institution's deep commitment to the cause of liberal education. Except in the faculty of medicine, professional or vocational educational was unknown and unwelcome. Latin and Greek flourished, and English language, literature, and philosophy commanded prestige. Even the motto, and other signs on which the image of the university depended, were couched in Latin. This kind of curriculum, however, reckoned without the powerful economic realities of the Nigerian situation. The graduate in classics was soon to realize that the ability to read Euripides and Horace in the original, so much respected within the walls of the university, counted for nothing in the real world of jobs and bread-winning. Rather it was the engineer, the accountant, teacher, pharmacist, doctor, nurse, librarian, architect, and business manager that seemed to have a real place in that world.

If the Nigerian university were to become the battleground where rationalism opposes realism, there would be virtually no contest. This is the issue of relevance, and no developing nation can afford exclusively liberal arts institutions. The virtual demise of the department of classics at Ibadan, and the fact that no other Nigerian university has found it worthwhile establishing a department of classics, illustrate the extent of the movement from pure rationalism toward practical realism in Nigerian higher education in the last few years. More of this is likely in the future.

Some of the other liberal arts departments could consider a phased deemphasis of the older and obviously arid aspects of their curriculum. Language and linguistics departments, for instance, could begin to wonder whether the age-old concern about the forms of primitive Germanic and the syntactics of Old and Middle English, both so close to the heart of dear old Professor Brosnahan in the 1950s, are quite as relevant to the Nigeria of the 1970s as the structure and use of Hausa or Efik. There is so much to do that to continue to dabble in the relative frivolities of Xenophon and Chaucer amounts to almost an act of sabotage against Nigeria's national aspirations. After all, probably the best Hausa dictionary in use today was compiled by a Russian.

Goals of the University Revisited

It is no longer original to define the purposes of higher education in Nigeria, or any other developing nation, in terms of its close relevance to the needs of the society concerned. The Ashby Report

(1960), countless leaders of thought including Dr. Azikiwe, and leading Nigerian educationists such as Professor Fafunwa, have done this very clearly. Several international conferences, such as the one sponsored by UNESCO and held at Tananarive in 1962, have spent a lot of time on this important problem. The Nigerian people themselves have always demanded this sort of identification with their goals and problems from their universities. This was the basis of much of the criticism against Ibadan in its early days. More recently, in 1969, the conference on curriculum held in Lagos put the national stamp on this perennial concern.

The aim here, therefore, is not to go over this ground so well covered by such able individuals and groups. It is rather to attempt to provide newer insights into the implications of the central issue of relevance, and to suggest a few practical steps that can be taken to achieve these purposes.

The main purposes of the Nigerian university may be classified as follows:

1. teaching and research;
2. public service;
3. meeting the nation's psychological needs.

The question here is: What things should the Nigerian university do, within the scope of these purposes, or what should it avoid doing, in order to remain visibly relevant to the Nigerian situation?

Teaching and Research

Teaching and research are the core tasks of all universities throughout the world. Some do more of one than the other. The great multiversities of the United States lean more toward research than teaching, while the latter is done more in the state colleges. This has its own problems. Student unrest is very often linked to the feeling among students that professors bury themselves in their research and neglect their academic needs. Besides, the subject of research has often raised philosophical issues connected with academic freedom. There is a very real doubt as to whether a responsible scientist has the moral right to do research in more powerful mass-destruction weapon systems and lay his findings at the disposal of the national war-machine. The answers are not easy. Perhaps Hiroshima and Nagasagi will always hang like twin albatrosses around the neck of M.I.T.

In Nigerian universities, teaching and research must go together. At its best, university teaching has to be invigorated by constantly updated research. These are commonplaces. The big question here concerns the type of research that will meet the criteria of relevance. If Dr. Azikiwe's enunciation of better living standards for all Nigerians is accepted as a worthwhile goal of the university, the matter boils down to the types of research that will directly contribute to better living standards throughout Nigeria. We will call those that do "Research Type A," and those that don't "Research Type Z." This classification allows for subtypes and overlappings in between.

Let us illustrate the point. A researcher is digging into the earth, examining rock layers, and testing samples of soil in some area of southeastern Nigeria. If he is trying to test for the possible ocurrence of uranium, that is Research Type A. If he is looking for remains of some ancient Ibibio empire that someone thinks probably existed there around the fifth century B.C., that is Research Type Z. The former, if proved, could lead directly to new industries, jobs, better income, and higher living standards for thousands of people. The latter, if proved, will change nothing materially for any Nigerian in the here and now.

The usual excuse for undertaking research activities of Type Z is that it contributes something to the total pool of world knowledge. It undoubtedly extends the boundaries of knowledge to discover, after years of research, that there are maybe five or six varieties of combustible gases floating about on Saturn, or, to borrow Fafunwa's contemptuous example, that Shakespeare was Shakespeare. But how this can even remotely improve the lives of Nigerians would still remain a question; and that is the criterion of relevance. What Nigeria needs at this stage is practical answers to problems related to the people's food, health, safety, sources of wealth, manpower, and so on, in order to raise the living standards of the people. Type-Z research will not provide this.

The Public Service Function

A lot of the public service functions of the university are usually taken for granted. They are expected to train manpower for the various levels of national activity, to promote extension programs in education and agriculture among the masses, to criticize fearlessly and constructively any public policies as they see fit, to provide ideas and leadership for national guidance, to engage in Type-A research, and so on. There is one item in this group that deserves closer attention. This is the function of preserving the culture, and transmitting it enriched to the new generation. Some Nigerian universities seem to see culture in terms of what is produced, and seek to perform their function by merely adding drama or fine arts to their curriculum. This is a halfway measure.

What is culture? And how does the university help to preserve and transmit it? Simply, culture is the sum total of a people's way of life. Culture, it has been said, is as people do, and the people's art, language, music, poetry, religion, food, and occupations are aspects or manifestations of it; also included are their ways of thinking, their perceptions, and their attitudes. Some of these the university can, and does, teach in the traditional ways. Nigerian languages, for example, are now receiving some attention in the universities. Colonialism had devalued the indigenous languages and made literacy and facility in English the hallmark of education. The universities must reverse this. Unfortunately not enough is being done. Nigerian universities generally set up departments of modern languages, where French, German, Spanish, Russian, and other European languages are taught. Nigerian languages are usually not considered "modern." They are treated, rather apologetically, under a sort of global African studies arrangement. If these languages are worth preserving, they are worth the prestige of use, analytical study, and research. Full departments and chairs of Nigerian languages seem long overdue.

It is perhaps in the areas of attitudes, values, and perceptions that the universities have failed most to preserve, not to mention transmit, true Nigerian culture. In fact, by some of the policies they adhere to, and by neglecting to try out others that could be temporarily unpopular, the universities inculcate in the students values and attitudes that run counter to the culture of the Nigerian peoples.

One obvious example is the attitude to work. Most Nigerians are very hard workers, spending most of the daylight hours on their farms every day during the farming season, or sitting in their market stalls selling from dawn to dusk, or peddling their wares almost round the clock on the city streets. One often hears that educated Nigerians, especially the students, have been educated out of their cultural context and despise manual work, preferring white-collar jobs. The way the universities are carrying on, this could prove to be so in the future, but there may be hope that in the future some of the young people who come to the universities bring with them the characteristic values of the Nigerian peasant with respect to productive manual work. Ashby (1964) reports that at Nsukka, which happens to be the only Nigerian university where work-study programs have been made available, students jump at the opportunity to engage in all sorts of manual work, even for as little as three shillings a day to help pay for their education. In 1963 alone as much as £5,000 was earned in this way.

Unfortunately no other Nigerian university has thought it necessary to set up similar programs to create opportunities for some students to learn, and others to reinforce, those attitudes to work that are consistent with Nigerian culture. On all campuses, especially the newer ones, a lot of construction work goes on much of the time. Yet neither during term nor during vacation are students employed there. They could work at clearing new sites, carrying sand or cement, mixing concrete, digging trenches, or building roads, and so earn a little money. The earnings would be useful, but the practical lesson that university education does not raise anyone above manual work would be an invaluable contribution. Our university students are not employed part-time as cleaners, library assistants, lawn mowers, or anything. They do not even wash dishes after their meals. During vacation, students either find jobs in government offices and schools or do nothing. With the scarcity of such jobs on the increase, the numbers of able-bodied young people who spend three months every year contributing nothing to the economy that supports them increase correspondingly. If the Nsukka example is anything to go by, thousands of these idle young people would be glad to do anything for minimal wages. If the universities are prepared to take their moral and cultural responsibilities more seriously, they will consider work-study programs as an important part of their educational commitment. It cannot be urged too strongly that Nsukka's modest example be copied and expanded upon by all the universities. In a country where hard work is the basis of culture, and of survival, to do otherwise would be a great disservice to the nation.

Other attitudes the university can help students absorb include tolerance of the other person or point of view that happens to be different; respect for merit in the making of choices and decisions; justice; fair play; and the national spirit. One does not have to "teach" these things at lectures and seminars. Creating the opportunities for students to absorb these values unconsciously, and making these values evident in the policies of the universities themselves, may be all that is necessary. Often this is lacking, and students draw value conclusions that corrupt the culture.

Meeting the People's Psychological Needs

The hunger of the Nigerian people for education at all levels is attested to by the ever-increasing number of primary, secondary, and university institutions in the country. The development of university education, as has been seen, has been phenomenal within the first decade of independence. But to the Nigerian people as a whole, the university is something more than an educational institution; it is a symbol of the new growth and prestige. There can be no doubt that the university feeds this new sense of national pride and sustains the growing self-confidence of the Nigerian nation.

Its high-rising buildings and modern architecture represent progress and high national goals. The growing participation of indigenous intellectuals in its halls of knowledge is a source of pride. Its robed ceremonies in which Nigerian men and women march together symbolize a new reaching out together of the sexes. Its libraries and archives are perceived as storehouses of time-tested wisdom and knowledge, available to whoever wants them. That the new knowledge gained within its walls will help obliterate the many unflattering stereotypes about the black man that have been created by the white man for his own selfish ends is cause for hope. In short, the university is an embodiment of a new-found pride, hope, and changing self-image. This is a vital psychological function, and the university will do well to remain constantly aware of its role in this area. If the university were to fail, or if the people were to become doubtful about its real value, the nation could see its heavy emotional investment in the institution as misplaced, and there is no knowing what harm this would inflict on the national psyche. This is where the Oxford and Harvard models break down. The expectations and perceptions of the Nigerian peoples, however, are different.

BIBLIOGRAPHY

Ashby, Eric. African Universities and Western Tradition. Cambridge, Mass.: Harvard University Press, 1960.

_____. Investment in Education. The Report of the Commission on Post-School Certificate and Higher Education in Nigeria. Lagos: Federal Ministry of Education, 1960.

_____. "The functions of West African Universities," in The West African Intellectual Communities. Ibadan: Ibadan University Press, 1962.

Azikiwe, Nnamdi. Footprints on the Sands of Time. Apapa: Nigerian National Press, 1963.

Fafunwa, A. Babs. A History Of Nigerian Higher Education. Lagos: Macmillan and Company, 1971.

_____. New Perspectives in African Education. Lagos: Macmillan and Company, 1967.

Ibadan University Calendar, 1970-71. Ibadan University Press.

11

Toward the end of the 1970-71 academic year, President
Joseph Mobutu of the Zaire Republic (formerly Congo, Kinshasha)
applied one of the most extreme measures ever taken by a government
to deal with the problem of student unrest. In response to a demonstration marking an earlier protest in which several students had been
killed, Mobutu drafted into the army for several months the entire
3,000-member student body of the then Luvanium University. Subsequently the leaders of the campus disorder were sentenced to life
imprisonment. Shortly after the Luvanium disturbance, President
Kenneth Kaunda closed Zambia University in a crackdown provoked
by a letter sent to the head of state by ten students critical of national
policies, using troops and police to roust 1,500 students out of bed in
a 4:00 a.m. raid. These moves are indicative of the punitive reaction
of many governments in tropical Africa to the growing incidence of
student unrest. Kenya, Ethiopia, Senegal, Tanzania, Ivory Coast, and
Nigeria have likewise met student ferment with swift government
sanctions.

It is extraordinary that in a continent marked by diversity and
division on a number of other timely issues, public authorities share
virtually the same outlook on the subject of student dissent. Despite
ideological differences, contrasting colonial backgrounds, and dis-
similar educational systems, African leaders generally take the position that student dissent is an intolerable luxury that new nations
cannot afford, a sign of the deteriorating values and lack of national
committment of the younger generation.

Condemnation of student unrest by public leaders is, however,
a relatively recent development in Africa. Prior to independence,
many of these same leaders had welcomed youthful protest as part
of the nationalist resistance to colonial rule. Since then the role of
African students has become more complicated. As part of a privileged

class generally representing far less than 1 percent of their societies, university students continue to be "uncritically regarded as pre-ordained members of the second- or third-generation successor elite."[1] At the same time, in their present circumstances as an aspirant elite unabsorbed by the establishment, they function as a highly visible interest group, a potential counterelite whose remonstrations are seen to be at variance with the interests of public order. University students have therefore inherited a dual and contradictory status in post-colonial Africa, as both probable successors to and possible subverters of existing political regimes.

This chapter presents the findings of research undertaken in Nigeria to probe the political attitudes, values, and opinions of university students in order to (1) compare the continuities and changes in the attitudes of students before and after the Nigerian civil war, and (2) assess the actual propensity for radicalism that exists among a politically significant section of the country's student population.

METHODOLOGY

The research approach adopted for this study was a replicated social survey of first-year students in the school of social Studies at the University of Lagos. Nearly all of the students who participated in the survey were from the six southern states. Two samples were drawn, in December 1966 and May 1971, from introductory political science classes. The 1966 sample consisted of 98 students; the 1971 sample consisted of 113.

These samples focused on a limited section of the Nigerian student population, but a section considered to be politically significant for three reasons. First, the majority of university students in the country come from the southern states. In 1966, for example, all but 369 out of 4,532 Nigerian university graduates originated in the south.[2] Second, by field of study, social science majors represent one of the largest proportions of students, claiming 25 percent of the total Nigerian university population in 1966.[3] Third, social science students tend to have a relatively high degree of political interest and awareness, and they are among the most occupationally insecure students, conscious of the growing frustrations that await them after graduation when they must compete for jobs against graduates in technical fields and those returning from universities abroad. Thus they are not only aware of the socioeconomic forces at work in their society but they are increasingly concerned about the direct impact of these forces upon their personal lives.

In view of the fact that stratified samples were used in this study, however, it should be stressed that the findings presented are not representative of Nigerian student opinion generally. Rather the major value of this research lies in suggesting attitudinal tendencies of a defined segment of the student community and in offering explanatory hypotheses about their possible behavioral consequences.

Data were gathered through questionnaires administered during class hours. Respondents were informed that the purpose of the survey was "to obtain a statistical evaluation of student opinion for academic research purposes." Since the questionnaires were unsigned, individual identities remain unknown.

The political atmosphere in the country differed considerably at the times the two surveys were conducted. In December 1966 Nigeria was on the verge of political collapse; within the preceding twelve months the country had experienced two military coups d'état, widespread communal rioting, and a mass migration of Ibos from urban areas back to the then Eastern Region, which was rapidly moving toward secession. An ad hoc constitutional conference had failed one month earlier and preparations were underway for an eleventh-hour summit meeting of military leaders in Aburi, Ghana—the only hope left after a chain of disappointing attempts to avert an outbreak of hostilities. Nigeria was only five months away from the Biafran declaration of independence and only seven months away from civil war.

At the time of the second survey, in May 1971, the Nigerian civil war had been over for fourteen months. Since then, substantial progress had been made toward reconciliation, the 12-state structure created in 1967 had began to function throughout the country, an ambitious four-year development plan had been launched, and large oil revenues were resuscitating economic life. However the country was facing mounting social and economic problems, including runaway inflation, labor unrest, rising unemployment, high military expenditures, an increase in violent crimes, and widespread corruption in private and official circles. In addition political dissatisfaction was emerging out of specific postwar problems, such as unresolved claims for abandoned property in the war-affected areas, boundary disputes, agitation for more states, labor immobility, and a delay in the return to civilian rule. Thus, whereas the first survey was conducted against a background of prewar hostility, violence, and insecurity, the second was conducted during the era of postwar reconstruction, against a background of smoldering social discontent.

CHARACTERISTICS OF THE SAMPLES

The first sample included students from the faculty of business administration and social studies who were specializing in five major fields—economics, political science, sociology, business administration, and accounting. All were then required to take the introductory political science course, a subject also offered as an option for mass communications students. By 1971 the faculty was split into two separate schools, of business administration and social studies. As a result the second sample included fewer business and accounting students, for whom political science was made an elective subject.

These changes naturally affected the composition of the samples and the stated career objectives of the respondents. The occupational goals of students in the 1966 sample were, in order of preference, business (43 percent), accounting (24 percent), teaching (9 percent), the civil service (7 percent), politics (1 percent), and other (16 percent, primarily journalism or broadcasting,-7 percent). Occupational preferences were more evenly distributed in the 1971 sample, with the civil service (27 percent) taking precedence, followed by accounting (22 percent) and teaching (22 percent), business (21 percent), and other (8 percent). Due to administrative and curriculum revisions, these responses obviously cannot be regarded as valid measures of shifting occupational aspirations. However it is significant that out of 211 students surveyed among the five fields at two different periods, only one expressed an interest in choosing politics as a profession!

Another difference in the characteristics of the two samples was also a product of external influences. Owing to the disturbances in the country that uprooted many residents in Lagos, the samples differed in regional and ethnic composition. The 1966 sample was almost evenly divided between students of the then Western Region (45 percent) and Mid-Western Region (41 percent), the remaining students coming from the Eastern Region (12 percent) and Lagos (2 percent). After the civil war, the second sample revealed a much heavier Western Region dominance (65 percent), followed by the Mid-Western Region (19 percent), Lagos (6 percent), the Eastern Region (6 percent), and the Northern Region and students from outside Nigeria (3 percent). The Yoruba proportion rose from 47 percent in 1966 to 71 percent in 1971. Surprisingly the proportion of Ibos did not decline dramatically (from 11 percent in 1966 to 9 percent in 1971), as compared to the decline in southern Nigerian minority groups from the Mid-West, Rivers, and South-Eastern states (from 41 percent in 1966 to 19 percent in 1971). The data seem to suggest that the civil war hit the minority groups in the university harder than the Ibos, who returned with greater speed after the end of hostilities. The data also indicate clearly the paucity of northern representation in the university. The three northern students in the 1971 sample originated from the Yoruba-inhabited Kwara State; there were no Hausa-Fulani, Kanuri, or other far northern ethnic groups in either sample.

All other socioeconomic indicators of the two samples were strikingly similar, showing strong consistencies in the patterns of student recruitment. Taking both samples together, the median age group was 24 to 26, though one third of the students were between 21 and 23 years of age. Males vastly outnumbered females, accounting for approximately 90 percent of both groups. More than 65 percent of the students were single, and 20-30 percent were married with children. Some 80 percent were Christain, less than 8 percent Muslim, and under 10 percent indicated that they either followed a "traditional religion" or were nondenominational, agnostic, or atheist.

Information on family backgrounds indicates that a larger proportion of students than expected had modest social origins and were not children of the Nigerian elite. Some 71 percent of the first sample and 65 percent of the second sample reported that the total household income of their families was under £500 ($1,400), and several students penciled in an annual income as low as £50 or £60 per annum. Roughly 25 percent reported a total household income of £500-2,000 ($1,400-5,600), and approximately 5 percent reported incomes of £2,000 ($5,600) or more. Over half of the students' fathers were farmers or fishermen, having no formal education. About 25 percent of the students' fathers had acquired some primary education and were self-employed traders, merchants, contractors, or artisans; 10 percent had attended or completed secondary school and held salaried jobs as teachers, government employees, or office workers. Approximately 6 percent of both samples consisted of students with indisputable upper-class origins; that is, whose family incomes exceeded £2,000 per annum, and whose fathers were professionals, businessmen, or civil servants with post-secondary technical or university education. About 60 percent of the students' mothers worked, mainly in farming or trading; no more than 5 percent of the mothers were salaried wage-earners and over 65 percent had no formal education whatsoever.

Over 40 percent of the respondents in each sample stated that they depended upon their families or parents as their main source of financial support. This dependency constitutes a heavy burden on the poor, since fees for resident students amount to £171 10s. 6d., or approximately $475 per year. More than one-third stated that they lived off personal savings or earnings from present employment, some with their spouse's assistance. Less than 20 percent depended on scholarships or loans as their major source of support.

Students were asked to place their families in one of five social groups, ranging from lower class to upper class. About 6 percent of both samples described their families as belonging to the upper- and upper-middle-class categories, an evaluation that was consistent with the objective indexes of social class. Similarly about 20 percent of the respondents described their families as middle class, a designation that varied only slightly with figures on income, occupation, and educational backgrounds. At the bottom of the social scale, however, wider disparities were discernible between perceived self-images and objective classifications. According to the students' own reporting on their family backgrounds, at least 50 percent had peasant origins; yet no more than 38 percent of each sample described their families as belonging to the lower class. Instead many students assessed their families as lower-middle class—30 percent in 1966 and 36 percent in 1971.

Two possible explanations may account for the discrepancy between perceived and objective class evaluations at the lower levels. First, despite the fact they were told that this study was for academic research, some students might have felt that it was actually being conducted on behalf of the government or university administration to determine the need for awards and scholarships for indigent students. On this premise some may have deliberately slanted the socioeconomic data downward in order to indicate that they were deserving of financial assistance. However, because of the consistency of the data, there would have to have been a remarkably high degree of similar reactions of this kind among the respondents on several questions to support this explanation. The second and more likely explanation is that many students, reflecting on their position in society and hopes for the future, found it difficult to admit that they had lower-class origins when confronted with the question directly—an indication of how high status and achievement motivations may influence student perceptions.

This explanation gains further credence from the responses to questions concerning mobility aspirations. Students were asked: "Generally speaking, with respect to your father's level of achievement, how would you compare your own ambitions?" Some 85 percent of the first sample and 65 percent of the second replied: "I want to do better than my father and raise myself above his standing." And 13 percent of the first sample and 21 percent of the second replied: "I want to be independent of any type of comparison." Less than 10 percent indicated that they would "like to follow in their father's footsteps." Only one or two individuals in each case replied that they did not feel they could match their fathers, would be happy to do just as well as their fathers, or did not care whether or not they did better. Students were also asked what range of income they expected to earn and how soon after graduation they expected to achieve this income level. The results again indicate high mobility aspirations: about 75 percent of the students expected to be making up to £2,000 per annum within one to five years after graduation, while approximately 25 percent expected to be making £2,000-5,000 within six to ten years. The ambitions of students may be better appreciated by contrasting these expectations against the £720 ($2,000) standard starting salary for a federal civil servant with a university education, and the £3,000 ($8,400) superscale income for a federal permanent secretary (the highest career classification in the public service that experienced officers regard as the peak of their career). Many students added further comments, such as there was "no limit" or "the sky is the limit for a businessman." Some described their career ambitions "to become a business tycoon" or "to pass my accounting exam and later become chief accountant of a big organization or a university lecturer."

VALUE ORIENTATIONS

To probe students' social and personal values, respondents were asked to rate different occupations on the basis of respect or prestige, and to rate different personality traits on the basis of importance or desirability. The technique used to measure these ratings was based on a common grading scheme used in several previous studies.[4] Items in a given list are evaluated against a five-point scale ranging from "very high" to "very low." Each of the five categories in the scale is given a numerical value, permitting a computation of a weighted average or mean rating for each item. From this score a single hierarchy can then be established, showing comparative ratings of the listed items relative to each other. In this study the numerical values range from 5.0 for "very high" to 1.0 for "very low," and mean ratings were computed on the basis of the sample number in each survey. The results are presented in tables 11.1 and 11.2.

The hierarchy of occupational prestige was fairly constant over time, indicating an established pattern similar to Western values. Doctors were accorded by far the greatest prestige, followed by university lecturers and government ministers. Surprisingly, in both the first and second surveys, building contractors were ranked fourth and fifth, respectively, probably because they are regarded as examples of business or entrepreneurial success. Civil servants and lawyers completed the top grouping of highly respected professional or white-collar occupations. It is interesting to note that on the basis of these ratings the prestige of government ministers and civil servants was not reduced by the turbulent events in the country over the past several years. In fact they even rose in esteem in contrast to university lecturers who appear to have lost a measure of respect in the eyes of their students over this period.

Regarding middle-income occupations, teachers and store managers declined in relative prestige, while traders, nurses, artists, and social workers increased. Traders were rated unusually high, probably because—like building contractors—they are seen as having a high degree of economic opportunity. Among the low-income workers, farmers were—curiously—ranked higher than office clerks, factory

191

TABLE 11.1

Prestige Ratings of Occupations
Mean Rating

Occupation	1966a	1971b	Occupation	1966a	1971b
Factory			Artist	3.13	3.23
worker	2.68	2.51	Teacher	3.48	3.06
Clerk	2.70	2.74	Social		
Doctor	4.93	4.51	worker	2.93	3.23
Trader	3.15	3.43	University		
Civil			lecturer	4.45	4.25
servant	3.52	4.05	Farmer	2.85	2.77
Carpenter	2.10	2.26	Store		
Herbalist	1.79	1.86	manager	3.26	3.07
Laborer	1.50	1.71	Messenger	1.47	1.64
Lawyer	3.49	3.53	Plumber	2.23	2.56
Nurse	3.18	3.43	Building		
Government			contractor	3.83	3.68
minister	3.84	4.16			

Note: Items listed here and in subsequent tables are presented as they appeared on the questionnaire, not as they were ranked on the prestige hierarchy computed from the mean ratings.

[a]98 students.
[b]113 students.

workers, plumbers, and carpenters. Predictably at the very bottom of the prestige scale were herbalists, laborers, and messengers.

More inconsistencies were evident in the personality ratings than in the ratings of occupational prestige. Out of a list of 20 items, hard work, honesty, intelligence, and courage were selected in that order by both sets of respondents as the four most desirable characteristics for a person to exhibit. These were followed, in varied sequence, by success, respect for authority, higher education, and integrity. On the basis of these preferred qualities alone, students might be said to display a high degree of personal ethics and a fairly strong sense of individualism. Indeed the only value linked with social obligation or awareness that they stressed is respect for authority, and they showed declining admiration for patriotism, generosity, and sociability, while good looks and sensitivity became more important,

TABLE 11.2

Desirability Ratings of Personality Characteristics
Mean Rating

	1966a	1971b		1966a	1971b
Good looks	3.74	3.89	Honesty	4.69	4.61
Physical			Sociability	3.53	3.32
strength	3.95	3.85	Thrift	3.18	3.30
Generosity	3.80	3.73	Intelligence	4.57	4.53
Higher			Wealth	3.12	3.21
education	4.46	4.44	Sensitivity	3.03	3.53
Respect for			Integrity	4.31	4.35
authority	4.36	4.45	Patriotism	4.21	4.19
Shrewdness	3.21	3.48	Family		
Courage	4.47	4.46	attachment	3.53	3.74
Hard work	4.81	4.62	Success	4.47	4.39
Independence	3.88	4.25	Fame	3.35	3.47

a98 students.
b113 students.

the latter substantially. Some interesting ambivalences could be
identified as well. For example, although students said that they
valued independence over family attachment, both attributes increased
in importance over time, suggesting continuing conflict between modern
and traditional values. Similarly they rated fame, shrewdness, thrift,
and wealth uncommonly low—evaluations that in themselves could lead
one to conclude that there was little concern among the students for
the pursuit of material rewards or public acclaim. Yet these evaluations stand in direct contradiction to the high rating given to success
and, more importantly, to the high income and career aspirations
expressed in previous questions.

These inconsistencies provide some insight into the complexities
of the status of this aspirant elite and the tensions that arise from the
imcompatible values they hold. While students may express a youthful
idealism and intellectually endorse the virtues of modesty and morality,
they are at the same time driven by a strong sense of success and
represent an upwardly mobile class emotionally committed to the
pursuit of personal privilege and material security. This latter
aspect of the students' personalities was also displayed through their
responses to questions about Lagos, the nation's bustling capital, to

which about 40 percent of the students had come for the first time
when they entered university. About 65 percent of both samples were
struck favorably by the big city, describing it as "an exciting and
sophisticated place to live," a city that "generally offers opportunities
to get ahead in life" and a "place to further economic advancement
and career." However 13 percent of the first sample and as many as
25 percent of the second sample did feel that Lagos was "crowded,
dirty and corrupt." A young Yoruba student aptly expressed the sense
of priorities that enables the young to resolve such contradictions:
"It is obvious that Lagos is crowded and dirty," he wrote. "All the
same, the city is exciting and as the Yorubas say, 'If you live in Lagos
and you are not wise then you will be a fool forever.' You have to
know and have experience to live in Lagos."

POLITICAL ATTITUDES

Three major political orientations were tested in this study:
(1) political alienation, (2) political liberalism, and (3) attachment to
democratic principles. Each was measured through responses to
statements scored on a five-point scale similar to that used in the
occupational prestige and personality ratings. Tables 11.3, 11.4, and
11.5 present the results, including breakdowns of responses for each
statement as well as the average of the aggregate responses from
which conclusions on overall attitudinal trends are based. To amplify
the data, students were also asked specifically about (4) their criteria
for leadership selection, and (5) their perceptions of the causes of
Nigeria's political problems. The results of these queries are presented in Tables 11.6 and Table 11.7.

Political Alienation

Political Alienation was examined through four questions probing
students' feelings about citizen impotence, disillusionment with the
party system, the role of personalities in politics, and political corruption.

As Table 11.3 indicates, the majority of students in both samples
were highly alienated, more so in 1971 than in 1966. Greatest dissatisfaction appeared on the question of citizen impotence; nearly 50 percent
of both samples indicated they agree strongly that citizens rarely
influence policy. Disillusionment with the party system was much
stronger in 1971 than in 1966, in spite of the fact that the earlier
group of students was much closer to the events that exposed the
weaknesses of the party system under the civilian regime. In view

194

TABLE 11.3

Political Alienation

	Mean Score*	
Question	1966	1971
1. "Most decisions in government are made by a small group of people and the average citizen rarely gets any opportunity to influence policy."	3.85	3.94
2. "It doesn't really matter what political party gets elected in most cases. They never follow their manifestos once they get in power anyway."	3.41	3.84
3. "Political success depends mainly upon personality."	3.56	3.94
4. "Politics is a dirty game and no politician who wants to succeed can really avoid getting involved in corrupt practices."	2.90	3.34
Average aggregate	3.55	3.76

*Alienation score: maximum alienation = 5.0; minimum alienation = 1.0.

of the nation's experience over the past few years, where the assassination of top politicians revolutionized the political system, it is not surprising that students also believed that political success depended mainly upon personality as opposed to, say, political skills, ideology, resources, etc. In sum, students indicated that they feel that their government is run, without public participation, by a small group of notables who owe their positions of influence to personal political connections. This image seems to have grown stronger over time, so that by 1971, 68 percent of the students held negative attitudes about political processes generally.

Curiously, on the fourth item regarding political corruption, students departed somewhat from this trend and displayed rather remarkable attitudinal patterns. In 1966 they were nearly evenly divided over the statement that argued that politicians had to be corrupt to succeed; 41 percent agreed and 42 percent disagreed, with the majority of the latter evidencing unusually strong opposition in this regard. Viewed in the context of the time this is an astonishing response, since political corruption was one of the major public grievances that brought down the old political regime. By 1971 the tenor of opinion had shifted, with 51 percent of the students now agreeing with the proposition against only 29 percent in disagreement. However, compared with the strong alienation expressed on other issues, even this may be seen as a relatively mild response, again somewhat puzzling in view of the extensive public criticism of corruption that was widespread at the time.[5]

This ambivalence about political corruption may possibly be explained by the students' faith in the future. While they were clearly disenchanted with the former political leadership, they may nevertheless have felt that the next generation—perhaps their own generation—could avoid the mistakes of the past and succeed in politics without necessarily getting involved in corrupt practices. This would account for the reservations they expressed about endorsing the proposition fully, though agreeing with it as a description of existing conditions.

Political Liberalism

Political liberalism of students was examined through seven questions, the responses to which were measured on a continuum ranging from high ("perfect liberalism") at one end to low (illiberalism or "perfect conservatism") at the other. Liberal political values are indicated here by a high regard for individual rights, political freedoms, and political equality; conservative or illiberal political values are thus indicated by a low regard for individual rights, political freedoms, and political equality.

As can be seen from the aggregate data in Table 11.4, 50 percent of the students in the first sample and 48 percent in the second sample had conservative responses, while only 39 percent of the first and 43 percent of the second had liberal responses, the remainder being uncommitted or not sure. The strongest conservatism was manifested on questions regarding electoral freedoms ("In a city referendum, only people who are well informed about the issue being voted on should be allowed to vote." "Voting is an individual matter, and organizations or groups should not be allowed to attempt to get members to vote as a block." "In a city referendum on tax matters, only taxpayers should be allowed to vote."). A substantial proportion of the students in both samples agreed strongly that voting privileges should be reserved for the informed, taxpaying members of society; that is, for the educated, politically articulate, law-abiding, or relatively wealthier citizens. Electoral activities of voluntary associations, they felt, should be curbed, probably because of a deep-seated suspicion that organizational leaders tend to mislead the uninformed masses. Liberal responses, however, were registered in questions regarding individual liberties

TABLE 11.4

Liberalism and Conservatism

Question	Mean Score* 1966	1971
1. "In a city referendum, only people who are well informed about the issue being voted on should be allowed to vote."	4.21	4.15
2. "If a person wanted to make a public speech against church and religion, he should not be allowed to do so."	2.46	2.66
3. "Voting is an individual matter, and organizations or groups should not be allowed to attempt to get members to vote as a block."	4.26	3.84
4. "An atheist should not be allowed to run for public office."	2.82	2.51
5. "In a city referendum on tax matters, only tax-payers should be allowed to vote."	3.59	3.61
6. "In any election, only people who are literate should be allowed to vote."	2.33	2.04
7. "The more educated a man is, the more ethical or moral he is likely to be."	2.78	2.90
Average aggregate	3.0	3.10

*Liberalism score: perfect liberalism = 1.0; perfect conservatism = 5.0.

("If a person wanted to make a public speech against church and religion, he should not be allowed to do so." "An atheist should not be allowed to run for public office."). Thus, while students would restrict public participation by less privileged elements of society and limit the activities of pressure groups, they reacted strongly against impingements upon individual freedoms—particularly freedom of speech and freedom of religion, rights that directly affect their own political liberties.

On the question of voting rights for nonliterates ("In any election, only people who are literate should be allowed to vote."), students opposed disenfranchisement, seemingly contradicting earlier prejudices against the "ill-informed" or nontaxpaying population. Apparently they felt that the masses should be guided or restricted, but not excluded entirely, from political participation, an attitude that could be described as a kind of political noblesse oblige, allowing an educated elite to concede certain democratic privileges to the masses.

As before, when required to make self-evaluations, students expressed ambivalence. Asked about the moral impact of education ("The more educated a man is, the more ethical or moral he is likely to be."), the largest proportion of students in both samples said they were not sure about the statement, but slightly more disputed than agreed with it.

Attachment to Democratic Principles

Students' attachment to democratic principles was examined through three questions focusing on leadership, party politics, and the role of an opposition. As Table 11.5 suggests, students in both samples strongly condemned authoritarian leadership ("Countries which do not have a long experience with democracy must have authoritarian leaders

TABLE 11.5

Attachment to Democratic Principles

	Mean Score*	
	1966	1971
1. "Countries which do not have a long experience with democracy must have authoritarian leaders to force the people to obey the law."	2.43	2.78
2. "Once elected, a party's main objective should be to remain in power at all costs."	1.46	1.81
3. "Though the existence of an opposition provides for an alternative government in a democracy, it should not be tolerated if all it does is criticize the party in power."	2.78	2.81
Average aggregate	2.22	2.47

*Democratic Score: maximum attachment to democratic principles = 1.0; minimum attachment to democratic principles = 5.0.

who force the people to obey the law.") and party domination ("Once elected, a party's main objective should be to remain in power at all costs."). But they were less convinced of the necessity to tolerate a political opposition ("Though the existence of an opposition provides for an alternative government in a democracy, it should not be tolerated if all it does is criticize the party in power."). Overall indications thus point toward a relatively strong commitment to democracy on two out of the three items tested. Regarding the third—the role of an opposition—38 percent of the students in 1966 felt that it would be justifiable to suppress an opposition that was critical of government, against 48 percent who felt such action would be wrong; but by 1971 the distribution of democratic and undemocratic responses on this issue were nearly equal, with the greatest increase occurring in the undemocratic responses. This is possibly due to longer experience with military rule, or possibly to growing disillusionment with the party system.

Perhaps the most important trend revealed by this data is the students' diminishing attachment to democratic values. The proportion of students opposed to authoritarian leaders dropped 10 percent within the five-year period, so that by 1971 students were more closely divided on this question—41 percent agreeing that authoritarianism was justified in new states (as opposed to 33 percent in 1966) and 11 percent being not sure. Reactions against a party attempting to stay in power at all costs were still strong in 1971, but the minority that supported party domination nearly doubled in strength over the five years, from 10 percent to 19 percent. Similarly the percentage of students who agreed that a critical opposition should be suppressed rose from 38 percent to 48 percent. Collectively, therefore, the proportion of students expressing an undemocratic response increased from 27 percent in 1966 to 36 percent in 1971, while the proportion of those expressing a democratic response fell from 64 percent in 1966 to 58 percent in 1971—a disquieting and perhaps unavoidable trend linked to the high incidence of political alienation.

Criteria for Leadership

Turning to more specific political perceptions, students were asked to select from a given list the most important criteria that would determine their votes in a national election. As Table 11.6 indicates, on the question of leadership criteria, students stated that a candidate's sympathy for the common people and his leadership capabilities were the two most important factors. Party affiliation was their third electoral consideration, despite the cynicism expressed earlier about party politics. Although tribal and regional origins have

TABLE 11.6

Criteria for Leadership

Answers to Question*	Most Important Factor, 1966		Second Most Important Factor, 1966		Most Important Factor, 1971		Second Most Important Factor, 1971	
	Number	Percent	Number	Percent	Number	Percent	Number	Percent
1. Candidate's party	13	13.2	14	14.2	24	21.2	16	14.1
2. Candidate's ethnic group	0	0	1	1.0	1	0.8	1	0.8
3. Candidate's educational qualifications	4	4.0	11	11.2	7	6.1	3	2.6
4. Candidate's shrewdness	4	4.0	2	2.0	7	6.1	2.	1.7
5. Candidate's prestige or social position	3	3.0	2	2.0	0	0	6	5.3
6. Candidate's hometown or province	0	0	1	1.0	1	0.8	1	0.8
7. Candidate's record as a liberal or conservative	2	2.0	1	1.0	2	1.7	5	4.4
8. Candidate's sympathy for the common people	39	39.7	28	28.5	33	29.2	36	31.8
9. Candidate's personality	1	1.0	4	4.0	3	2.6	8	7.0
10. Candidate's leadership capabilities	32	32.6	34	34.6	35	30.9	35	30.9

*Question: "Generally speaking, in a national election what two factors would be most important in determining your vote?"

influenced both student and national politics, they roundly rejected
these criteria. They also thought that a candidate's political record
as a liberal or conservative, as well as his personality, educational
qualifications, prestige, and shrewdness, were relatively unimportant
considerations.

Causes of Political Difficulties

In naming the factors most responsible for the country's political
difficulties, students felt that the "irresponsibility and corruption of
politicians" was far and above the most important. As Table 11.7
shows, over 50 percent of the second sample condemned the old political class. Among other common explanations offered, students felt
that the "illiteracy and ignorance of the masses," and "irreconcilable
cultural conflict" ranked second and third.

The selection of these three factors reveals a great deal about
student political attitudes and opinions. First, it is evident that students
share the popular viewpoint in Nigeria that responsibility for the country's turmoil can be laid squarely at the doorstep of a corrupt civilian
leadership, which misled the unknowing public by appealing to its basic
primordial instincts and loyalties. Second, the political importance
attached by students to the nonliteracy and ignorance of the masses
betrays again their paternalistic sense of noblesse oblige toward the
ordinary public, which was expressed earlier. This also partially
explains their choice of leadership criteria. Because they felt that
the ignorance of the masses was in large part responsible for Nigeria's
upheavals, students stressed that future leaders had to have sympathy
for the common people, not necessarily for ideological reasons, but
more fundamentally as a safeguard against continued political exploitation. Third, students did not feel that constitutional or historical
factors were important; few attributed the country's problems to the
nature of the federal system or to policies of the former colonial
rulers. Tribal domination, held to be relatively significant in 1966,
was considered far less important in 1971. Fourth, while students
seemed to appreciate some of the immediate causes of political unrest,
they downplayed remote factors that were at the root of the nation's
problems. They rightly dismissed conspiratorial theories of foreign
subversion or minority tribes striving for power as significant. But
they almost totally dismissed factors pointing to inequities and injus-
tices arising out of rapid social change and modernization. In 1966
not a single student conceived that class conflict was important and
only one identified exaggerated aspirations for development as of
secondary importance; in 1971 only eight students singled out either
of these two factors.

201

TABLE 11.7

Responsibility for National Political Problems

Answers to Question*	Most Important Factor, 1966		Second Most Important Factor, 1966		Most Important Factor, 1971		Second Most Important Factor, 1971	
	Number	Percent	Number	Percent	Number	Percent	Number	Percent
1. High rate of illiteracy and ignorance of the masses	19	19.3	16	16.3	18	15.9	20	17.9
2. Irresponsibility and corruption of the politicians	37	37.6	18	18.3	59	52.2	26	23.0
3. Irreconcilable conflict between widely different cultural groups	14	14.2	15	15.3	6	5.3	29	25.6
4. Exaggerated aspirations for economic development and modernization	0	0	1	1.0	1	0.8	1	0.8
5. The nature of the federal system which existed during the First Republic	9	9.1	15	15.3	5	4.4	7	6.1
6. The colonial power which never properly prepared Nigeria for independence	4	4.0	8	8.1	8	7.0	8	7.0
7. Domination of the country by one tribal group	13	13.2	19	19.3	6	5.3	11	9.7
8. Class conflict between the elite and masses	0	0	0	0	4	3.5	2	1.7
9. Conspiracy and subversion by foreign interests	0	0	5	5.1	1	0.8	5	4.4
10. Minority tribes striving for power	0	0	0	0	5	4.4	1	0.8
11. Other	2	2.0	1	1.0	0	0	3	2.6

*Question: "In explaining or attempting to understand the political problems in Nigeria today, what two factors would you say are most responsible or important?"

It is worthy of note that, with one exception, breakdowns by sex, region of origin, ethnic affiliation, religion, career objectives, mobility of residence, and father's education showed no significant correlations between these socioeconomic variables and particular political attitudes. The only meaningful deviation from the normal distribution of responses appeared among easterners of the Catholic faith who, unsurprisingly, expressed strong conservative views on the two questions dealing with religion; they largely felt that an atheist should not be allowed to run for public office and that a person who wanted to make a public speech against church and religion should likewise not be allowed to do so.

CONCLUSION

Although, as indicated at the outset, the findings of this study are not conclusive, they do suggest several interesting and in some respects disturbing attitudinal and behavioral patterns. First, the Nigerian civil war does not appear to have fundamentally transformed the political orientations of university students. The students have more or less regarded the war as part of a protracted crisis that began during the civilian regime when their basic attitudes toward modern politics were shaped. The civil war intensified these existing orientations, in particular by increasing their sense of political alienation and weakening their commitment to democratic principles.

Second, it is clear from the data that the primary factor underlying student reactions is their class position as an emerging or aspirant elite. It is on this basis that their political attitudes and political action may be best understood. In the past, students have demonstrated most frequently and most violently on private issues, such as campus living conditions, university appointments, and administrative sanctions against campus protests. Only rarely, and generally with less intensity, have they demonstrated over wider social or political issues unrelated to their specific interests. The basically conservative political attitudes that condition student behavior were evident in this study, which showed, for example, that students would restrict public participation by the masses but would defend their own political rights. In view of this, the presumed propensity for student radicalism and the severity of response by the authorities are based on misconceptions about the sources of student disorders. Students may be expected to be "radical" not so much because of ideological opposition to a particular regime or administration but because their class or group interests are threatened. As has proven to be the case in many countries, repressive sanctions against student demonstrations (even those arising out of elitist motivations) often radicalize conservative or moderate students, unduly escalating a private matter into a political one and drawing unnecessary public attention and publicity to what originated as a limited issue.

Third, given the dominance of class or status considerations among students and the high political alienation they expressed in this study, student nationalism in Nigeria may be expected to grow, especially as university expansion progresses at its currently rapid rate. The intake of social science students at the University of Lagos alone nearly doubled from 1970/71 to 1971/72. Within the eight-year period extending from 1962 to 1970, the total student population of Nigeria's universities soared from 3,600 to 14,518, and would have probably reached about 17,000 if the University of Nigeria campus at Nsukka had not been closed during the civil war.[6] Yet Harbison noted in 1966 that "over half of the students in Nigerian universities . . . were studying subjects for which effective demand, in the south, at salary levels hitherto considered to be ensured for degree-holders, is becoming satiated. The resulting situation of graduates employed at levels and salaries below their expectations may have serious political and social consequences."[7] Aware of these conditions, students may be expected to form a more solidly cohesive group whose anxieties and frustrations are bound to lead to dissent unless their lofty expectations are brought closer into line with reality, and university and curriculum development are planned more rationally in relation to societal needs.

Finally it is important to stress the political uncertainties and contradictions surrounding the students' position. While they are highly conscious of their elite status and expect their education to catapult them from poverty to prosperity and from impotence to influence, they are at the same time evidencing less attachment to the "system" they expect to inherit and are therefore capable of being turned against it. Whether their energies and talents will ultimately be channeled into system opposition or system support will depend upon the rate of production and qualifications of future university graduates, the ability of the society to absorb them, and perhaps most importantly the foresight of government authorities who, as indicated earlier, generally oversimply the problem. For them to continue to conceive of student unrest as a luxury is to be blind to the inevitable social forces in the society fostered in large part by government educational policies; and for them to continue to feel that student dissent is a sign of deteriorating values of the young is to be ignorant of the emerging class interests of an impatient generation eager to share, as fully as their predecessors did, in the fruits of national development.

NOTES

1. James S. Coleman, ed., Education and Political Development (Princeton: Princeton University Press, 1965), p. 4. In Nigeria, university graduates represented a mere 0.4 percent of the total labor force in 1965. See Nigerian Human Resource Development and Utilization, Education and World Affairs Committee on Education and Human Resource Development, Nigeria Project Task Force Report prepared for USAID, December, 1967, Frederick H. Harbison, Chairman, p. 45.

2. Ibid., p. 161.

3. Annual Abstract of Statistics (Lagos: Federal Office of Statistics, 1967), p. 153.

4. See J. C. Mitchell, "Aspects of Occupational Prestige in a Plural Society," in P. C. Lloyd, ed., The New Elites of Tropical Africa (London: Oxford University Press, 1966), pp. 256-71.

5. See Labanji Bolaji, Anatomy of Corruption in Nigeria (Ibadan: Daystar Press, 1970); "A Sick Nation?" Daily Sketch, June 7, 1971, p. 1; and Ola Balogun, "Money Business is the Best Business," New Nigerian (July 3, 1971), p. 5.

6. Chief Obafemi Awolowo, Nigerian Tribune, July 5, 1971, p. 12.

7. Nigerian Human Resource Development and Utilization, p. 129.

12

**NIGERIAN POLITICS:
CLASS ALLIANCES AND
FOREIGN ALIGNMENT**
Philip V. White

PREWAR FOREIGN POLICY

Nigerian nonalignment was the professed cornerstone of foreign policy in the years immediately preceding and following independence. Initially the National Council of Nigeria and the Cameroon (NCNC) alone among the three major political parties came out for a truly nonaligned foreign policy. The Northern Peoples' Congress (NPC) and the Action Group (AG) were pro-West. But as federal elections approached, the NCNC modified its foreign policy position and brought it into line with that of the other two parties. In August 1959 Azikiwe gave assurances that foreign investment would be encouraged in Nigeria and that no business in existence before October 1, 1960 (Independence Day) would be nationalized. In October, two months before the election that would put Nigeria's first independence government into office, the NCNC promulgated a policy statement aligning Nigeria squarely with the West, and, also in accordance with the other two parties, rejecting Pan Africanism as an immediately attainable goal while endorsing membership in the United Nations and the British Commonwealth.[1]

After the 1959 elections the AG, now the opposition to a coalition government of the NPC and NCNC, drastically reversed its position on many issues. It insisted that the government support Lumumba, undertake efforts in behalf of Pan Africanism, and more forcefully oppose the South African regime. One of the most controversial reversals, however, came in regard to the defense pact with Britain.

In April 1960 Chief Obafemi Awolowo, federal president of the Action Group and leader of the opposition in the House of Representatives, shocked the house when he declared that the initialling of the draft agreement of the Anglo-Nigerian Defence Pact by himself, the other two party leaders (Azikiwe and Sir Ahmadu Bello, Sardauna of Sokoto), and Prime Minister Abubaka Tafawa Balewa in 1958 had been a pre-condition for Nigerian independence.

A few days after Awolowo's disclosure, the prime minister stated that he would not commit the country to any treaty obligations without the prior approval of the house, and in November 1960, the pact came up for debate. At the urging of NPC Minister of Defense Alhaji Ribadu, the pact was passed by a vote of 166 to 38.

Nigeria followed equally conservative economic policies during this period. By early 1960 the mercurial Awolowo indicated that he was now in favor of nationalization of foreign-owned firms, and the government agreed to debate the issue of nationalization. Awolowo spoke essentially for the radical elements that were vocal at the All-Nigeria Peoples' Conference. Chief Festus Okotie-Eboh, the NCNC federal minister of finance, defended the government's position.

What is significant about the debate is that the government felt under enough pressure to discuss the nationalization issue in the house, and that it chose to answer its critics in purely economic terms without raising directly the ideological implications of the argument.[2]

Nigeria's economic relations with the Soviet Union and Communist-bloc nations were minimal. Exports to the Soviet Union increased from less than $55,500 (50,000 new rubles) in 1955 to $7.3 million in 1959 (a fraction of 1 percent of Nigeria's total trade); two-way trade commenced in 1960 when the federal government imported less than $55,500 worth of Soviet goods and exported about $7 million worth of goods to the Soviet Union.[3] In March 1963 the Soviet Union and Nigeria signed a bilateral trade agreement providing for most-favored-nation treatment regarding trade and navigation.[4] Throughout 1964 several unofficial invitations were extended to the Soviet Union to offer Nigeria economic aid. In fact the problem was not one of the Soviet Union refusing aid to Nigeria, but of the Nigerian government refusing to accept such aid. Nigeria had already been offered $14 million in credits by Czechoslovakia, $9.1 by Yugoslavia, and $32 million by Poland.

Essentially, then, prewar policy was characterized by two strains. The conservative strain of the NPC-dominated government was avowedly nonaligned but in fact pro-West. It was typified by membership in the Commonwealth and the United Nations, and encouragement of foreign investment. It was undergirded by the desire to make as few foreign commitments as possible. The more radical strain developed among those on the periphery of political power—the students, trade union leaders, some members of the opposition, and radicals within the NCNC and minor parties such as the United Middle Belt Congress (UMBC) and the Northern Elements Progressive

Union (NEPU). This strain was more consciously ideologically informed, had roots in the experience of Nigeria under colonial rule, and was more Pan Africanist, being particularly concerned with Nigeria's image among other African nations.[5]

FACTORS CONTRIBUTING TO MILITARY INTERVENTION

Vulnerability of the Political Economy

An important factor in the coups d'état and the subsequent civil war that convulsed Nigeria was the vulnerability to instability of the federal structure with its relatively impotent central administration in Lagos and strong regional governments. This instability had two dimensions—the political and economic imbalance of a federal structure in which one component had more potential power than the combination of the others, and intra- and inter-class conflict compounded by ethnic antagonisms.

The potential for political instability because of the predominance of the Northern Region has been widely noted. The Northern Region was represented with 92 seats in the house, while the east and west had 42 each; of the remaining eight seats, six went to the Southern Cameroons and two to Lagos. Under the statutes of the independence constitution, which became effective in 1959, single-member constituencies were limited to one representative per 100,000 people, and the Northern Region was allocated 174 of the 312 seats.[6]

Attempts to change boundaries or create additional states during the series of constitutional conferences during the 1950s were futile. Northern leaders demanded and got this political leverage in return for remaining within the federation. In other words the first threats of secession were made by the Northern Region, even before Nigeria secured its independence. Because of northern hegemony, a purely technical matter such as the taking of the census could become the basis of a serious constitutional crisis, as it did from 1962 until 1964.

Economic and educational imbalance have accompanied the political and demographic imbalances. While the Northern Region accounted for about half of the gross domestic product before the discovery of oil in the east, it was the Western Region that had the highest per capita income—almost twice that of the Eastern Region—and that introduced universal free primary education in 1955.[7] The two southern regions have far outpaced the north in terms of education, which has led to the northern fear of southern domination. These factors have not operated in a vacuum, however; what made them so

potentially volatile was their interaction in complex ways with the
realities of ethnicity and class.

Ethnic and Class Conflict

While much has been made of the primacy of "tribalism" in
understanding Nigerian politics, it is my belief that confining an
analysis of Nigerian politics solely to ethnic conflict yields a distorted comprehension.* It must be emphasized that ethnic conflict
did not always play a part in Nigerian politics. Ethnic conflict became
politically salient only in the late 1940s, when it emerged as tribal
nationalism. Indeed the NCNC's president was a Yoruba, Herbert
Macaulay, and its general secretary was an Ibo, Nnamdi Azikiwe.
Moreover Macaulay brought his overwhelmingly Yoruba constituency
with him from the Nigerian National Democratic Party into the NCNC.[8]
What Aristide Zolberg calls the "politicization of primordial cleavages"
did not occur until Yoruba elites decided that the best way to advance
their own particular interests was by building a political party based
on a common cultural heritage.[9]

One of the reasons for the emergence of ethnic conflict into
the political arena was because of the uneven rate of development
and modernization among the regions. Of all the Nigerian tribes
the Yorubas were the first to benefit from Western education, because
of sustained and early contact with the British. The primary reason
then for the emergence of nationality associations among the Ibos,
Ibibios, and other groups was for the purpose of education and group
advancement.

Tribal nationalism arose in the south with the birth of the Egbe
and the belief by Azikiwe that it represented a direct threat, on the
basis of ethnicity, to the NCNC membership in Lagos. When the Egbe
did form its political arm, the Action Group, it was able to recruit

---

*I use "tribalism" in the popular sense as being the basis for
discrimination against a person or group outside one's ethnic group,
where the principal reason for the discrimination is membership in
an ethnic group different from one's own. Membership in a different
ethnic group usually carries with it the implication of possessing
derogatory attributes. "Ethnic nationalism" is used to indicate the
perception of one's own ethnic group as having the attributes of nation-
hood or attempting to invest one's group with the attributes of nation-
hood. It does not imply any particular feeling toward members of
other ethnic groups. "Tribal nationalism," on the other hand, is used
to designate ethnic nationalism reinforced by "tribalism." Thus ethnic
nationalism emerged among Yorubas and Ibos before tribal nationalism
did in the late 1940s.

successfully among the indigenous Lagos Yorubas only after the ascendance of a pro-Action Group Oba in Lagos.[10]

It is difficult to discuss the role of tribal nationalism in Nigerian politics without also discussing the role of class. The differential rate of development of potentially antagonistic classes, largely identifiable along ethnic lines, was rooted to a great extent in the interaction of the traditional cultures and British colonialism. Embryonic ruling classes existed in the Western Region before the advent of European penetration. Although the traditional Yoruba society was hierarchical, there were genuine checks and balances on the rulers, the subjects were not tied in a feudal productive relationship to the land, and social relationships were not antagonistic. Class antagonisms in the Yoruba community grew up as the slave trade developed, creating a wealthy slave-trading class in the coastal areas.[11]

The situation in the north and east was quite different. In the Northern Region, the jihad of Usuman dan Fodio in the early nineteenth century established a truly feudal rule of the Fulanis over the Hausa and other indigenes. The emirs saw in British indirect rule a method for maintaining and broadening their own power, and cunningly cooperated. One of the bargains struck with the British in return for the emirs' cooperation was the banning of missionaries; since the missionaries were also teachers, a very small educated class indeed developed in the north. In the east, on the other hand, there existed no hierarchical social or political framework into which the various clans of Ibos fit. Traditional rulers played a much smaller part in Ibo society than in either Yoruba or Hausa society, and Ibos resisted the imposition of indirect rule by the British more effectively than the other tribes. At the same time certain elements of Ibo culture—competitiveness, aggressiveness, radical democracy— predisposed them to adopt with alacrity and notable success many of the habits and attitudes common to modern Western society.

Social Basis of the Political Parties

The genius of the political parties in Nigeria has been the remarkably successful manner in which they have been able to integrate the goals of their militantly nationalistic emergent bourgeois founders with those of the traditional rulers and trading class to develop a more or less uniform class outlook. Control over the regional marketing boards and, through them, the development corporations and banks, gave the parties a near monopoly on the sources of capital for indigenous entrepreneurs. The parties used this control to help create and influence a new constituency of upwardly mobile, likeminded elites, especially in the south.

213

With hindsight it is now possible to discern that the events surrounding the creation of the NPC as a political party presaged the later intense conflict that occurred between the leaders of the north and south. The NPC originated as a cultural organization in 1949. The first declared political party in the north, the Northern Elements Progressive Union (NEPU), was formed in Kano in 1950 and had originally planned to operate within the framework of the more conservative NPC. Since this was a period of constitutional review, the north would have to be represented at conferences by a political party; it was important therefore for the emirs and other traditional rulers to have a party. Rumors circulated among the civil servants and teachers who founded the NPC that the emirs were planning to start their own party. In order to make the NPC attractive for the traditional rulers, all members of NEPU were purged. When several members of the NPC lost to NEPU candidates in the primary voting phase of the 1951 parliamentary elections, the NPC promptly announced that it had become a political party, that all civil servants in the NPC "including the General President, Dr. Dikko, had been advised to resign their NPC offices, that Alhaji Sanda, a Lagos merchant, had been elevated from the office of Deputy General President to Acting General President, and that the Sardauna of Sokoto and the Hon. Abubakar Tafawa Balewa had become members."[12] In one masterful stroke the party of the ruling class established firm control over the region by the expedient of becoming the administration.

Two factors of significance emerge from this brief recount of the founding of the NPC as a political party: (1) the middle-class bureaucrats and teachers denied their own class interests and effectively handed over the party to the feudal aristocracy, and (2) the party came into being as a direct result of a challenge mounted by the progressive bourgeois elements in the NEPU—precisely those same elements that were spearheading the nationalist drive in the south and with whom the NEPU would later form an alliance.

Of the three major parties the Action Group was probably the most representative of the interests of the rising bourgeoisie. While the Action Group did not begin as mass party like the NCNC, it did have mass support. As the Action Group leader of the opposition in the federal house of representatives in 1957, Chief S. L. A. Akintola, wryly noted that "as a member of the Government once told me, when they look around the Opposition from the bench they see some reactionary Members, some middle of the road Members, and they also see some people whom they regard as extreme firebrands. If any group is truly democratic in the sense that they have extreme right and extreme left, and we are not lacking in either, there are also those who travel the middle of the way, then it is the Opposition in the Federal House."[13] Indeed it was this very diversity that played a major role in the Action Group crisis of 1962, which led to the ability of the NPC for the first time to establish a major bulwark in the south.

Proximate Causes of Military Intervention

The breakdown of the federal system was largely a result of a realignment of the political parties along ideological lines, abetted by the inherent political weaknesses embodied in the Constitution. Tribalism itself played a pernicious but usually subsidiary role. The NPC, the major partner in the federal government, violated the tacit understanding about the rules of the political game in Nigeria when it interfered in Western Region politics to exploit the ideological split within the Action Group. This enabled the factions to realign with their true class confrères.

The Action Group Crisis

If a single significant factor can be accorded primary responsibility for leading to the collapse of the federation it is probably the challenge to the principle of noninterference by the federal government in regional politics and the NPC's subsequent exploitation of ideological bifactionalism in the Action Group.

The rift in the Action Group started in 1961 when Awolowo presented his blueprint for "democratic socialism." Chief Akintola, deputy leader of the party and premier of the Western Region, wanted the party to join in a national government with the NPC; he did not like the possibility of the Action Group being cast in the role of a permanent opposition at the center. At the annual AG congress in February 1962, Awolowo again advocated the adoption of democratic socialism and rejected the idea of national government with the NPC. Characterizing the factions within the party as "inside-left and inside-right," he so angered Akintola that Akintola, Chief Ayotunde Rosiji (the secretary of the party), and a few others walked out. Akintola's post as deputy leader was abolished, the Marxist Samuel Ikoku (leader of the opposition in the Eastern Region house) was appointed party secretary, and the Federal Executive Committee removed Akintola as premier as punishment on twenty-four charges that had been placed against him at an earlier date and to which he had pleaded guilty.

Akintola went to court to challenge the legality of his removal as premier, since the legislature had not returned a vote of "no confidence." The court upheld him. The Action Group in the meanwhile had designated a new premier, Alhaji Dauda S. Adegbenro, and called a session of the legislature to procure a vote of confidence. Chaos reigned during the two attempts to convene the legislature, and Prime Minister Balewa declared a state of emergency in the Western Region. He also appointed an administrator, who restricted the movements of the principals in the dispute to limited areas within the region and assumed control of the government. After the emergency was lifted, Chief Akintola formed the United Peoples Party (UPP) and eventually reconvened the legislature, now a coalition government composed of the UPP and NCNC opposition. The Action Group boycotted the legislature.

During the state of emergency, searches by the police force were carried out all over the country and large quantities of smuggled arms were found. Balewa announced in the second anniversary of independence speech that Chief Awolowo and his supporters were planning to overthrow the federal government. Among those charged and convicted were Awolowo; Joseph Tarka, whose United Middle Belt Congress was allied with the Action Group; Chief Anthony Enahoro, the Action Group's vice-president; and Samuel Ikoku. Ikoku and Enahoro fled to Ghana. Awolowo was sentenced to ten years in prison; Enahoro was eventually recaptured and sentenced to fifteen years. Ikoku was extradited to Nigeria after the Ghana coup.

Alienation between the NPC and the NCNC

The immediate cause of the rift between the NPC and the NCNC was the results of the census of 1963, which again gave the Northern Region overwhelming population superiority over the entire southern third of the country and hence entitled the north to more representation in the federal legislature than the east and west combined. The census results, announced on February 24, 1964, gave the Northern Region 29.8 million; the Eastern Region 12.4 million; the Western Region 10.3 million; the newly-created Mid-West Region 2.5 million; and Lagos 700,000.[14]

Neither the Action Group nor the NCNC would accept the new census figures. Akintola did. He gave the Western Region branch of the NCNC, aligned in a coalition government with the UPP, an ultimatum on March 14, 1964 to either join his new Nigerian National Democratic Party (NNDP) or resign from the government. Twenty-seven of the 31 former NCNC members joined the NNDP, giving the new party 58 of the 90 seats in the Western Region House of Assembly. Akintola's NCNC vice-premier, Remi Fani-Kayode, was among those who crossed the carpet to join the new party.

In preparation for the 1964 federal elections, two broad-based coalitions were formed: the Nigerian National Alliance (NNA), composed of the NPC, NNDP, MWDF, Dynamic Party, and Niger Delta

Congress, and the United Progressive Grand Alliance (UPGA), composed of the AG, the NCNC, and the Northern Progressive Front (NEPU, United Middle Belt Congress, and the Kano Peoples Party). The electioneering and voting were characterized by beatings, ballot box stuffing, prevention of voters from registering, buying of votes, unilaterally declaring candidates unopposed, and destruction of voting papers. Three weeks before the election, President Azikiwe first broadcast his fear of the possibility of secession:

> Whether our beloved Nigeria will continue to remain
> united as one country or will become disintegrated into
> minute principalities depends now upon two factors:
> whether our politicians would desist from inciting our
> communities to liquidate themselves and whether our
> politicians would co-operate so that the law-abiding ele-
> ments in this colossus of Africa will experience a free
> and fair election. . . . I have only one request to make
> from our politicians, and in this I hope I have the support
> of the other leaders of this nation: if this embryo Republic
> must disintegrate, then, in the name of God, let the oper-
> ation be a short and painless one. Let it not be featured
> by violence, which we shunned during the dark days of
> our national humiliation. . . . Should the politicians fail
> to heed this warning, then I will venture the prediction
> that the experience of the Democratic Republic of the
> Congo will be child's play, if it ever comes to our turn to
> play such a tragic role. . . . I have made my observations
> not necessarily as an alarmist but as a realist who is in
> a position to read the handwriting on the wall of our
> destiny.[15]

Two days before the elections were scheduled to be held, the UPGA called a boycott. But voting took place on December 30, 1964, and the crisis passed. Elections were held in the boycotted constituencies; a carefully balanced coalition government was formed, which included the NCNC but not the AG.

The Western Region elections of October 1965 were characterized by the same sort of activity that typified the federal elections of 1964. The UPGA, which had announced that a merger of the two main parties would become effective after the Western Region elections, won only 17 of the 94 seats, while the NNDP won 74.[16] After the election results were announced, the UPGA declared that it rejected them and Alhaji Adegbenro, the AG leader, proceeded to form a government based on the UPGA's interpretation of the election returns. What differentiated this election from the previous federal

217

election, however, was the chaos into which the Western Region plummeted. Akintola imposed dusk-to-dawn curfews, but that did little to quell the sporadic violence (more than 160 people were killed) and riots that broke out all over the region. This violence was perpetrated by both supporters of the victorious NNDP and supporters of the UPGA.

On January 14, 1966 Premier Akintola met with the Sardauna in Kaduna to discuss the possibility of using the army to quell the disturbances in the west.[17] On January 15 a coup d'état occurred in which the prime minister, the premiers of the Western and Northern regions, and the federal minister of finance were the most prominent Nigerians killed. The army took over the government.

THE ESTABLISHMENT OF MILITARY RULE

The Coup of January 15, 1966

It can be asserted that tribalism was not the primary motive behind the coup, despite the fact that twelve of the fourteen identified leaders were Ibo and the only important Ibo killed was Colonel Arthur Unegbe. Rather, Nzeogwu "claimed to have commanded the support of the Northerners involved who, he said, were a majority of his force. 'It was truly a Nigerian gathering and only in the army do you get true Nigerianism.'"[18] This claim is all the more significant since northern troops participated in killing the Sardauna—the spiritual as well as political leader of the north.[19]

The army coup represented the reestablishment of a type of administrative-traditional rule that was characteristic of the days of colonial rule in Nigeria:[20]

> The pattern of rule which [was] emerging [was] military-bureaucratic in type, politically repressive, espousing conservative finance and free enterprise, culturally null. The formal homology between this pattern and the old colonial administration is striking: an irresponsible executive, feeble communication or consultation, departmental policy-making, proliferation of committees, sanctions against normal forms of political association.[21]

It was Ironsi's general political ineptitude that proved his final undoing. He attempted to unify the civil service, a move particularly resented by senior civil servants in the north who still feared southern domination.* His last egregious error was announcing on May 23 the abolition of the federation and commencement of unitary rule, even before the Constitutional Review Study Group had made its recommendations.[23] Anti-Ibo riots broke out in Kano the following weekend, and about 90 people were killed. Katsina tried to mollify the northerners with assurances that the civil service and governmental unification decrees were temporary measures that would be subject to change after definite constitutional arrangements had been worked out. Ironsi was killed in a countercoup on July 29 in Ibadan, where, coincidentally, he had journeyed to address a gathering of 24 traditional leaders whose support he hoped to win in filling the vacuum created by the removal of the politicians.[24]

Ultimately the countercoup resulted from Ironsi's underestimation of the strength of traditional factors in Nigerian politics- in this case the power of the northern emirs and the fear of southern domination. It also resulted from his failure to realize that capitalizing on the corruption and inefficiency of the civilian regime, coupled with attempts to win over the untainted elements of the civil service, are insufficient to establish political legitimacy.[25] Finally he banned politics without coopting the politicians into the government and before he could effectively mobilize support among traditional leaders.

Countercoup and the Road to Secession

Lieutenant Colonel Yakubu Gowon emerged as leader of the new government by default.[26] He had the three most important attributes that the armed forces commanders and coup leaders thought mandatory: he was from the north; he had not participated in the coup; he was not a member of a major tribe. With Gowon in charge it would be difficult to claim that the coup represented Hausa revenge against the Ibos.[27]

Among Gowon's first and highly significant acts was the release in August of Chief Awolowo, Chief Enahoro, and Chief Joseph Tarka. He also released the former premier of the Eastern Region, Michael Okpara, and appointed Colonel Robert Adebayo to replace the dead military governor of the Western Region.

---

*The northern leaders also probably could not forget that it was Ironsi who was an early advocate of the virtues of army recruitment solely on the basis of merit and without regard to regional origin. Because of the large number of educated Ibos and the favor with which they viewed military careers, such a policy would (and did until it was later modified) result in a largely Ibo officer class.[22]

Gowon called an all-Nigeria constitutional conference for mid-September in Lagos. The composition of the delegation to the conference was revealing. Representing the Western Region was Chief Awolowo; his old Action Group deputy, Chief Enahoro, represented the Mid-West Region. The north was represented by Joseph Tarka of the United Middle Belt Congress, which had been agitating for its own region, and by the progressive Alhaji Aminu Kano of NEPU. Only the Waziri of Bornu, Sir Kashim Ibrahim (former governor of the north), who presided, was representative of the traditional NPC leadership.[28]

General agreement was reached on the need for creating a federation with minimum centralized power, but discussions broke down on the question of the creation of additional regions. The east was against more regions because it feared that in the face of agitation for separate regions in eastern minority areas, its region would likely be subdivided. Moreover these new regions would contain a large part of the oilfields and would probably be under the leadership of Awolowo's close friend and Action Group politico E. O. Eyo. Given the impact that the anti-Ibo pogroms in the north must have made, eastern reluctance about creating additional regions was understandable. Significantly the Awolowo-Enahoro axis persuaded the north's delegation, through Tarka, to endorse the creation of additional regions in the north, despite the region's previous adamant opposition to what had been viewed as an attempt to destroy northern political hegemony.

Anti-Ibo riots in the north were also a cause for the adjournment of talks. That they began September 18, shortly after the northern delegation agreed to the creation of additional regions, and that the outbreaks occurred almost simultaneously in several cities across the north, has led to speculation that the riots were instigated by traditional leaders angered at the prospect of the diminution of their power and bent on forcing the dissolution of the federation through anti-Ibo acts.[29] On September 29 northern soldiers mutinied and killed twenty-five Ibos aboard a plane in Kano. Rioting, pillaging, and killing continued for several weeks,during which an estimated 18,000 Ibos were killed and nearly 1.5 million were driven back into the Eastern Region.[30] The riots, and especially the participation of soldiers in anti-Ibo atrocities, demonstrated that Gowen had yet to consolidate power in Lagos.

In mid-March Ojukwu called a press conference in which he announced his intention to decentralize the federation by assuming regional control of certain functions heretofore controlled by the federal government. A few days later Gowon promulgated his Constitution (Suspension and Modification) Decree: the army would govern the country through a Supreme Military Council under the chairmanship of the commander-in-chief of the armed forces and head of the federal military government; all decrees passed since May 1966 that diminished regional power in any way would be repealed; consent of the head of the federal military government and all the regional commanders would be needed to enforce legislation on most items on the exclusive and concurrent lists of the Constitution, including those affecting regional integrity.

What Ojukwu rejected out of hand was the revision of particular sections of the Constitution that allowed the Supreme Military Council to take certain steps after declaring a state of emergency and to enact legislation with only three of the four regions concurring. This objectionable clause was included in the decree upon the insistence of Gowon's civil servants.

From then on events rapidly deteriorated. The east withheld revenue from the federal military government starting March 31; the Central Bank of Nigeria blocked the transfer of foreign currencies to the east; the Eastern Region assumed control over the branch offices of many federal agencies. Biafra was declared born on May 27, 1967; the federal military government announced the creation of twelve states and declared a general state of emergency a few hours later.* War broke out within a few weeks.

The Soviet Union and the Civil War

There is no gainsaying the significance of Soviet aid to the federal military government. Whether Soviet aid was decisive for the federal victory or for a more rapid ending of the war is ultimately less important than the fact that the federal military government and the Nigerian people perceived the aid as being in fact decisive. Unlike Western powers who either had refused Nigeria's request to purchase arms (the United States) or procrastinated in fulfilling the request (Great Britain), the Soviet Union responded swiftly and unequivocally.[31] Moreover the federal military government also expressed regret that the previous Nigerian governments had been so short-sighted as to reject previous Soviet offers of assistance.

One can well wonder why the Soviet Union chose to become involved in the Nigerian civil war. The reasons for aiding the federal military government had become compelling by late August 1967, and,

---

*The Eastern Region was subdivided into the East Central, South East and Rivers states; the North into North East, Kano, Kwara, North Central, North West, and Benue-Plateau states; Lagos, the Mid West, and the West completed the twelve.

interestingly (perhaps characteristically), were strictly practical: "This, then, is the crucial implication of the commitment: the federal government captured the Soviet interest because it controlled one of Black Africa's most important countries, not because it was one of Black Africa's most progressive regimes."[32]

This indeed is the crucial point, for it relates directly to the question of Nigeria's commitment to leftist policies in the postwar era. Furthermore the Soviet Union's decision to aid Nigeria indicates a departure from previous primary concern with Mali, Guinea, the United Arab Republic (UAR), Ghana, and Algeria—states that the Soviets declared had skipped the phase of "bourgeois-democratic" revolution and had embarked directly upon the road of "scientific socialism."[33] What is particularly ironic is that the Soviet Union's pragmatic response to the Nigerian civil war was grounded in a resurgent neo-orthodoxy that envisaged class struggle developing within the small, politically active segment of the population—bureaucrats, military, politicians, plantation owners, traditional leaders—around the issue of the direction of further socioeconomic progress in the post-independence situation. The Soviets hoped to give the more progressive elements in the Nigerian government the ideological foundation needed to guide the country into the revolutionary socialist camp.

POSTWAR POLICY AND THE APERTURA À SINISTRA: AN ASSESSMENT

Postwar Foreign Policy

More leftist (or militantly nationalistic) trends are discernible in three areas: in utterances regarding the white minority governments in southern Africa; in decisions to regulate the foreign-controlled petroleum industry; in relations with socialist nations.

Nigeria is an important member of the Organization of African Unity's Liberation Committee dealing with South Africa. In October 1970 Nigeria rejected South African Prime Minister Vorster's offer of September 15 that he was prepared to enter into a nonaggression pact with any African nation.[34]

Since the countercoup the country has taken several significant steps toward nationalizing the petroleum industry. Most important in this respect is the Petroleum Decree of 1969: by the end of the decade, 60 percent of the workers would have to be Nigerian, and 75 percent of the total managerial, professional, and supervisory grades would also have to be Nigerian. In February 1970, two months after the Petroleum Decree was promulgated, the federal commissioner for mines and power, A. R. B. Dikko, announced that the government would participate in the oil industry on the basis of a previously agreed percentage in each license granted to oil companies; that it reserved the right to purchase up to 12.5 percent of total crude production of any company, or its total requirements for internal consumption; that it would fix the prices of petroleum products sold in Nigeria. Dikko also announced restrictions for prospecting the 5,000 square miles of offshore reserves, and that henceforth licenses would be required for the construction of refineries and for engaging in marketing petroleum products in Nigeria.[35]

Furthermore, while Nigeria, second largest exporter of oil in Africa (after Libya) and tenth largest in the world, is not a member of the Organization of Petroleum Exporting Countries (OPEC), she has recently concluded a new taxation agreement with Shell-British Petroleum (the largest exporter of Nigerian oil) that will bring her earnings from oil much more closely in line with those of the OPEC nations.[36] Assurances from both Gowon and Dikko have been given to the various petroleum companies that nationalization is not contemplated, but recent policies have certainly been moving in that direction. It is around the question of nationalization that divisions are evident between a left and right in the domestic political arena.

Finally, Nigeria's historic position of nonalignment has been given more substance since the conclusion of the civil war as contacts with socialist or communist nations have been broadened. Thus in March 1970 Radio Lagos indicated that, while the government was anxious to maintain its friendship with the West, it was also eager to make more friendships among the communist nations, especially since those nations had supplied certain arms that Nigeria could obtain from no other countries. The broadcast further implied that the government was no longer convinced by Western admonitions about the dangers in dealing with communist countries.*

---

*The lineup of foreign countries indirectly involved in the civil war was indeed strange. At the end of 1968 Czechs were sending arms to Biafra, as were the Communist Chinese and the French. Portugal cooperated by allowing São Tomé to be used as a staging base for planes flying equipment and supplies into Uli airstrip. American and Swiss mercenaries flew American aircraft for Biafra. On the side of the federal military government, of course, were the Soviet Union, Britain, and Egypt (which donated pilots to fly Soviet aircraft). Yet it was ulterior motives, not great dislike for Biafra or Lagos, that prompted many of the countries to participate. Thus France would have like to see a balkanized Nigeria because of fear

Many agreements with the Soviet Union have been concluded. In November 1968 a technical and economic cooperation agreement was signed. It provides for the exchange of experts, trainees, and apprentices in various fields; for extension of credit to finance development and survey projects; and for the delivery of equipment and materiel to execute projects.[37] A new cultural pact expanding upon the agreement of 1967 was concluded in April 1970. In June 1970 Moscow and Lagos signed an agreement for joint cooperation in geological research and metal prospecting, and for the establishment of a geological laboratory and training center for skilled industrial workers. Between 1967 and 1970, Soviet imports (excluding arms) have also increased by about 35 percent.[38]

Relations with other socialist countries are also being cultivated. Nigeria received her first Bulgarian ambassador in early June 1970, shortly after the Nigerian visit of Rumanian Foreign Minister Corneliu Manescu. New initiatives with the Maghreb countries, especially with Algeria and the UAR, have been undertaken, and a joint Algerian-Nigerian communique of August 28, 1970 stated that a joint committee for scientific, cultural, trade, and technological cooperation between the two countries would be established.[39] On the other hand, Lagos has kept up relations with France despite that country's de facto recognition of Biafra, and continued sending students to study in France during the height of the war.[40]

The evidence available from Nigerian foreign policy to date in the areas briefly discussed is not compelling enough to conclude that there has been a definite shift in emphasis toward policies that would find Soviet support as a matter of conscious policy. Nigeria has become more truly nonaligned, but this shift toward the left has been motivated more by pragmatic reasons than by ideological ones. Apart from the cultural pact of 1970 with the Soviet Union (the pact of August 1967 provided the rationale for selling arms to Nigeria then), the agreements between Nigeria and the socialist countries have been principally of a technical nature. Indeed it is probably closer to the truth to assert that the new "opening to the left" discernible in Nigerian foreign policy is the result of a reassessment of Nigeria's interests as a nation: what is tempting to define in terms

---

about the influence a united and prosperous Nigeria would have over smaller, less viable (French-speaking) African states; Czechoslovakia and Communist China saw an opportunity to irritate the Soviet Union by aiding Biafra. See Africa Confidential, December 20, 1968, p. 1; and Walter Schwarz, "Foreign Powers and the Nigerian War," Africa Report, XV, 2 (February 1970), 12-14.

of ideological considerations should be defined in terms of a re-
definition of perceived national interest.

Postwar Domestic Politics

The significance of postwar domestic politics is that it has
been characterized by a certain degree of conflict between a "right"
and a "left" around three issues: the creation of additional states;
free primary, secondary, and post-secondary education; and nationalization of the oil industry.[41] The political right is usually represented by Gowon, most elements of the armed forces, and the Lagos
bureaucracy; the left consists of some of the former politicians—
Awolowo, Kano, Ikoku, Okunnu—and some of those associated with
the trade unions, such as Wahab Goodluck (president of the Nigerian
Trade Union Confederation), Sam Bassey (general secretary of the
confederation), Michael Imoudu (a leader of the Labour Unity Front),
and Tunji Otegbeye.

In his book, The People's Republic (1968), Awolowo declares
the necessity of creating a state for each linguistic group. He and
his supporters argue that the Yoruba-speakers of Kabba and Ilorin
provinces, now part of Kwara State in the former Northern Region,
must be incorporated into the West State. Both the federal military
government and the remaining leaders of the NNDP are against the
consolidation of all Yoruba-speaking areas. Lagos is opposed on
principle to political support based on tribal allegiance, and views
the desire to incorporate the two provinces as essentially an attempt
to broaden support for the Action Group in preparation for a return
to civilian rule. Gowon has declared, however, that he favors the
creation of additional states in general but would like to maintain
the status quo until 1974. The NNDP, on the other hand, favors the
creation of additional states in the West in order to diminish the
strength of the Action Group and consolidate its own.[42]

Another of Awolowo's proposals—universal free education—has
excited much comment and support from almost all shades of the
political spectrum. Gowon has announced that he is against it at this
time because of the cost involved. Ideological polemics aside, it
appears difficult for Gowon to endorse universal free education,
because of the lack of jobs. Indeed one reason for having to keep
the armed forces near full strength now that the war is over is the
paucity of employment opportunities for military personnel who
return to civilian life. The paradox is that the increased defense
expenditures could be channeled into education if there were jobs
to absorb graduates.

It is in this light then that the nationalization controversy should be viewed. Gowon has been solicitous of the foreign oil interests and has continued to reassure them that nationalization is not being contemplated. Yet, as has been indicated, the actions of the federal military government have been moving almost inexorably toward full nationalization. It may be that Gowon is attempting to defuse the education issue by yielding ground, piecemeal, on the question of nationalization. Nationalization would mean more white-collar jobs more quickly for Nigerian graduates than if the industry remained privately controlled.

Political discontent has been erupting in the west, indirectly expressing dissatisfaction with military rule. Riots started in 1968, provoked by increased taxes, austerity, import restrictions (particularly anathema to the Yoruba market women), and a compulsory savings plan. Twelve people were killed in November 1968.[43] The cocoa farmers have formed the militant Agbekoya ("the farmers will no longer be fooled"), a powerful pressure group completely outside the control of the government or the influence of the political leaders. They have been agitating over the failure of the government to pass on to them the high world price of cocoa. Meanwhile the civilian commissioner government that Brigadier Adebayo established in the West has assumed an increasingly military complexion as the former Action Group members have started dissociating themselves from it as popular discontent has mounted.

About the only area in which Soviet influence is apparent in domestic politics is the labor unions. The NTUC, which had formerly been prohibited from joining the communist World Federation of Trade Unions (WFTU)—although it received communist funds through the All-African Federation of Trade Unions—formally joined the WFTU at the latter's October 1969 congress in Budapest. The Advance, the erstwhile weekly of the NTUC, has become a daily with a large new printing works financed by Moscow.[44] Yet, even in this area, the Soviet Union is merely capitalizing on the earlier influence she exercised in the NTUC and its political offspring, the Nigerian Socialist Workers and Farmers Party (NSWFP). Still, given the fact that most unionized workers are employed in the public sector and given the precedent of labor union cooperation established by the general strike of 1964, infiltration of the labor movement could become an effective method for initiating revolutionary social change in Nigeria.

NOTES

1. Claude S. Phillips Jr., The Development of Nigerian Foreign Policy (Evanston: Northwestern University Press, 1964), pp. 15-21.

2. Ibid., pp. 108-12.

3. Alexander Erlich and Christian R. Sonne, "The Soviet Union: Economic Activity," in Zbigniew Brzezinski ed., Africa and the Communist World, (Stanford: Stanford University Press for the Hoover Institution of War, Revolution and Peace, 1963), p. 61.

4. Agence France-Presse, Africa: Interafrican News Survey, March 14, 1963, p. 19.

5. John P. Mackintosh, "Nigeria's External Relations," Journal of Commonwealth Political Studies, Vol. II (November 1964), pp. 208-10.

6. Kalu Ezera, Constitutional Developments in Nigeria (2nd ed., Cambridge, England-Cambridge University Press, 1964), pp. 64-263, passim. A total of 320 seats were actually allocated for the House of Representatives, but 8 of those were reserved for the Southern Cameroons. The allocation was 174 for the north, 73 for the east, 62 for the west, and 3 for Lagos.

7. John Grimond, "Nigeria Starts Again, A Survey," The Economist (special supplement) (October 24, 1970), p. xii.

8. Richard L. Sklar, Nigerian Political Parties (Princeton: Princeton University Press, 1963), pp. 41-64.

9. Aristide Zolberg, "The Structure of Political Conflict in the New States of Tropical Africa," American Political Science Review, LXII, 1 (March 1968), 70-87, passim.

10. Sklar, op. cit., pp. 69-72.

11. See Samir Amin, The Class Struggle in Africa (Cambridge, Mass.: Africa Research Group, n.d.), pp. 30-34. The pamphlet originally appeared as an article in the French magazine Revolution, Vol. 1, No. 9 (1964).

12. Ibid., pp. 96-97.

13. Sklar, op. cit., p. 261.

14. West Africa, February 29, 1964, p. 243.

15. Paul Anber, "Modernisation and Political Disintegration: Nigeria and the Ibos," Journal of Modern African Studies, Vol. V (September 1967), pp. 176-77.

16. West Africa, July 17, 1965, p. 795. For accounts of the irregularities surrounding the election, election coverage, and post-election disorders, see the September-December 1965 issues of West Africa.

17. Africa Institute of South Africa, "Nigeria: End of a Tragedy," Bulletin, VIII, 3 (April 1970), 92. Also see African Confidential, January 21, 1966, p. 1.

18. William F. Gutteridge, The Military in African Politics (London: Methuen & Company, 1969), p. 76.

19. Africa Confidential, February 4, 1966, pp. 1-3.

20. See Edward Feit, "Military Coups and Political Development: Some Lessons from Ghana and Nigeria," World Politics, XX, 2 (January 1968), 179-93.

21. Roger Murray, "Militarism in Africa," New Left Review, No. 28 (July-August 1966), p. 52.

22. See Feit, op. cit., pp. 189-91.

23. Kalu Ezera, "The Failure of Nigerian Federalism and Proposed Constitutional Changes," African Forum, II, 1 (Summer 1966), 28.

24. Gutteridge, op. cit., p. 90.

25. See Claude E. Welch Jr,, "Africa's New Rulers," Africa Today, XV, 2 (April-May 1968), 8.

26. Information about events surrounding the emergence of Gowon was obtained in an interview with Ade Oyejide at Princeton, New Jersey, December 30, 1970.

27. The army does not publish its ethnic composition, but Africa Confidential. December 23, 1966, p. 8 and Gutteridge, op. cit., p. 10 corroborate the overrepresentation of northern minorities. Alhaji Inuwa Wada, former NPC federal minister of works, is alleged to have started recruiting Hausas into the army after the countercoup, in an attempt to redress the imbalance. See Africa Confidential, October 25, 1968, pp. 2-4.

28. Africa Confidential, September 23, 1966, p. 6.

29. Robert Legvold, Soviet Policy in West Africa, (Cambridge, Harvard University Press, 1950), pp. 316-18.

30. Russell Warren Howe, "Nigeria at War," Editorial Research Reports, February 28, 1968, p. 155.

31. Africa Research Limited, Africa Research Bulletin (Political, Social and Cultural Series) [hereafter Research Bulletin (PSC)], VI, 3 (April 15, 1969), 1354A.

32. Legvold, Soviet-Policy, p. 329.

33. Robert Legvold, "Moscow's Changing View of Africa's Revolutionary Regimes," Africa Report, XIV, 3-4 (March-April 1969), 54; David Morison, The USSR and Africa: 1945-1963 (London: Oxford University Press for the Institute of Race Relations and the Central Asian Research Centre [1964]), pp. 3-5.

34. Research Bulletin (PSC), VII, 9 (October 15, 1970), 1863B.

35. Africa Research Limited, Africa Research Bulletin (Economic, Financial and Technical Series) [hereafter Research Bulletin (EFT)], VII, 1 (February 28, 1970), 1591C-592A.

36. See Africa Confidential, September 4, 1970, pp. 5-6.

37. Research Bulletin (EFT), V, 11 (December 31, 1968), 1214BC.

38. Research Bulletin (PSC), VII, 4 (May 15, 1970), pp. 1738C-1739A; and Research Bulletin (EFT), VII, 6 (July 31, 1970), p. 1749C.

39. Research Bulletin (EFT), VII, 8 (September 15, 1970), p. 1836B.

40. Research Bulletin (PSC), VII, 3 (April 15, 1970), p. 1711B.

41. Africa Confidential, August 7, 1970, p. 1.

42. Ibid., January 16, 1970, p. 8.

43. Ibid., December 6, 1968, p. 6.

44. Ibid., February 27, 1970, p. 4. For a somewhat polemical but still useful outline of the ideological orientation of the four major trade union federations see Eskor Toyo, The Working Class and the Nigerian Crisis (Ibadan: Sketch Publishing Company, [1967]), pp. 58-61, et passim.

13

SOVIET INVOLVEMENT
IN THE NIGERIAN
CIVIL WAR
George Obiozor

The Soviet Union welcomed Nigerian independence with mixed feelings. On the one hand there was the pessimism that was inspired by the assessment of Nigeria's internal structure. Basically this was the awareness that the achievement of political independence on October 1, 1960 was already compromised by Nigerian dependence on Western investment, Western advisers, and Western trade. The Soviets therefore saw Nigeria as being in no form or spirit any better than the Ivory Coast or Senegal. Nigeria's political independence, the Soviets maintained, rested on an economic superstructure controlled by British businessmen. The Soviet Africanist I. I. Potekhin has stated that "the whole economy of the country including foreign trade is controlled by foreign, principally British, capital."[1] The Soviet policymakers were further disturbed by the newly independent country's military pact with Great Britain. Guinea, having shown an example of total separation from a former colonial master (France, in 1958), was quick to condemn this military pact as an "absurd agreement," because it allowed the former colonial power (Britain) to maintain a military basis on Nigerian territory, to influence in no uncertain terms her economic development, and to plan an important role in her policy in international affairs. These and other factors formed the basis of the Soviet discontent with Nigerian achievement of independence and placed Nigeria among Africa's "unprogressive" states.

On the other hand there was the presence of a dynamic and "progressive" opposition party and of opposition elements within the other three major parties. These made Nigeria seem less hopelessly monolithic in its commitment to reactionary programs and policies.

Within a few years the leaders of the "progressive" African states, with the exception of Guinea, were overthrown. Even in Guinea, a falling out had occurred, and they broke diplomatic relations. If the

Soviet leaders were waiting for an issue to force them to reexamine their African policies it came with the overthrow of Nkrumah in Ghana on February 24, 1966. For the Soviets the first coup in Nigeria was warmly welcomed. The "coup had been directed against the reactionary feudal clique in Northern Nigeria whose rule weighed heavily on other regions and held back Nigeria's development as an independent state. This could only be considered a step forward."[2]

However a countercoup took place that was prompted by the remnants of the "northern, feudal, reactionary" elements. It was followed by massacres or pogroms against the peoples of Eastern Region (particularly Ibos). As the crisis heightened toward a war of independence on the part of the east, given a long-range Soviet protestation of commitment to "progressive" elements, it was almost a foregone conclusion that the Soviets would remain genuinely neutral or fight on the side of the "progressives." But this did not happen. As eventually happened the Soviets chose to fight against the section that they identified as "progressive" and in favor of the section that they had associated with the labels "feudal" and "reactionary"—hence improving the chances of "reactionary mischiefs." Why was such a contradictory shift necessary?

With the coup in Ghana, and the countercoup in Nigeria on July 29, 1966, a shift in Soviet perceptions of African realities became imperative. For the first time the Soviets had no doubt that "in fact the weakest forces in Africa were revolutionary and the strongest were traditional with no need of direct imperialist intervention." Thus the Soviet Union lost its aversion to Nigeria's new military government, shifted to an openly sympathetic attitude, and finally firmly rallied to the military government's side in the war against secessionist Biafra. This represented an overwhelming demonstration of Soviet readiness to adjust to the exigencies of policy.[3]

To encourage the Soviet change of attitude, the new Nigerian regime gathered around it all the known radical (progressive) elements of the early 1960s associated with the opposition chief. The presence of these men had been seized upon by the Soviet press to justify the Soviets' policy shift. The Soviets felt that, contrary to their first expectation, the situation was "irrevocably" changing the feudal north to the extent that it might be safe to assume that it was either weakened or dead. The result of this new perception was extremely significant. From now on Moscow played down such events as the massacre of the easterners or the discontent of the Eastern Region.

One Russian Commentator, Korovikov, "emphasizing the murderous storm in which the Ibo of the North had been caught,"[4] warned against speedy identification with the north, which, as it seemed, still remained unpredictable. After a brief period of neutrality, the Soviet policymakers' swing back to the support of the north became increasingly evident as the preparation for secession in the east intensified. The Soviets' method was superb; they moved cautiously, obviously courting the north but not condemning the east. On March 21 Kudryavtsev, a Pravda correspondent, endorsed Gowon, the northern leader, and the Soviet Union started identifying the east with Katanga. The Soviet Union had taken sides. On March 28 Nigeria and the Soviet Union signed an agreement promoting "cultural cooperation," the cover used four months later in negotiating an arms deal.

After the Eastern Region had declared its independence, the Soviet press returned to a neutral role; apparently the Soviet Union was not going to encourage war unless invited. If the Biafrans and Nigerians refused to fight, the Soviet Union had better remain friendly to both sides. Pravda preferred to blame Nigeria's troubles on the "ruling circles" of the United States and Britain. Radio Biafra appealed to Soviet Union to continue her neutrality and said that "Gowon [the northern leader] wants to tarnish the image of the Soviet Union in Africa by dragging it into a foreign war."[5] By mid-August 1967 Nigeria had successfully negotiated supplies of Soviet MIG-175s and Czech L-29 Delphin trainers, which began arriving in Nigeria with Soviet technicians to assemble and later to maintain them.[6]

Why did the Soviet Union ally herself with the side she had initially identified as belonging to the reactionary forces? Of all regions in Nigeria, the east had urged expanded contacts with the Soviet Union and Eastern Europe, and had most openly expressed interest in Soviet aid. "If before July 29, 1966 [the date of the second coup], the Soviet Union had preferred any region in Nigeria, it was the East."[7]

For the Soviet's decision to support Nigeria, Soviet commentators argue that the position of the east's leadership had been changed fundamentally; that Ojukwu (the east's leader), however much he had been the spiritual heir of Azikiwe and Okpara (all prominent eastern leaders at various times in the civilian days), had a basically different purpose; that, perhaps understandable, the east's decision to secede broke a long-held commitment to the federation of Nigeria and that Soviet commentators had never approved separatist tendencies; that the Soviet Union believed that after two military coups the northern "feudal" society had received a deadly shakeup or had been even transformed. Kudryavtsev challenged the idea that the "East was allegedly combating the dominance of the feudal north." He argued that "this was nonsense because socially the north is heterogenous, and numerically the feudal elements constitute an insignificant stratum there."[8] That these arguments were easier to make long after the Soviet Union had chosen sides destroys its significance. According to Legvold, such a defense of the "feudal" north came in November 1967, while three months earlier (August 1967) no Soviet writer had justified his government's choice in these terms. At that time (August 1967)

Legvold stated that, while the Soviets suspected that the northern political structure was changing, equally they had apprehensions concerning
the possible reappearance of the northern feudal emirs at the center
of political decisions. Again, having accepted that Gowon ruled at "the
sufferance of the northern officers associated with the 'feudal' emirs,"
to announce their insignificance as a political force was contradictory.
Even more, Gowon's helplessness in controlling the political tide, and
the propensity for violence in the north, which these same Soviet commentators believed were engineered, revealed the hollowness of the
argument.

Perhaps other factors make the Soviet decision to intervene on
the side of Nigeria more comprehensible. Nigeria is one of sub-
Saharan Africa's most important states, and the unsettled conditions
of its politics encouraged the Soviet Union to devote special efforts
toward strengthening its position there. The increasing presence of
the "progressive" elements (civilians) in the new Nigerian regime
helped the Soviet Union to decide fast enough which side to back in case
of a showdown. The Soviets, like most observers, believed that the
war would be over quickly and this time they wanted to be on the side
of a winner (compare the Middle East war of June 1967).

The Soviet policymakers may have reasoned that, even if Nigeria
lost and Biafra succeeded, the remnants of the Nigerian federation
could still be friendly. This meant that at no time did the Soviet Union
stand the chance of a total loss. The isolation of Biafra by other
powers and the African reaction to secession of any part of an existing
(African) state system were all in the Soviets' calculations to intervene.

After the loss of the "progressive" African states, particularly
Ghana, through coups, the Soviet Union was desperate for a foothold
in Africa no matter how shaky it may seem initially. And Nigeria was
a particularly strong or irresistible temptation. As a Nigerian
"progressive," Femi Okunnu (one of the civilians coopted by the military regime), put it, "the relations between Nigeria and the Soviet
Union which had considerably improved within the past four to five
months would generate unto something bigger to the mutual benefit of
both countries."9 Thus the Soviet leaders responded to more pragmatic considerations, such as the effect the civil war would have on
Soviet relations with other African countries, the supposed advantages
the Western nations would obtain in an independent Biafra, and the
advantages created by the Anglo-American refusal or delay to give the
Nigerian government every support it asked for. Another factor was
that as long as the Lagos (Nigerian) regime was willing to deal with
the Soviet Union, its general character (feudal or not) remained a
secondary issue. The Soviet Union simply needed a place in Africa
after her favorite states had been overthrown. As Legvold puts it,
the crucial implication of Soviet commitment was that "the federal

government captured Soviet interest because it controlled one of Black Africa's most important countries, not because it was one of Black Africa's most progressive regimes."

In the aftermath of both situations, compared to the United States, it appears that at least on the surface, Soviet pragmatism is paying a good dividend.

The Soviets' opposite roles in the Nigerian and Pakistani civil wars reflect a shameless inconsistency and self-serving purposes that will always be remembered by all observers and interpreters of the foreign policy of major powers. The chances are, however, that this manipulative propensity, as exhibited in both cases, leaves little room for confidence or predictability necessary in the conduct of foreign relations of major powers if future calamities are to be avoided.

NOTES

1. Robert Legvold, Soviet Policy in West Africa (Cambridge, Mass.: Harvard University Press, 1970).
2. Ibid., p. 272.
3. Ibid., pp. 276,312.
4. Ibid., p. 317.
5. Ibid., p. 323.
6. Ibid.
7. Ibid., p. 236.
8. Ibid., p. 326.
9. Ibid., p. 328.

14

MASS COMMUNICATIONS
IN NIGERIA
Alfred E. Opubor

There is a close relationship between the condition of the media, as institutions, and the nature of the society in which the media operate.

In this chapter we intend to examine the present state of the mass media in Nigeria and relate it to the structure of Nigerian society. We will look at the size of media operations, the location and focus of the media, their potential audience, and the content they offer. The concept underlying this exercise is access. We are interested in the question: Who obtains what kind of information from which media, how often and why, at what cost? We believe that an access approach to the study of mass media provides a more subtle view of the operation of the media in any society than would the mere statistical enumeration of the media facilities available in the society. In addition basic statistics of media growth are provided,[1] as in Tables 14.1, 14.2, 14.3, and 14.4.

What the figures in the tables obscure is the regional variation in the distribution of media facilities. Most of the national newspapers are based in Lagos and have their highest circulation there. For example four of the six "national dailies" designated in Graham and Gillies Media Guide (1970) are published in Lagos. Of these the largest circulation is recorded by the Daily Times, which in April 1971 sold an average of 185,000 copies daily, out of which 82,300, or nearly half, were sold in Lagos.[2]

Similarly the northern states, with just over half of the total population of Nigeria, have only one-third of the total number of radio receivers. The Mid West State has almost as many cinema seats as the Western State, which has about five times the Mid West's population.

TABLE 14.1

Growth of Daily Newspapers

Category	1952	1960	1965	1966
Number of newspapers	15	20	22	24
Total circulation	90,000	284,000	291,000	417,000
Number of newspapers per 1,000 population number	3	8	7	8
Adjusted for number of readers per copy (5)	15	40	35	40

Source: UNESCO, Statistical Year Book (1966-69).

TABLE 14.2

Growth of Radio Receivers

Category	1950	1960	1963	1964	1968
Total number of sets	15,000	143,000	400,000	600,000	1,500,000
Number of sets per 1,000 population	0.6	4	11	11	26.7
Adjusted for number of listeners per set (7)	4.2	28	77	77	166.9

Sources: 1968 data from Graham and Gillies, Media Guide (Lagos, 1968); other data from UNESCO, Statistical Year Book (1966-69).

TABLE 14.3

Growth of Television Receivers

Category	1960	1962	1964	1965	1970
Total number of sets	1,000	10,000	15,000	30,000	40,000
Number of sets per 1,000 population	0.03	0.30	0.30	0.5	0.7
Adjusted for number of viewers per set (4)	0.12	1.20	1.20	2.0	2.80

Sources: 1970 data from Graham and Gillies, Media Guide (Lagos, July 1970); other data from UNESCO, Statistical Year Book (1966-69).

TABLE 14.4

Growth of Cinema Facilities

Category	1960	1968	1970-71
Number of fixed cinemas	67	117	
Total seating capacity	65,400	122,470	118,210
Seats per 1,000 population	2	2.2	2.1

Source: Graham and Gillies, Media Guide (Lagos, July 1970).

Also obscured by the figures, but only to be expected, is the concentration of media resources in the urban areas. There is a centripetal tendency for the demands of urbanization to lead to the congregation of technological, political, and economic institutions, including media institutions, in the urban centers. Daniel Lerner, in his study of the Middle East, has suggested that a certain level of population concentration and economic activity is a prerequisite to the development of the mass media.[3] Newspapers get published where most of their readership will be found. Radio and television stations are sited where, among other things, there is easy access to power supply and a large, economically welloff population. In a largely illiterate and comparatively poor country, all of these factors are concentrated in a few cities and large towns.

MEDIA CONTENT

To what extent does he who pays the mass media piper call the tune? In Nigeria, as in most other countries, the content of the media is oriented largely toward urbanites. Although we have not undertaken a close analysis of media content, it is not untrue to suggest that over 50 percent of the content of the daily press is concerned with, and implicitly directed toward, the new urban elite and the traditional elite and their imitators. It is members of this group whose opinions are quoted, whose fortunes are featured in the papers. When rural or less privileged people are given prominence in the press, it is usually in connection with antisocial, sensational acts. A news item in the July 13, 1971 issue of New Nigerian is typical of the kind of behavior in which a member of the masses has to engage in order to be quoted in the press. A back-page story in the paper entitled "Man gets death verdict for culpable homicide," begins:

A 23-year-old cattle rancher, Ilu Garba of Ngelshongel village in Bama, was at Maiduguri High Court, sentenced to death after being found guilty of culpable homicide.
The prosecution State Counsel Mr. H. Wonsku told the court that on April 27, 1971, at Ngelshongel village in Bama, the accused committed the offence by causing the death of one Hammadu Adamu by shooting him with an arrow on the left side of his neck.

The front page of that same issue of the New Nigerian carried news of the resignation of the Lagos state commissioner for works and planning, and General Gowon's message of congratulation to King Hassan II of Morocco "rejoicing with him on the failure of the attempt made on his life."
This bias of media content away from the masses is probably a function of the logic of social stratification that has been reinforced by the traditional journalists' definition of news as "what important people do." What unimportant people do becomes important if it impinges significantly on the lives of "the great," if it is bizarre, or if the journalist self-consciously indulges in so-called human

interest. Therefore, consciously or latently, in the rules of the journalistic game, emphasis is given to the opinions of the elite class and other powerful minority groups.

In one sense this situation is imposed on the media by restrictions on the availability of media space and time. An editor of a newspaper has only so many column-inches available for editorial material and so many for advertising. And one of the crucial editorial tasks is decision-making about how much of the incoming information can be accommodated, and what priorities should govern the decisions made. Editorial policy or ideological orientation may provide adequate guidelines for the systematic winnowing out of certain kinds of content, as may factors of cost and profit. But the most basic constraint on choice is the capacity of the channel, especially where potential input is greater than available space. Thus it is possible to compare societies in terms of the total number of newspaper column-inches available for the presentation of news and views. The larger the ratio of such space to population size the greater the degree of access to newspapers as a potential source of self-expression.

But absolute quantity is only a crude index of access. A more sensitive index concerns the possibility of expressing alternative points of view. If, for example, a political party doubles the number of newspapers it publishes, we can say that the supporters of that party now have more access to opportunities for expressing their opinions. But the society as a whole cannot be said to have increased its members' access to such opportunities—unless of course it is a one-party state. Viewed against this background the increase in the number of daily newspapers in Nigeria (and their increased circulation) does not represent real increase in access. What we find is that much of the increase is absorbed either by new government-supported newspapers or by the expansion of earlier government-supported facilities. Reviewing the decade 1969-70 a distinguished student of Nigerian press history, Increase H. E. Coker, remarked that "the trend in the decade just ended, and indeed the prospect of the succeeding one, is that the media of mass communication have come more and more under control of the Governments of the Federation."[4]

In a 1971 study of the Nigerian press based on 1964-65 data, Marcia Grant discusses the relationship between types of newspaper ownership and constraints on the content of the press. She distinguishes three categories of newspaper owners: "political parties and politicians, foreign press groups, and governments. . . . Using these three ownership categories the Nigerian Press can be classified into four newspaper types, the last of which is a hybrid. They are 'overseas commercial', 'political party', 'government', and 'overseas commercial/political party'." She quotes the president of the Nigerian Guild of Editors on the question of "restrictions on the content of the overseas commercial paper": "A foreign-owned newspaper which wants to continue in business for long must play ball with the ruling party or parties and with the government of the country where it is making a profit."[5]

Grant's paper contains specific illustrations of how ownership factors imposed constraints on the reporting of events in 1964—events involving the formation of a new political coalition, the Nigerian National Democratic Party (NNDP), and tension over the results of the 1963-64 census. In much broader, and not quite so political terms, we can proceed to examine the content of the Nigerian media.

An analysis of the content of radio programs broadcast by Radio Nigeria in 1968-70 and the first quarter of 1971 yield the following breakdown by content categories: [6]

Category	Percent	Content
News	15.9	Bulletins and summaries in English and 9 Nigerian languages
Current affairs	2.6	Newstalk, Editorial review, Nigerian newsreel
Religion	7.0	Programs for Muslims and Christians
Features	17.0	English- and Nigerian-language programs; e.g., "Perspective,"
	17.0	"Nnoko ndi Igbo"
Public information	8.0	Radio Doctor; Radio Lawyer
Education	3.9	School broadcasts
Music	47.0	Piano music, juju music, Akpala, highlife, etc.

All of the Nigerian media show clear signs of the influence of the international arrangements that govern the production and dissemination of mass-communicated messages. The national newspapers subscribe to Reuters, AFP, United Press International (UPI), the Associated Press (AP), and Tass, although there is a great variability in the flow and use of material from these sources, and therefore in the picture of the world that emerges. Hachten states that he found "in a study of African news flow that for English-language African papers in Nigeria, Kenya, and South Africa, some 67 percent of foreign news items were from English-speaking or Commonwealth nations. Since Reuters was the prime news source for these papers as well as for the British Commonwealth, perhaps it is Reuters which overselects this kind of news."[7]

In its annual report for 1967-68, the Nigerian Broadcasting Corporation's Television Service listed its "main sources of foreign news" as Reuters, AFP, and the Associated Press. The report further states that "the full service of Visnews, a television newsfilm agency, to which NBC began to subscribe in 1966-67 has continued to come in handy for the compilation of news bulletins and other news programmes. With the aid of materials supplied by this Agency, NBC-Television's news service was able to stretch its tentacles to cover not only Africa, but other parts of the globe."[8] In 1971 Nigerian television stations broadcast an average of four hours per night of foreign material out of a total of six hours of broadcasting. Local programs usually took the form of newscasts, variety-type shows (e.g., "The Bar Beach Show" on NBC-TV in Lagos), traditional dancing, local dramatic performances, and panel discussion programs.

Cinema content is even more foreign-dominated. Although cinema has been in Nigeria nearly seventy years, it has largely been in the hands of foreign proprietors. The first film was exhibited in August 1903 at the Glover Memorial Hall in Lagos. The medium of film was itself still new in those days and still technically in its infancy. Content was largely documentary. The first showings in Lagos, according to the Lagos Standard, included scenes of a steamer moving through water; a conjugal dispute; a steeplechase; acrobats and other pictures . . . shown with the vividness of life; and scenes of the coronation of King Edward VII at Westminister Abbey (the royal procession alone, according to the newspaper, being worth the price of admission). In 1904 one of these newsreels gave a brief glimpse of the Alake of Abeokuta, a Yoruba king of western Nigeria, during a visit he made to England.

The newspapers report that over the next few years films continued to be shown to full houses in Lagos, and the European merchant who showed them, a man by the name of Stanley Jones, was commended for relieving the monotony of Lagos life through interesting and innocent entertainment.[9]

World War II saw the widespread use of film by the British government in its wartime propaganda effort. Mobile cinema vans operating in the open air traveled all over Nigeria bringing the war and news of the success of the Allies and the defeat of the Germans. But perhaps the most popular films were those starring Charlie Chaplin, that inimitable cinema great.

Also about this time commercial cinema houses, now greatly expanded in number and geographical location, were showing American Western and Tarzan films, both types of which were extremely popular.

Since then the growth of cinema has been largely predictable and uninteresting, with foreign domination of content, distribution, and ownership. The 1960s saw the influx of third-rate films from India's assembly-line productions of the spectacular fight-plus-dance genre and the low-budget sex-cum-violence products of Italy's film industry.

An ongoing study of film censorship in Nigeria by the present
writer shows that, out of a sample of 289 films viewed by the Federal
Board of Film Censors in 1970, nearly 90 percent came from India
and Italy; the rest came from Britain and the United States. Local
production has been largely by the Federal Film Unit and the film
units of some state governments interested more in short tourist-
promotion documentaries rather than feature films for the entertainment industry. Over the last couple of years, however, indigenous
enterprises in collaboration with foreign partners have taken a keen
interest in film production. Kongi's Harvest, an adaptation for the
screen of a play of the same title by the Nigerian playwright Wole
Soyinka, was produced in 1971 by Calpenny Nigeria Limited, an
international company with Nigerian, American, and European partners.
The company has also undertaken production of Bullfrog in the Sun,
an adaptation from two novels by the Nigerian writer Chinua Achebe.

Although audience response to Kongi's Harvest was mixed, the
experience of a film with Nigerian content and mostly Nigerian actors
will have far-reaching consequences for the Nigerian film industry,
as will the federal government's decree on the Nigerianization of
businesses, including ownership of cinema theaters and distribution
of films. It is too early to discern the combined effect of these events,
but it is doubtful that the foreign domination of cinema content will
change significantly.

An unconventional means of mass communication in Nigeria
involves pamphlets, chapbooks, and other ephemera. Usually referred
to as Onitsha Market literature, this genre has been well described
by Emmanuel Obiechina.

> The Onitsha Market pamphlets comprise literature par
> excellence for the masses. They are literature about
> common people by some of their members for everyone's
> enjoyment—though its staunchest consumers remain
> the common people. Among the most devoted readers
> of the pamphlet literature must be listed grammar and
> elementary school boys and girls, lower-level office
> workers and journalists, primary school teachers,
> traders, mechanics, taxi-drivers, farmers and the
> new literates who attend adult education classes and
> evening schools. University graduates and people with
> post-grammar-school education tend to ignore this
> literature in favour of the more sophisticated novels,
> drama and poetry.
>   The pamphlet authors have themselves a fair idea
> of the kind of audience for which they produce and they
> sometimes define this audience in the prefaces and

introductions accompanying their works. Thus, Cletus
Nwosu, author of Miss Cordelia in the Romance of
Destiny, says in the introduction to his book: 'I have
made the book as simple as possible so that an average
boy can enjoy it without his dictionary by his side.'[10]

There are no accurate figures on the circulation of these Onitsha
pamphlets or of other ephemeral materials that have become an
entrenched feature of the Nigerian communication scene. Political
pamphleteering in English and the major languages flourished in the
1950s and 1960s, and helped to launch and sustain the career of many
an entrepreneurial printer-publisher. Although this kind of ephemera
was not periodic, it tended to be topical, to be passed from hand to
hand, and to enjoy popularity and currency among devotees. Its
content, translated for the benefit of illiterate relatives and widely
discussed, helped to introduce many to the mores and complexities
of the modernizing forces in Nigerian society.

A more traditionally based form of mass communication is
provided by theatrical and folk opera performances. Among many
Nigerian ethnic groups, dramatic entertainment involving masquerad-
ing, miming, and dancing, has functioned as a means of social control
and religious expression. The village masked plays of the Ibo, Ijaw,
and Ibibio peoples stress traditional virtues and values, although
the more secular performances incorporate vignettes of contemporary
life. Since the performances are usually in the open air and are open
to the whole population, their value as a means of instantaneous
dissemination of relevant social knowledge is high.

The Yoruba of western Nigeria have developed and modernized
folk drama. In recent years, under the influence of church and school
concerts, professional and amateur traveling companies have emerged.
The pioneering company—and one of the best companies—is the Hubert
Ogunde Concert Party, founded in the 1940s by a former police
constable with a flair for music and theater. Hubert Ogunde's early
"plays" were dramatized versions of biblical stories with musical
interludes featuring one or more female saxophone players. Ogunde
toured Nigeria first in the late 1940s, and although his performances
were in Yoruba, they were usually well-received. The content of his
plays became more secular in the 1950s and 1960s as he commented,
often satirically, on the failures and foibles of man or the chicanery
of petty politicians. His political commentary became so telling in
the 1960, that his company was banned from performing in the West
State, following the appearance of his play Yoruba Ronu ("Yorubas,
Think!").

Following in Ogunde's footsteps but exploiting traditional drama
and humor as well as indigenous legends and history, a number of

Yoruba folk drama companies now regularly travel all over Nigeria. The most contemporarily oriented is the Alawada Group led by Moses Olaiya. Their performances to large audiences in the halls and auditoriums of the larger cities consist essentially of verbal repartee and slapstick based on the problems and opportunities that accompany modern life—coping with the extended family, polygamy, problems of making it in the big city without money, the battle of wits between creditor and debtor. Realising the popularity of his performances, Olaiya has undertaken to advertise commercial products and events during the intervals in his shows—a sort of on-stage commercial!

Again the potential of this kind of drama for social mobilization has yet to be exploited.

MEDIA COSTS

Another factor related to access is economic. What does it cost people to expose themselves to the media? What does it cost media operators to produce media content? These two questions are obviously related, but the equation between the two kinds of cost is solved differently in different countries.

For example the price at which a newspaper is sold is determined normally by the cost of production. But a government that has a policy that all its citizens must read a newspaper every day may be willing to distribute daily newspapers either entirely free of charge or at a nominal price.

In Nigeria a good transistor radio set costs about $45—that is, about half the average annual income of a Nigerian farmer, or the equivalent of one month's salary for a secondary school graduate working as a third-class clerk in government service. A television set costs about $300, which is equal to the national average yearly income per capita. A newspaper costs 3 or 4 cents a day; that is, between $1 and $1.50 a month. This is probably not a lot of money, but it is enough to prevent a good percentage of Nigerians from being regular readers of the daily newspaper. We would say that such people are denied access to the newspaper for economic reasons. But one should also state that the price of newspapers has been one of the few stable prices over the years. In over a century the price of newspapers has risen (in Nigerian currency) from one penny to fourpence. Growth in advertising revenue, which is dependent on size of circulation and in its turn on increase in literacy and general economic well-being, led to a situation where newspapers can make a profit without being unreasonably expensive. But how long this situation will last for many newspapers is an interesting question.

The cost of production is determined not only by the intrinsic cost of material but also by government regulations about tariffs, by the labor code regarding wages and salaries etc. Where, as in Nigeria, radio and television receivers are subject to high taxation because they are regarded as luxury items, access to them is limited to the economically well-off or to those whose needs for prestige among the less well-off motivates them to endure the hardship of purchasing receivers they cannot really afford. So that even where transmission facilities are improved, and the duration of transmission is increased, access may not be increased correspondingly.

Cost plays a more subtle role in determining access. The less economically secure Nigerian newspapers often carry, as news stories, what are obviously press releases from the various foreign embassies in Nigeria. This is probably how these newspapers respond to staff shortages. They do not have to expend staff time and energy chasing after stories. As a recent report has suggested, "Provided the opportunity to get something for nothing, many newspapers will take it."

LANGUAGE AND ACCESS

A basic fact of the communication situation in Nigeria is that it is multilingual. Of the nearly 300 languages spoken in the country less than 20 are employed by the mass media. And those which are used are employed for different purposes in different media, as demonstrated in the following tables.

What is demonstrated is the extent to which the media offerings in the major national and regional languages are more comprehensive than for the minor languages. There are no news bulletins in the smaller languages, no features, no dramas; just the occasional short story and record-request programs. The implication is that people who speak only these languages are denied access to extensive media coverage. We know though that the sociolinguistic fact is that minority people tend to be multilingual and to speak at least one of the major languages, usually the one geographically closest to them. So that the Angas people of the Benue Plateau State are to a large extent speakers of Hausa as well. The extent of functional bilingualism is not documented in Nigeria, but there are subjective reasons for believing that it is widespread, especially among people who speak the smaller languages.

The English-language media are more comprehensive in their coverage than are any in the Nigerian languages. On radio and television, news bulletins in English are three times as long as news bulletins in any other language.[11] This means that an English-speaking

TABLE 14.5

Language Use in the Media

Language	Editorial	Used in Letters	Advertisment	Magazines
English	X	X	X	X
Hausa	X	X	X	X
Ibo	X	X	X	-
Yoruba	X	X	X	X
Effik	X	X	-	-
Edo	-	-	-	-
Ijaw	-	-	-	-
Kanuri	-	-	-	-

TABLE 14.6

Language use in Radio Broadcasting in Mid Western Nigeria - N.B.C., Benin

	News	Talks	Features	Drama	Short Story	Request
Edo	X	X	X	X	X	X
Urhobo	X	X	X	-	X	X
Ibo	X	X	X	X	X	X
Itsekiri	X	X	X	-	X	X
Ijaw	X	X	X	-	X	X
Isoko	-	X	-	-	X	X
Ika (Agbor)	-	-	-	-	X	X

listener potentially receives more varied information, in greater detail, than a listener restricted to the Nigerian-language service. Perhaps in the northern states, because of the long-standing dominance of Hausa and its political importance, Hausa-language broadcasting is almost at par with English-language broadcasting in terms of variety of programming and depth of coverage.

TRAINING MEDIA PERSONNEL

A final factor affecting access to the media concerns the training of media personnel. It is clear that the professional quality of those who operate the media is related to the kind of content the media carry. The intellectual ability of media executives and their sensitivity to the logic of their society will greatly influence the role they accept for the media, as well as the efficiency with which they fulfill that role. But perhaps the most persistent influence of training and education on the performance of media personnel is in the area of judgment and decision-making. The world today is characterized by a so-called information explosion. The news editor on an average newspaper in Lagos is bombarded with thousands of words every day in news reports from the wire services, from news agencies, from his paper's correspondents and reporters, handouts from embassies, releases from business and industry. From all of this sea of words he is expected, if he is a radio journalist, to compile a ten-minute news bulletin. If he takes his job seriously he will also want to produce commentaries or news talks that attempt to put events and places in the news in some kind of perspective.

He cannot do the necessary editing and synthesizing well unless he possesses the mental discipline and has had practice in digesting and collating information, and unless he can respond quickly and intelligently to new information. The challenge of professional and academic training for media personnel is to produce people who can respond with the appropriate mixture of flexibility and competence.

The training of media personnel in Nigeria is largely accomplished through the universities and media institutions. University training at both the University of Nigeria at Nsukka and the University of Lagos leads to a bachelor's degree at the end of three or four years of study. It is designed to provide both a broadly based liberal arts-social science background and substantial professional knowhow. In addition the Institute of Mass Communication at the University of Lagos operates a one-year diploma program for middle-level media personnel with three years experience or more—people who typically have had little or no university training and are therefore in need of the kind of broadening and updating that a university experience can give.

The Institute of Journalists, which opened in Lagos in 1971, concentrates on short skill-oriented workshops. A joint project of the Nigerian Guild of Editors and the International Press Institute, it is intended to upgrade the professional standard of lower-level journalists, as well as provide professional skills for newcomers to the profession.

On-the-job training is also provided by the larger newspapers and the broadcast media. From its earliest days Radio Nigeria had attempted to upgrade the quality of its staff through periodic training courses and workshops. It established its own training school for junior production and engineering staff, and sent its more senior people overseas for attachments, usually to the British Broadcasting Corporation (BBC).

While training enhances the performance of individual media people, the professionalization of the media will be enhanced through creation and development of professional associations. The Nigerian Union of Journalists has emerged in the last ten years as a powerful force, a champion of press freedom and better professional standards.

But much of the training is directed toward those working in English-language media. Early results from recent surveys carried out by the present writer show that people involved in the vernacular media are generally less well educated and have had inferior professional training than those who work in English. This means that, on the average, they are less capable of making the kinds of sound professional judgment that media people have to make increasingly now. The result is that, for example, Irohin Yoruba, the Yoruba-language weekly newspaper, carries trivial headlines and news stories even when events of national importance are available. It is possible that over a period of a few years someone who reads only Irohin Yoruba would have a vastly different perception of Nigerian life than someone who reads, say, the Daily Times. Because their education is basically poor, vernacular newsmen are less likely to qualify for admission to institutions of higher learning. Yet because of the sociolinguistic situation in Nigeria, the vernacular media reach the overwhelming proportion of the population. That those who work in the vernacular media need at least as good training as anyone else in the media is clear.

But universities are jealous of their academic standards. They will almost certainly deny admission to such poorly educated professionals. Therefore professional media institutions such as the Institute of Journalists will be the obvious place for providing specific, short, workshop courses and training for upgrading the level of vernacular media personnel.

The critical question is not *where* media personnel are trained; but *what* they are trained *for*. That will ultimately determine the kind of training they get, and even where they get it.

What can be done?

RECOMMENDATIONS

We have tried to analyze the working of the mass media in Nigeria and to show some of the forces that affect access to the media.

This last section presents a number of recommendations of a positive nature designed to correct some of the imbalances that exist in the distribution of access to mass media. There are nine basic recommendations:

1. There must be more consciousness of the built-in bias against the so-called masses in the mass-communications process. The denial of access to this segment of the population is almost institutionalized by the way media operations are structured.

2. This requires deliberate planning of communication facilities and their allocation in order to create more deliberate ways of integrating mass media communication with interpersonal communication, so that access to media content can be increased for those who for many reasons cannot gain direct access themselves to the media. This will be in one sense conscious exploitation of the "two-step flow," and is comparable to the organization of social communication that has proved effective in China, and in experimental situations in India.

3. More reading matter—newspapers, magazines, books, and pamphlets for new literatures—must be provided. This will help maintain and improve literacy skills, reinforce the reading habit, and ultimately facilitate access to national newspapers and magazines.

Furthermore the national effort to combat illiteracy must be sustained and intensified. This is particularly important in view of the fact that, under the influence of such international agencies as UNESCO, African governments seem to be accepting radio as the only road to public education and are giving up widespread literacy as an possible goal, even in the long run. This fatalistic attitude is short-sighted. Literacy skills are important for national development, and they must be cultivated.

4. There is a need to increase broadcasting time and to diversify the content of programs for the minority languages. Perhaps what is needed is general adoption of the practice of the Broadcasting Company of Northern Nigeria, which has instituted two radio channels, one for the General Service in English and Hausa, the other for the Selected Language Service, which gives more prominence to programming in selected minority languages of the area.

249

5. The media must help create a climate in which people want
to be involved in the national communication network. People like
to read and hear about themselves, their neighbors, and other people
like themselves. They like to share stories of success, not just
stories of anti-social behavior. There are few opportunities at the
moment for sustained localized media content. A greater decentralization of media facilities would go a long way toward solving this
problem. Perhaps radio (NBC) is the most decentralised medium
in this regard. Local community-oriented newspapers and radio
stations can help create the necessary climate of involvement.

6. Media content could be geared more closely to the needs
and level of understanding of the masses. This need not mean lowering
standards of professionalism or good taste.

7. Greater attention must be given to eliminating the de facto
censorship of cinema by Lebanese and other proprietors whose operation restricts access to different styles of film-making and different
content other than sword-fire-and-sex.

One possible solution is government ownership of cinema houses
and indigenous control of film importation and distribution. Also the
Board of Film Censors must be vigilant in ensuring that the widest
possible variety in films is presented to the Nigerian public. If
necessary the board should indicate where distributors are failing in
meeting this need for variety, and instruct that in any one quarter or
six-month period a specified percentage of films of certain categories
must be shown.

8. In order to increase access to the broadcast media for
people in the rural areas and for less privileged Nigerians, government could remove all tariffs, taxes, and license fees on electronic
equipment, especially those connected with radio manufacturing.
Also more communal radio and television sets could be provided.
The trend in Nigeria in the past ten years has been toward government
ownership of the media. Radio and television have been government-
owned from the start. With the creation of more states, each of
which wants to operate broadcasting institutions, government ownership will be consolidated. The indications are that the new states
will also establish newspapers and magazines sponsored by government.

One must view this government influence on media with alarm
as it threatens access to nongovernmental and independent points of
view. There is no doubt that he who pays the media piper will want
to call the tune. African governments especially are sensitive to
anything that sounds even faintly critical of their actions. They will
almost certainly prevent unfavorable comment appearing in media
owned or sponsored by them, so that, although in a few years one
will be able to say that newspaper circulation has increased and more
broadcast channels have been added with more diversified programming,

we may find that access has not increased significantly in terms of the presentation of alternative approaches to questions of public policy.

The answer is not necessarily private ownership of the media, for the business establishment can be just as intolerant of opposition as government, and just as restrictive of access. Perhaps one solution is to establish media institutions as publicly owned business— with shares on the stock market, and care being taken to diversify ownership of the shares. This possibility is likely to be publicly discussed seriously in the years ahead.

NOTES

1. The source of the data presented, is, unless given otherwise, UNESCO, Statistical Year Book (1966-69). [See also the following bibliography].

2. Timestaff, April 1971.

3. Daniel Lerner, The Passing of Traditional Society (Glencoe, Ill.: The Free Press, 1958).

4. Increase H. E. Coker, "The Media of Mass Communication," Nigerian Morning Post, October 1, 1970.

5. Marcia A. Grant, "Nigerian Newspaper Types," Journal of Commonwealth Political Studies, IX, 2 (1971), 95-114.

6. I. A. Olatunji, "A Study of NBC Radio Programme Contents" (unpublished bachelor's degree honors thesis, Institute of Mass Communication, University of Lagos, 1971).

7. William A. Hachten, Muffled Drums - The News Media in Africa (Ames - Iowa State University Press, 1971), p. 68.

8. Nigerian Broadcasting Corporation, Annual Report (1968), p. 32.

9. Lynne Leonard, "The Growth of Entertainment of Non-African Origin in Lagos From 1866-1929 (With special emphasis on Concert, Drama and the Cinema)" (unpublished master's thesis in drama, University of Ibadan, 1967).

10. Emmanuel Obiechina, Literature for the Masses (Enugu Nwankwo-Ifejika Publishers, 1972).

11. Olatunji, op. cit.; Andrew A. Moemeka, "NBC Igbo Language Programmes: Audience Preference Involvement and Benefits" (unpublished bachelor's degree honors thesis, Institute of Mass Communication, University of Lagos, 1972).

BIBLIOGRAPHY

Coker, Increase H. E. Landmarks of the Nigerian Press. Lagos: Cornell University Press 1968.

_____. "The Media of Mass Communication," Nigerian Morning Post (Lagos), October 1, 1970.

Colle, Royal, ed. Perspectives on Media Systems: India, Japan, Nigeria, USSR, Worldivision. Ithaca, N.Y.: Department of Communication Arts, Cornell University, Bulletin No. 4, 1968.

Grant, Marcia A. "Nigerian Newspaper Types," Journal of Commonwealth Political Studies, IX, 2 (1971), 95-114.

Hachten, William A. Muffled Drums: The News Media in Africa. Ames: Iowa State University Press, 1971.

Leonard, Lynne. "The Growth of Entertainment of Non-African Origin in Lagos From 1866-1929 (With special emphasis on Concert, Drama and the Cinema)." Unpublished master's degree thesis in drama, University of Ibadan, 1967.

McKay, Ian. Broadcasting in Nigeria. Ibadan: Ibadan University Press, 1964.

Moemeka, Andrew A. "NBC Igbo Language Programmes: Audience, Preference Involvement and Benefits." Unpublished bachelor's degree honors thesis, Institute of Mass Communication, University of Lagos, 1972.

Nigerian Broadcasting Corporation, Annual Report.

Obiechina, Emmanuel. Literature for the Masses. Enugu: Nwankwo-Ifejika Publishers, 1972.

Olatunji, I. A. "A Study of NBC Radio Programme Contents." Unpublished bachelor's degree honors thesis, Institute of Mass Communication, University of Lagos, 1971.

Timestaff (staff newsletter of the Daily Times of Nigeria), Lagos.

UNESCO, World Communications, 1964.

UNESCO, Statistical Year Book, 1966-69.

UKANDI G. DAMACHI is a research fellow in industrial relations at Princeton University. He has been a research associate at the Russell Sage Foundation, 1969-70, and an instructor at the New School for Social Research. In 1967 Damachi was an English-Speaking Union scholar to the European Economic Community countries. He has done field work in Ghana.

He received his Ph.D and an M.A. from Princeton University, an M.A. from the University of Illinois, and his B.A with honors from the National University of Ireland. He has published a number of articles. He is also the author of Nigerian Modernization: The Colonial Legacy, and a teacher's manual, From Black Africa.

H. DIETER SEIBEL is chairman of the Sociology Department at Manhattanville College. He has published several books (among them Industriearbeit und Kulturwandel in Nigeria) and numerous articles.

He has done extensive field research in Nigeria and Liberia as well as comparative studies in Germany and the United States. He has been chairman of the African Studies Department of the Arnold Bergstraesser Institut in Freiburg; chairman of the Department of Sociology and Anthropology at the University of Liberia; a visiting lecturer at Princeton University and a visiting professor at the University of Münster.

He holds a Dr. phil. degree in sociology from the University of Freiburg and a Dr. habil. degree from the University of Münster.

WILLIAM RUSSELL BASCOM is professor and director of the Robert H. Lowie Museum of Anthropology at the University of California at Berkeley. He received his Ph.D. from Northwestern University. Among the several positions and fellowships he has held at one time or another are the following: Social Science Research Fellow to Nigeria, 1937-38; Wenner-Green Foundation for Anthropological Research grantee, 1948; Fulbright grantee to Nigeria, 1950-51; NSF senior postdoctoral fellow in England, 1958; president of the Central States Anthropological Society, 1950-51; executive member of the American Anthropological Association, 1961-64, and of the American Association of Museums, 1962-67. He is also a member of the Advisory Board of the Museum of African Art, a position held since 1964.

Dr. Bascom is the author of several articles and books, among which are (with Paul Gebauer) Handbook of West African Art, 1953,

1964; The Sociological Role of the Yoruba Cult Group, 1944; Ponape, A Pacific Economy in Transition, 1965; and African Arts, 1967. He is the co-editor (with M. J. Herskovits) of Continuity and Change in African Cultures, 1959.

MICHAEL KOLL teaches at the University of Munster, and is the author of several books (among them Crafts and Cooperation in Western Nigeria) and articles. He holds a Dr. phil. degree in sociology from the University of Freiburg. He was a research fellow at the Arnold Bergstraesser Institut in Freiburg; a research fellow at the Nigerian Institute of Social and Economic Research; and a lecturer at the Ahmadu Bello University at Zaria.

ROBERT MELSON is associate professor of political science at Purdue University. He received his Ph.D. from the Massachusetts Institute of Technology, and has taught at Michigan State University. He has done field work in Nigeria and has been a faculty fellow of the Center for Advanced Study at the University of Illinois. His publications appear in The American Political Science Review and elsewhere. He is the co-editor (with Howard Wolpe) of Nigeria Modernization and the Politics of Communalism.

M. O. KAYODE is a lecturer in economics at the University of Ibadan and author of several articles. He received his Ph.D. from the University of Ibadan.

ALAN PESHKIN studied at the University of Illinois (1948-54) and the University of Chicago (1957-62). He taught high school social studies for several years before completing his doctoral research on a project of planned education change in East Pakistan. After two years of teaching and field work in Bornu, Nigeria, he joined the University of Illinois, where he is professor of comparative education and was, until recently, director of African studies. His research interests include education in Islamic societies, political socialization, and the effect of schooling on traditional-modern value orientations. He is the author of Kanuri School Children: Education and Social Mobilization in Nigeria.

AKPAN ESEN is a lecturer in education at the University in Nigeria. Esen has published numerous articles in various professional journals. He holds a Ph.D. from Columbia University.

PAULINE H. BAKER is lecturer in the Institute of Social Studies at Lagos University. She is the author of several articles. She holds a Ph.D. from the University of California at Los Angeles.

PHILIP V. WHITE is a Ph.D. candidate in the Politics Department at Princeton University. He received an M.B.A. from Columbia University in 1968, with a concentration in international business. After he completed his degree, he worked at Columbia as assistant to the dean in the School of General Studies, and later as associate director of the Council for Opportunity Graduate Management Education. He attended Williams College, where he earned the B.A. in political science in 1966. He spent the year 1964-65 at the University of Ibadan, Nigeria. He is the author of a number of articles.

GEORGE OBIOZOR is currently working toward his Ph.D. in political science at Columbia University. He was born in Awo-Omamma, Orlu, in eastern Nigeria. He attended Community Grammar School, Awo-Omamma, for his secondary school education and also taught there briefly. He served as a public relations officer before he left Nigeria for further studies. He studied for two years in Switzerland before going to the University of Puget Sound in Tacoma, Washington where he received his B.A. in political science in 1969. He received his M.I.A. from the School of International Affairs at Columbia University in 1971.

ALFRED E. OPUBOR is director of the African Studies Center at Michigan State University. He was born in Kaduna, Nigeria. He attended the University of Ibadan, graduating with honors in English. After a brief period with Radio Nigeria in Lagos, and graduate studies at Ibadan University, he took an M.A. in linguistics at the University of California at Los Angeles. He received his Ph.D. in communication research at Michigan State University. His research interests include the study of traditional verbal art, the ethnography of communication, and communication planning strategies in national development. Dr. Opubor has taught at Duquesne University, the Institute of Mass Communication at the University of Lagos and Michigan State University.

ARMS AND AFRICAN DEVELOPMENT:
Proceedings of the First Pan-African Citizens' Conference
Edited by Frederick S. Arkhurst

EDUCATIONAL PROBLEMS OF DEVELOPING COUNTRIES:
With Case Studies of Ghana, Pakistan and Nigeria (Expanded and
Updated Edition)   Adam Curle

A SOCIOECONOMIC PROFILE OF SOUTH AFRICA
William Redman Duggan

PLANNED CHANGE IN A TRADITIONAL SOCIETY:
Psychological Problems of Modernization in Ethiopia
David C. Korten with Frances F. Korten.

AID TO AFRICA:
A Policy Outline for the 1970s   Paul Streeten